Reasoning
Olympiad

Class 05

Reasoning

Olympiad

Class 05

A must have book for all Olympiads & Talent Search Exams...

by
Prachi

BLOOM CAP
Bloom Cap Edu Ventures Pvt. Ltd.

Bloom Cap Edu Ventures Pvt. Ltd.

卐 **Administrative & Production Office**

'Ramchhaya' 4577/15, Agarwal Road, Darya Ganj, New Delhi -110002
Tele: 011- 47630600, 43518550

卐 **ISBN :** 978-93-25519-04-6

卐 **PRICE :** ₹100.00

卐 **PO No :** TXT-XX-XXXXXXX-X-XX

For further information about the books log on to
www.bloomcap.org

Follow us on   

Preface

"Future belongs to those Who prepares for it today"

School Olympiads are National & International level competitions conducted by different Government, Non-Government & Educational Organisations with the purpose of making the children ready to face competitive exams. The challenging Questions asked in Olympiads motivate them to learn more & more and bring out the best result with improved academic performance. The Awards & Scholarship offered by Olympiads motivate children to aspire & strive for doing better and emerge out to be the best.

Reasoning Olympiads

Reasoning or Logical thinking is the ability of mind that helps in dealing with complex situations. It is also directly related to evolving careers like Software Development, Coding, Mobile App Development etc.

Reasoning Olympiads are targeted to induce & enhance the logical thinking skills and Analytical Approach in students which further aid to improve their academics.

'Bloom Reasoning Olympiad Study Book Class 5' is a perfect resource to Study & Practice for Olympiad Exams and other National & State Level Talent Search Exams & Other Competitions.

Some Special Features of Bloom Reasoning Olympiad Study Books are;

- Complete coverage of all the aspects of Reasoning; Verbal, Non-Verbal, Analytical & Logical Reasoning etc.
- Chapterwise Exercises having different types of Objective Questions at par with the Olympiad Level.
- Detailed Explanation for each question.
- Olympiad Pattern Practice Sets at the end.

This book is prepared by Expert Panel with the utmost care, still if you have any suggestions regarding its improvement then feel free to contact us at olympiads@bloomcap.org. We will try to inculcate your suggestions in the further editions.

Contents

Matching Pairs

The concept of 'Matching Pairs' can be understood easily by following example.

EXAMPLE 1 The figures in the first pair are related to each other in a certain way. Find the figure which will complete the second pair in the same way as the first pair.

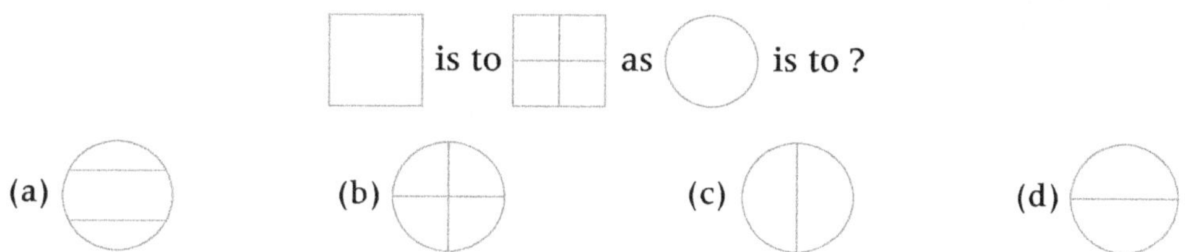

Sol. *(b)* In first pair, the square is divided into four equal parts to obtain the second figure. Similarly, in second pair, the circle must be divided into four equal parts to obtain the second figure. So, option figure (b) will complete the second pair.

Hence, option (b) is correct.

In 'Matching Pairs', following types of questions are generally asked.

EXAMPLE 2 'Cool' is related to 'Cold' in the same way 'Pretty' is related to what?

    (a) Ugly   (b) Beautiful

    (c) Good   (d) Glowing

Sol. *(b)* As the synonyms of Cool is Cold similarly, synonym of Pretty is Beautify.

Hence, option (b) is correct.

EXAMPLE 3 Identify the relationship of the first pair and then find the missing term in the second pair.

BEH : DGJ :: NQT : ?

    (a) PSV   (b) MRU

    (c) LSU   (d) QRV

Sol. *(a)* The pattern is

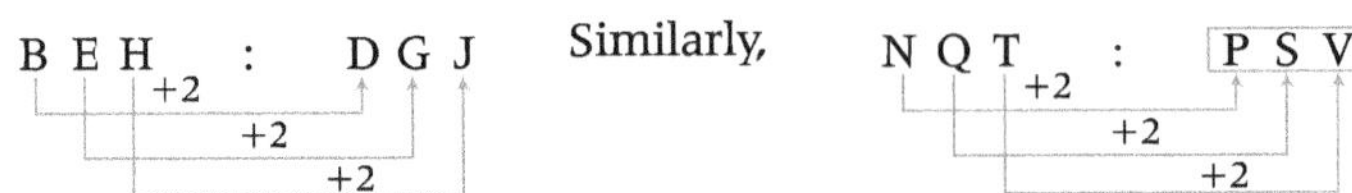

So, PSV will complete the second pair. Hence, option (a) is correct.

EXAMPLE 4 Find the number that will replace the question mark(?).

5 is to 40 as 8 is to ?

(a) 16   (b) 20

(c) 64   (d) 40

Sol. *(c)* Here, the first number is multiplied by 8 to get the second number.

As, $5 \times 8 = 40$ Similarly, $8 \times 8 = 64$

So, 64 will replace the question mark. Hence, option (c) is correct.

EXAMPLE 5 Complete the second pair in the same way as first pair.

Question Figures

 : 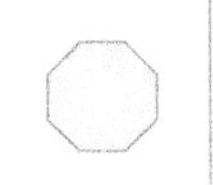 ::  : ?

Answers Figures

(a) 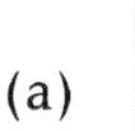   (b) 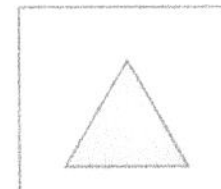   (c) 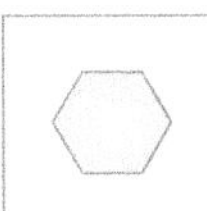   (d) 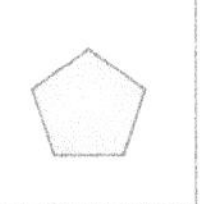

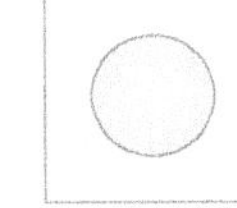

Sol. *(d)* In first pair, as the number of legs of the spider is eight, similarly the number of edges of the given shape is eight. In second pair, the number of arms of the star fish is five, similarly the number of edges of the shape will be five. So, figure in option (d) will complete the second pair.

Hence, option (d) is correct.

⏰ Let's Practice

1 Mark Questions

1. Wax is related to candle in the same way clay is related to
(a) Kite (b) Pot (c) Paper (d) Pen

2. Cat is related to kitten as dog is related to
(a) Puppy
(b) Bark
(c) Child
(d) Cub

3. Dates are related to calendar in the same way words are related to what?
(a) Paper
(b) Dictionary
(c) Time
(d) Clock

4. Find the letters which will complete the second pair in the same way as the first pair.

AC : ZX :: BD : ?

(a) ZT (b) KU (c) YW (d) XU

5. Find the letters that will replace the question mark(?).

EGH is to EHG as TLU is to ?

(a) ULT
(b) TUL
(c) UTL
(d) LTU

6. What letters will come in the last balloon following the same pattern which first two are following?

KMFD : DFMK :: SMRT : ?

(a) SRMT
(b) RSMT
(c) TRMS
(d) MSRT

7. Choose the alternative which will replace the question mark(?).

99 : 90   80 : 71   100 : ?

(a) 109
(b) 90
(c) 89
(d) 91

8. Complete the following analogy.

7 : 50 :: 9 : ?

(a) 80
(b) 82
(c) 90
(d) 100

9. Find the missing number in the second pair.

8034 : 0843 :: 2918 : ?

(a) 1892
(b) 8129
(c) 9281
(d) 8219

10. Find the missing number in second pair.

G : 7 :: J : ?

10	11	9	8
(a)	(b)	(c)	(d)

11. Complete the second pair in the same way as first pair.

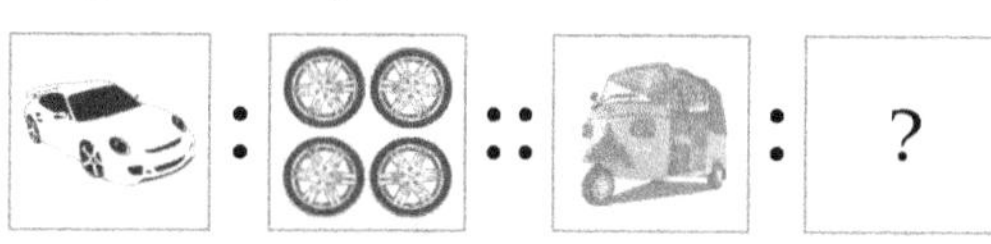

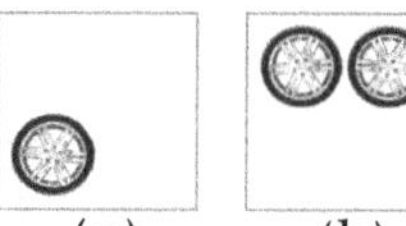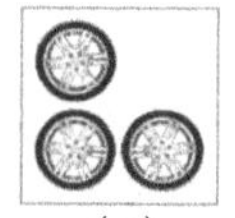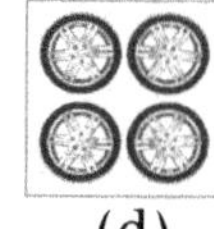

(a)   (b)   (c)   (d)

12. Which shape completes the second pair?

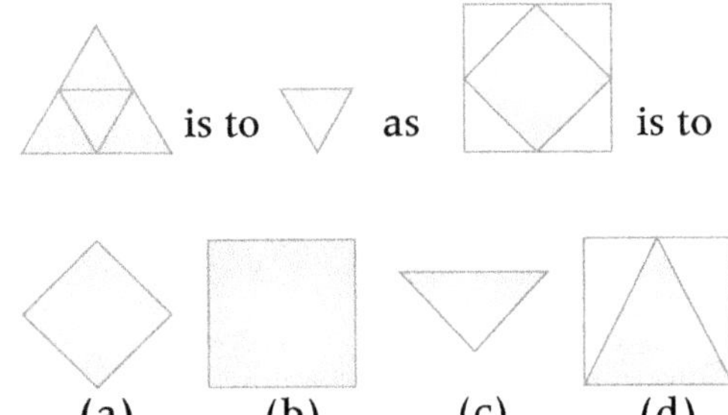

(a)   (b)   (c)   (d)

13. Find out the missing figure that will complete the second pair.

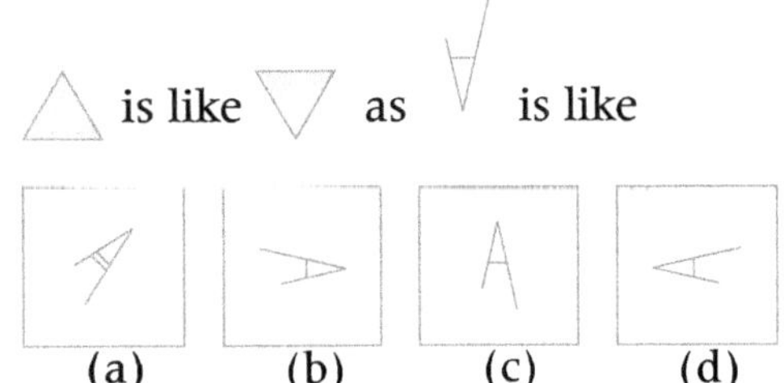

(a)   (b)   (c)   (d)

14. Complete the second pair in the same way as the first pair.

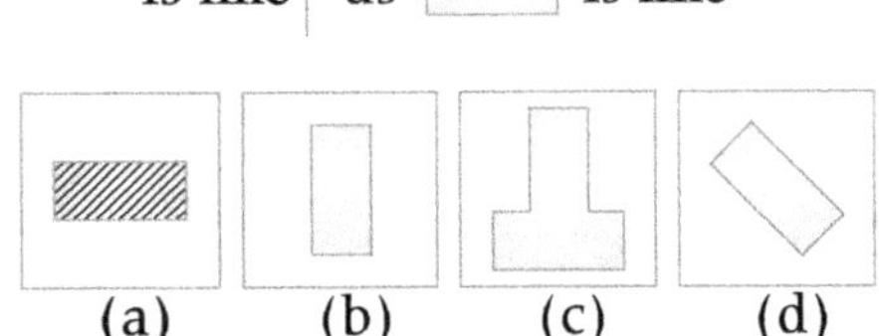

(a)   (b)   (c)   (d)

15. Find the figure which will complete the second pair in the same way as the first pair.

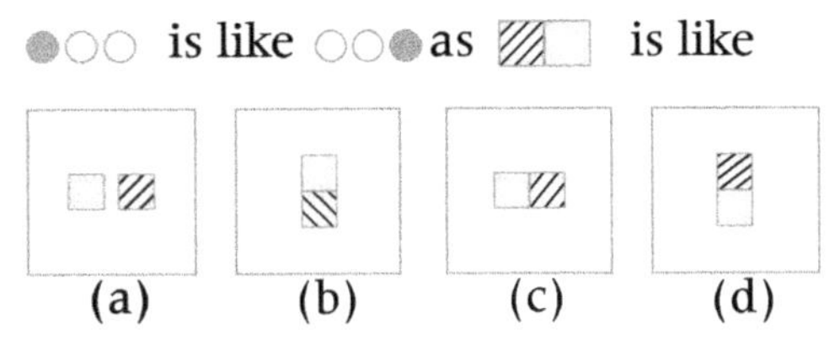

(a)   (b)   (c)   (d)

16. Find the figure which will complete the second pair following the same rule that first pair follows.

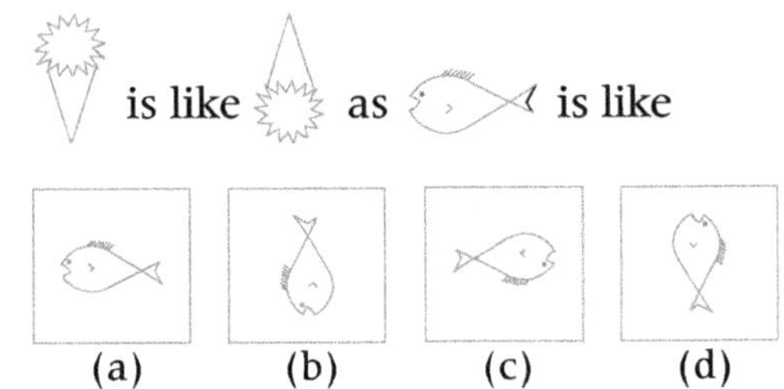

(a)   (b)   (c)   (d)

2 Marks Questions

17. Choose the alternative which will complete the second pair in the same way as the first pair.

TPQ : WQV :: PLM

(a) SMR   (b) RST
(c) QMT   (d) TNQ

18. Find the term which replaces the question mark(?).

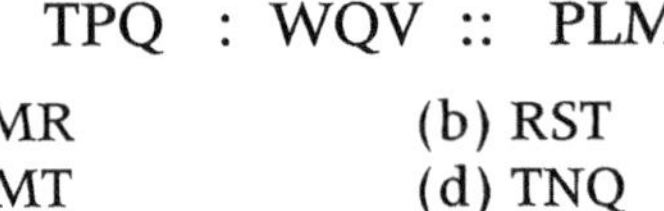

WXY is to TUV as PQR is to ?

(a) TUV   (b) MNO
(c) OPQ   (d) JKL

Directions (Q. Nos. 19 and 20) Identify the relation between each of the given pair on either side of : : and find the missing figure/term.

19. S E R I E S : Ƨ Ǝ I Я Ǝ Ƨ :: M U S I C : ?
(a) MUSIC   (b) ƆIƨUM
(c) M U Ƨ I C   (d) M U I Ƨ Ɔ

20. 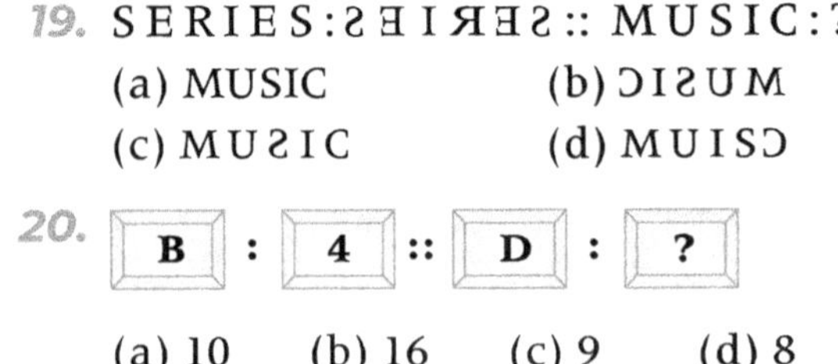

B : 4 :: D : ?

(a) 10   (b) 16   (c) 9   (d) 8

Directions (Q. Nos. 21 and 22) Find the term which will replace the question mark(?).

21. 7 : 57 : : 9 : ?
   (a) 98   (b) 99   (c) 89   (d) 95

22. 7 : 75 : : ? : 85
   (a) 6   (b) 8
   (c) 7   (d) 9

23. If $\begin{array}{cc} E & K \\ Z & N \end{array}$ is related to $\begin{array}{cc} 6 & 12 \\ 27 & 15 \end{array}$ is some way, then in the same way $\begin{array}{cc} U & P \\ J & C \end{array}$ is related to ....

(a) $\begin{array}{cc} 4 & 17 \\ 11 & 21 \end{array}$ (b) $\begin{array}{cc} 17 & 4 \\ 11 & 21 \end{array}$

(c) $\begin{array}{cc} 22 & 17 \\ 11 & 4 \end{array}$ (d) $\begin{array}{cc} 4 & 22 \\ 11 & 17 \end{array}$

24. Find the term which will replace the question mark(?).

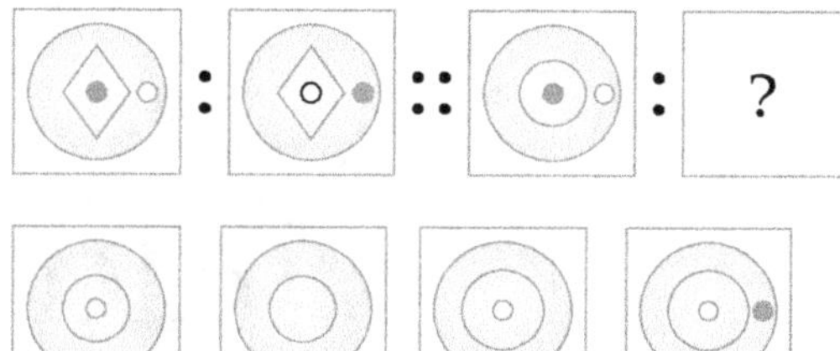

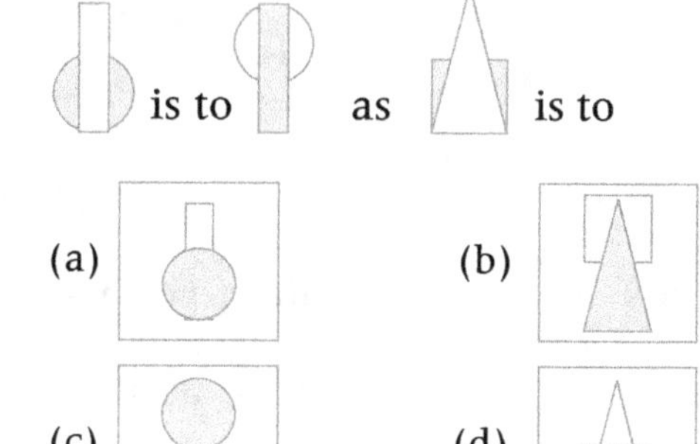

   (a)   (b)   (c)   (d)

25. Find the figure which will complete the second pair in the same way as the first pair.

is to   as   is to

(a)   (b)

(c)   (d)

Odd One Out

Let us consider the following example to understand the concept of 'Odd One Out'.

Which one is different from others?

(a)   (b)   (c)   (d)

Sol. *(c)* Except option (c), the number of sides in each figure is even.

In 'Odd One Out', following types of questions are generally asked

EXAMPLE 1 Four different months are given below. Choose a month which is different from others.

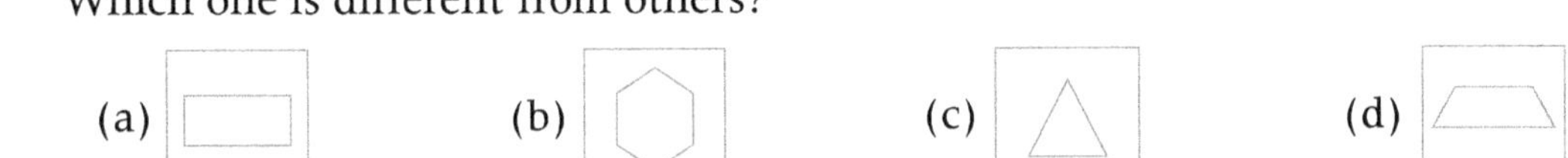

(a)   (b)   (c)   (d)

Sol. *(b)* If we analyse the number of days in the given months, we find that, March has 31 days, April has 30 days, December has 31 days and July also has 31 days.
So, except April all others have 31 days. Thus, April is different from others.
Hence, option (b) is correct.

EXAMPLE 2 Amongst the following, which boat is different from others?

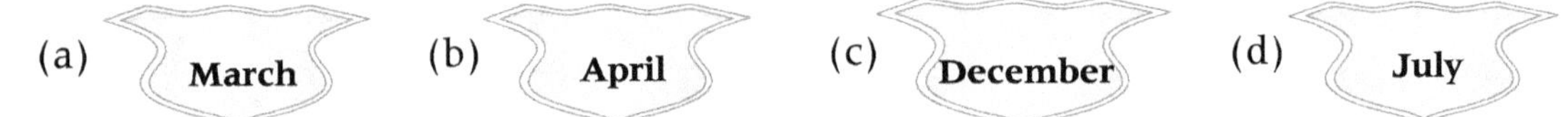

(a)   (b)   (c)   (d)

Sol. *(a)* Here, boats (b), (c) and (d) show an odd number but boat (a) shows an even number. So, boat (a) shows different number from others. Therefore, boat (a) is odd one out.
Hence, option (a) is correct.

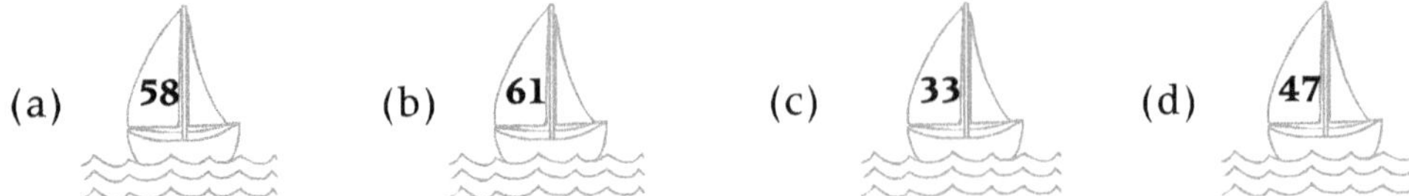

EXAMPLE 3 Choose the odd one out.

(a) EJOT   (b) GLQV   (c) CHMR   (d) BDFH

Sol. *(d)* The letters follow below pattern

$$E \ J \ O \ T \qquad G \ L \ Q \ V \qquad C \ H \ M \ R \ \text{and} \ B \ D \ F \ H$$
$$+5 \ +5 \ +5 \qquad +5 \ +5 \ +5 \qquad +5 \ +5 \ +5 \qquad +2 \ +2 \ +2$$

It is clearly seen that, except BDFH all others follow similar pattern but letters' group BDFH follows different pattern. So, BDFH is odd one out.

Hence, option (d) is correct.

EXAMPLE 4 Four different lockers are shown below. Each locker represents a combination of a letter and a number. Choose the one which represents different combination from others.

(a) 14 / N   (b) R / 18   (c) 27 / U   (d) E / 5

Sol. *(c)* Here, all lockers consist of a letter and its positional value (in English alphabetical series), whereas locker in option (c) consists of letter 'U' whose positional value is '21' not '27'. So, it is odd one out.

Hence, option (c) is correct.

EXAMPLE 5 A Maths teacher draws four different figures on blackboard. Among these four figures, three are similar in certain way. Choose the figure which is different fro

(a) 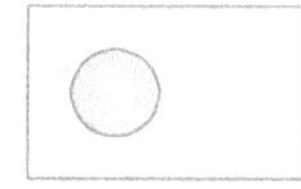   (b) 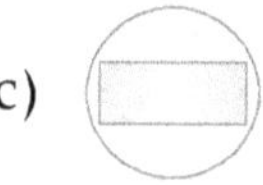   (c) 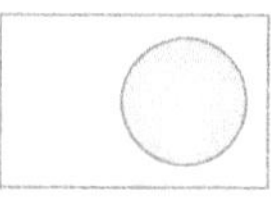   (d)

Sol. *(c)* Here, in all the figures except figure (c), the circle is enclosed by a rectangle. But in figure (c), the rectangle is enclosed by circle. So, figure (c) is odd one out.

Hence, option (c) is correct.

⏰ Let's Practice

1 Mark Questions

1. Joy writes the name of parts of body. Choose the one which is different from others.

Ear	Nose	Tongue	Throat
(a)	(b)	(c)	(d)

2. Which word does not belong to the group?

Curd (a)   Butter (b)

Cheese (c)   Oil (d)

3. Sakshat likes four things which he eats. Three of them are similar in a certain way. Choose the one which is different.

Honey   Apple   Brinjal   Pomegranate

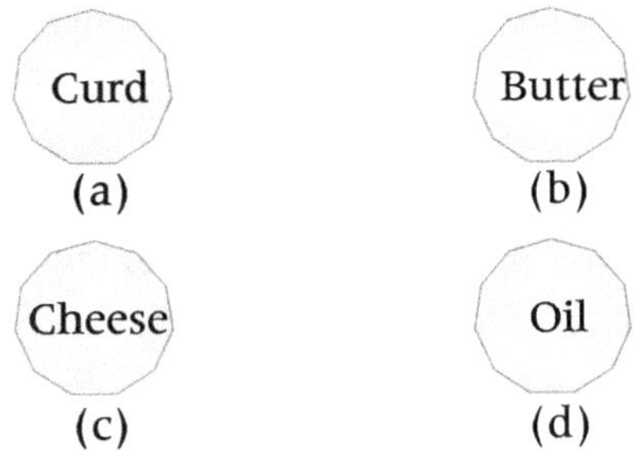

(a)   (b)   (c)   (d)

4. Which word does not belong to the group?

Scissors	Knife	Axe	Hammer
(a)	(b)	(c)	(d)

5. Choose the odd word pair.
(a) Square : Four
(b) Triangle : Three
(c) Rectangle : Five
(d) Pentagon : Five

6. Choose the odd one out from the following.

ACE	PRT	UWY	MNO
(a)	(b)	(c)	(d)

7. Which one is different from others?

EGIH (a)   QSUT (b)   LNPQ (c)   HJLK (d)

8. Find the number which is different from others.

36 (a)   26 (b)   24 (c)   54 (d)

9. Choose the spectacle which is different from others.

3–10 (a)   2–5 (b)   5–20 (c)   4–17 (d)

10. Four different combinations of letters and numbers are given below. Choose a combination which is different from others.

$\frac{15}{O}$ (a) $\frac{20}{T}$ (b) $\frac{10}{J}$ (c) $\frac{26}{Y}$ (d)

11. Amongst the following, choose the figure which is different from others?

(a)   (b)   (c)   (d)

12. Choose the figure which is odd one out.

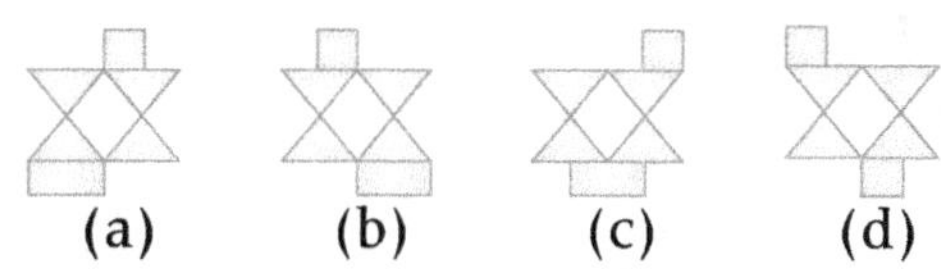

(a) (b) (c) (d)

13. Amongst the following, choose the figure which is different from others?

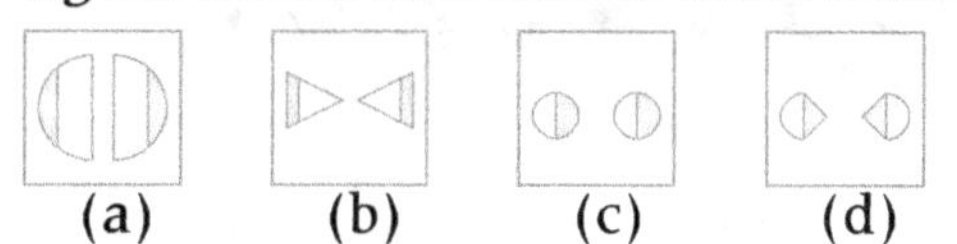

(a) (b) (c) (d)

14. Which pattern is different from others?

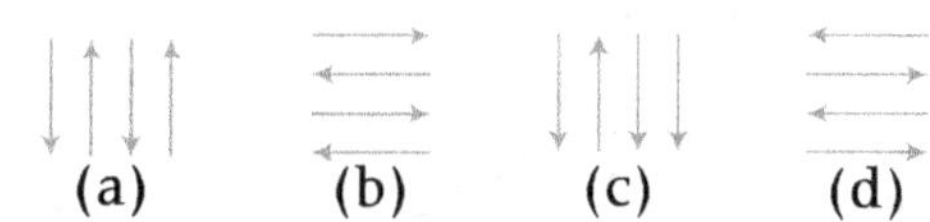

(a) (b) (c) (d)

15. A group of children is playing with four small cubes. Among these four cubes, three are alike in some way.

Find the one which is different from others.

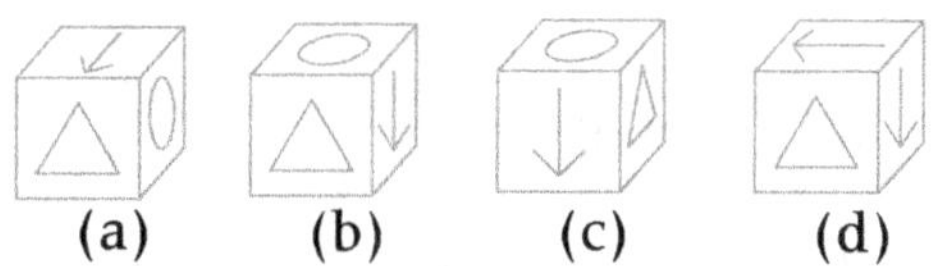

(a) (b) (c) (d)

16. Find the odd one out.

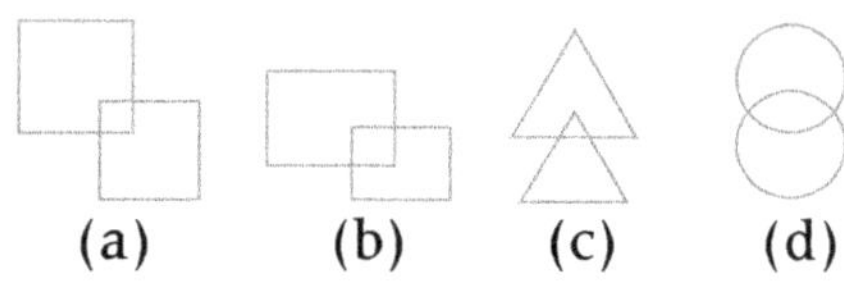

(a) (b) (c) (d)

17. In a drawing competition, four friends draw certain figures. These figures are shown below. Choose a figure which is odd.

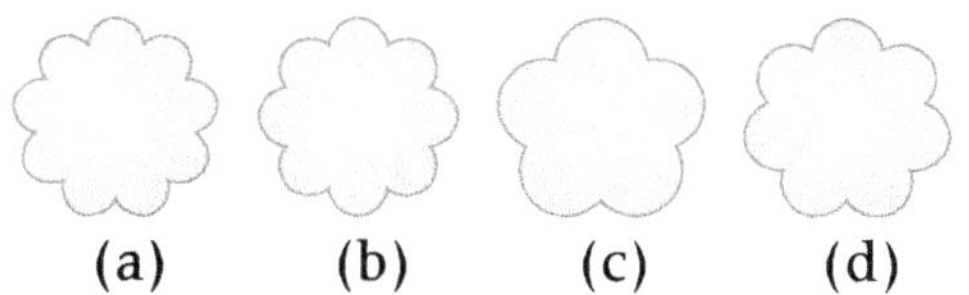

(a) (b) (c) (d)

2 Marks Questions

18. Amongst the following four, three are alike in a certain way. Choose the one which is different from others.

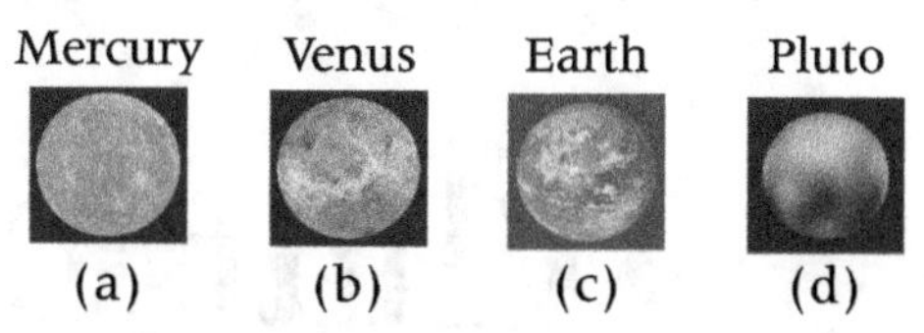

(a) (b) (c) (d)

19. The given options show the number on four different buses. Which bus number is different from other?

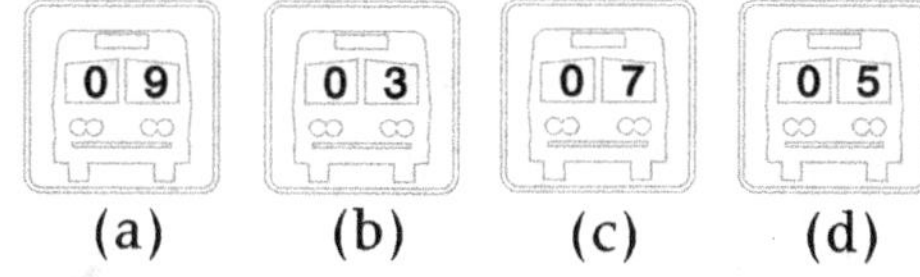

(a) (b) (c) (d)

20. Identify the number which does not belong to the group.

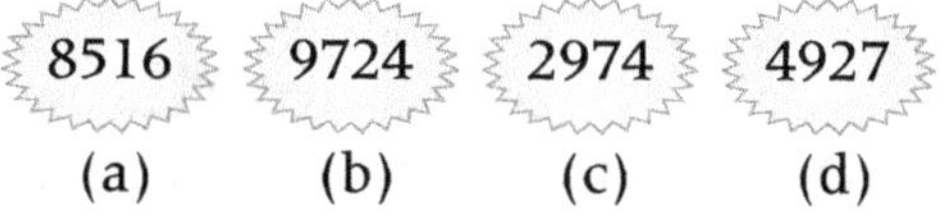

(a) (b) (c) (d)

21. Which number does not belong to the group?

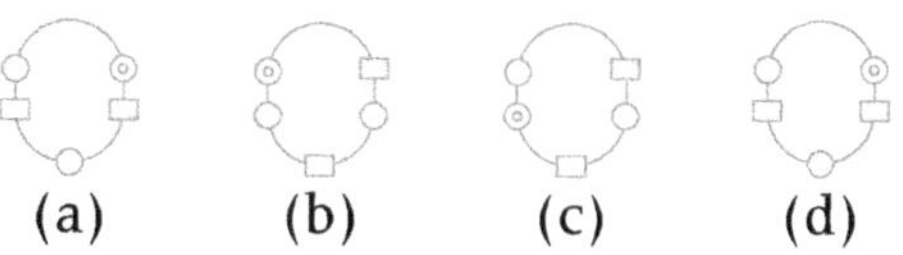

(a) (b) (c) (d)

22. Sudiksha wears four necklaces on four different days. Choose a necklace which is different from others.

(a) (b) (c) (d)

23. Select odd one out.

(a) H 9 17   (b) F 13 19

(c) L 4 19   (d) U 2 23

What Comes Next?

Consider the following example to understand the concept of 'What Comes Next?'

In the following sequence, find the next figure.

Question Figures   **Answer Figures**

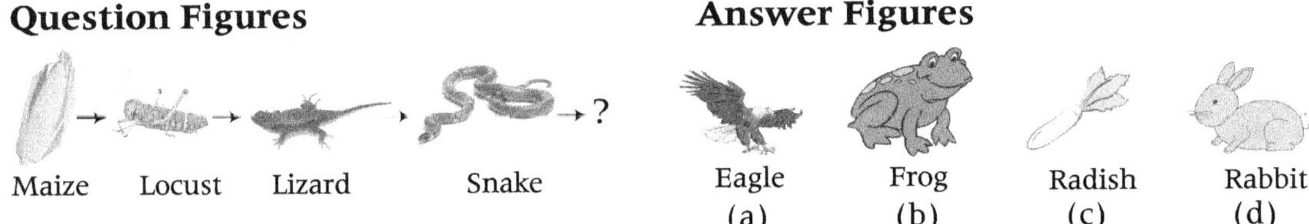

Sol. *(a)* When we carefully observe the above sequence we see that, it represents a food chain. Maize is eaten by Locust, Locust is eaten by Lizard and Lizard is eaten by Snake. Now, who eats Snake. Eagle is the bird, who eats Snake. So, Eagle will come next.

Hence, option (a) is correct.

In 'what comes next?', following types of questions are generally asked

EXAMPLE 1 Five cats are labelled with five different tags. These tags show five different alphabets. One new cat joins the group. Find the alphabet that will be written on the tag of this new cat.

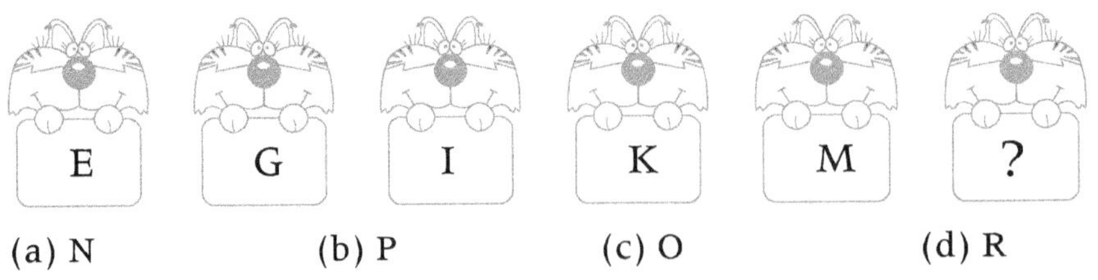

(a) N   (b) P   (c) O   (d) R

Sol. *(c)* Pattern is as follows $E \xrightarrow{+2} G \xrightarrow{+2} I \xrightarrow{+2} K \xrightarrow{+2} M \xrightarrow{+2} \boxed{O}$

So, the next alphabet will be M + 2 = O, as shown above.

Hence, option (c) is correct.

EXAMPLE 2 If the pattern continues, which letter is at the 90th position?

ABCDE ABCDE ABCDE

(a) A   (b) C

(c) D   (d) E

Sol. *(d)* Here, 5 letters i.e., ABCDE are repeated.

A B C D E	A B C D E	A B C D E	....

1 2 3 4 5   6 7 8 9 10   11 12 13 14 15

So, the letter at 90th position will be E as follows

A B C D E

86 87 88 89 90

Hence, option (d) is correct.

EXAMPLE 3 What is the missing term in the series given below?

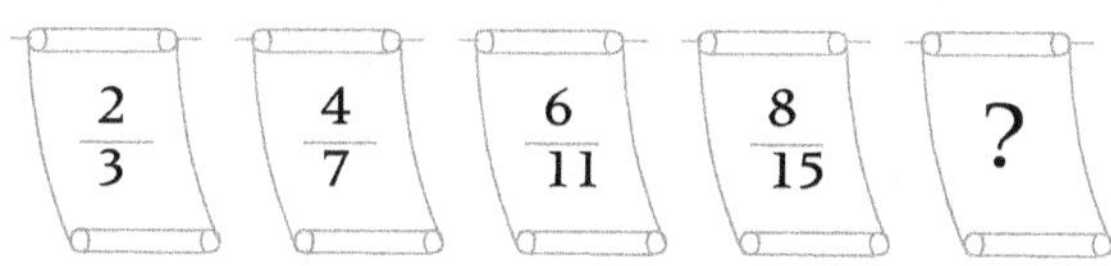

$$\frac{2}{3} \qquad \frac{4}{7} \qquad \frac{6}{11} \qquad \frac{8}{15} \qquad ?$$

(a) $\dfrac{14}{20}$ (b) $\dfrac{13}{19}$

(c) $\dfrac{10}{19}$ (d) $\dfrac{16}{18}$

Sol. *(c)* The pattern is $2 \xrightarrow{+2} 4 \xrightarrow{+2} 6 \xrightarrow{+2} 8 \xrightarrow{+2} \boxed{10}$

$3 \xrightarrow{+4} 7 \xrightarrow{+4} 11 \xrightarrow{+4} 15 \xrightarrow{+4} \boxed{19}$

So, the next term will be $\dfrac{10}{19}$.

Hence, option (c) is correct.

EXAMPLE 4 How many squares will be there in pattern 60?

Patten 1   Patten 2   Patten 3

(a) 120   (b) 122

(c) 118   (d) 119

Sol. *(b)* Number of square in pattern $1 = 4$, Number of squares in pattern $2 = 6$
Number of squares in pattern $3 = 8$
The sequence follows below pattern, $(1 \times 2 + 2), (2 \times 2 + 2), (3 \times 2 + 2).....$
So, the number of squares in pattern $60 = 60 \times 2 + 2 = 120 + 2 = 122$
Hence, option (b) is correct.

EXAMPLE 5 Find out the next term in the following series.

Question Figures   **Answer Figures**

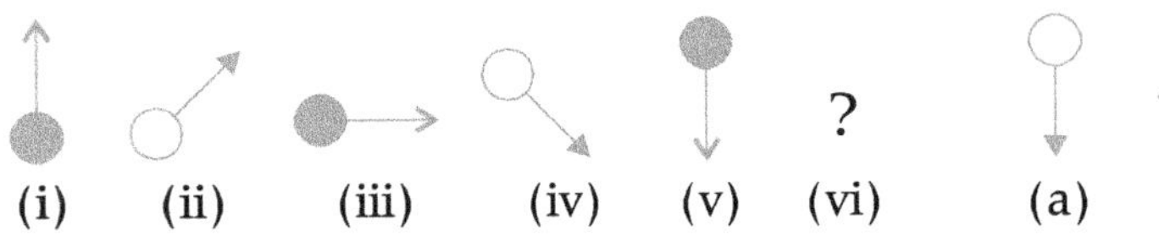

(i)   (ii)   (iii)   (iv)   (v)   (vi)   (a)   (b)   (c)   (d)

Sol. *(d)* In each step, the arrow rotates 45° in clockwise direction.

The arrowhead remains same in each alternate figure. And, the circle becomes unshaded and shaded in each alternate figure. On following this pattern, option figure (d) will complete the series.

Hence, option (d) is correct.

⏰ Let's Practice

1 Mark Questions

1. Complete the following letter series.

T	R	P	N	L	J	?

(a) H   (b) P
(c) E   (d) F

2. Find the next two letters for the series given below.

(a) CB   (b) CA
(c) AB   (d) BA

3. Choose the term which will complete the following series.

(a) TJ   (b) VH
(c) UI   (d) RL

4. What will come in place of question mark?

(a) 30   (b) 28   (c) 34   (d) 29

5.

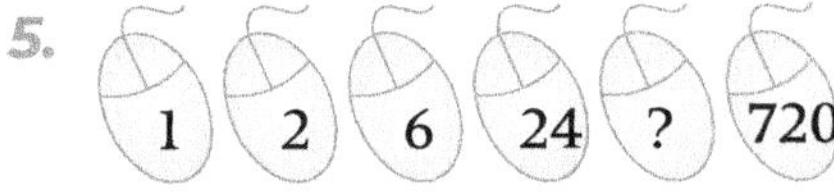

The value of the missing number in the given pattern is
(a) 110   (b) 100   (c) 300   (d) 120

6. Observe the pattern and find the next term.

53670	53770	53570	53670	?

(a) 35870   (b) 53870
(c) 53470   (d) 53570

7. Which number will replace the question mark?

(a) 12 (b) 11
(c) 20 (d) 28

8. Complete the following series.

(a) $\dfrac{160}{30}$ (b) $\dfrac{108}{33}$ (c) $\dfrac{152}{36}$ (d) $\dfrac{162}{33}$

9. Which of the following terms will continue the given series?

| 3 | D | 6 | G | 12 | J | 24 | M | ? |

48 P	40 P	30 Q	36 D
(a)	(b)	(c)	(d)

10. Which of the following options will complete the given series.

4 Z   7 X   11 V   16 T   ?   29 P

(a) 22R (b) 20T
(c) 20R (d) 22T

11. If the pattern continues, which letter is at the 91st position?

P Q R S T P Q R S T P Q R S T P Q R S T
(a) P (b) Q
(c) R (d) S

12. How many circles will be there in pattern 98?

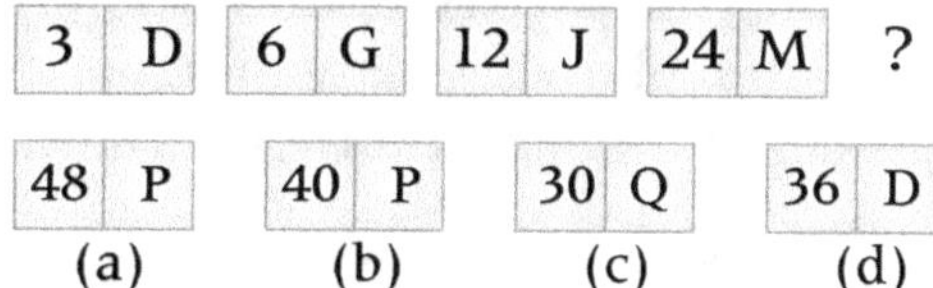

Pattern 1   Pattern 2   Pattern 3   Pattern 4

(a) 200 (b) 198
(c) 197 (d) 99

13. A piece of paper is torn, in which column did the number 80 appear?

I	II	III	IV
1	2	3	4
5	6	7	8
9	10	11	12
13	14	15	16
17			

(a) I (b) II (c) III (d) IV

14. A couple is celebrating their marriage anniversary. They decorate the party hall with various frills. Among those frills, one frill is given below. The two designs of this frill are missing. Observe the pattern and find out the missing designs.

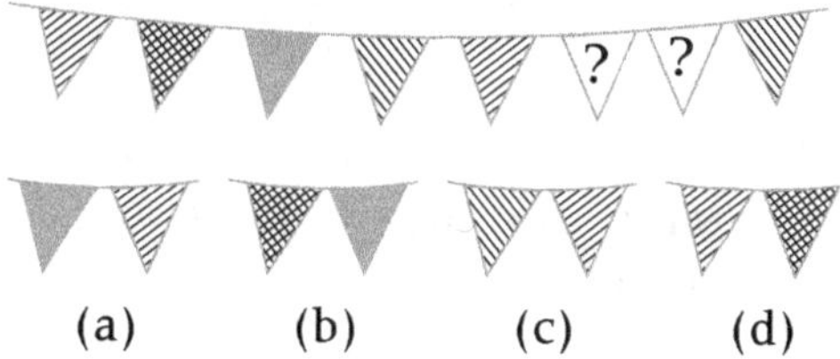

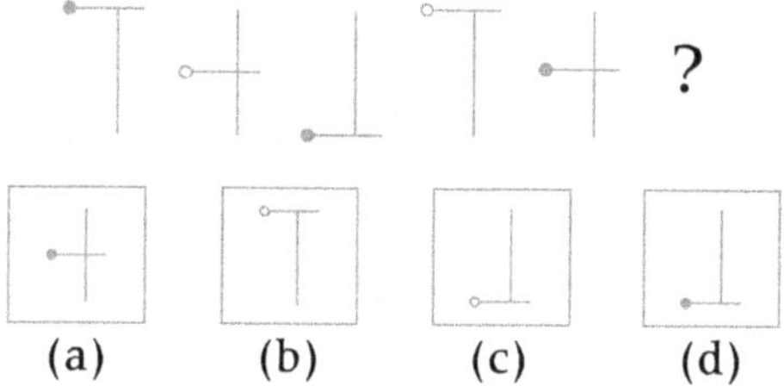

(a) (b) (c) (d)

15. What comes next in the following series?

(a) (b) (c) (d)

16. Which shape is the next in the below series?

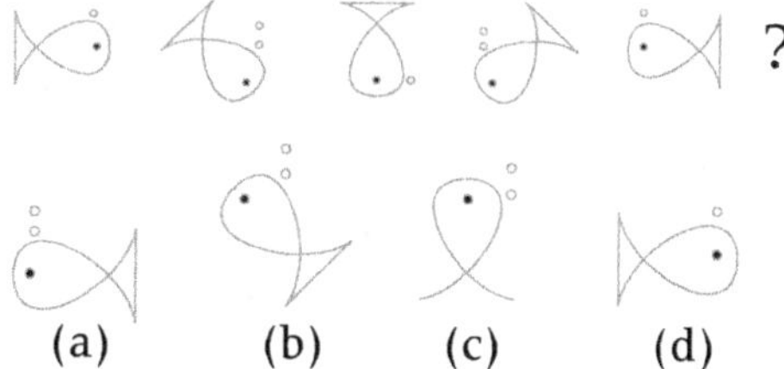

(a) (b) (c) (d)

17. Which figure will come next?

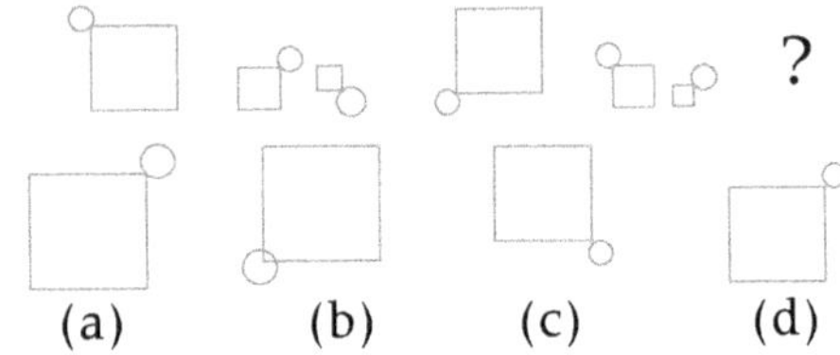

(a)   (b)   (c)   (d)

18.

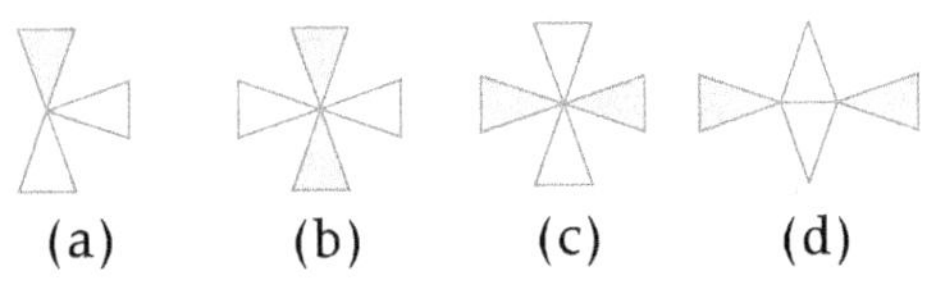

What continues the above sequence?

(a)   (b)   (c)   (d)

19.

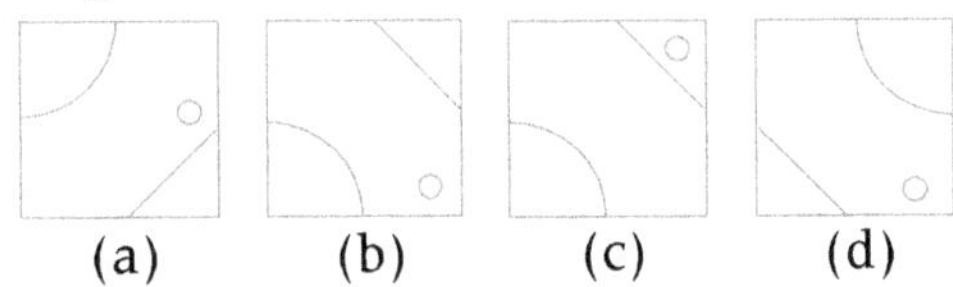   ?

What comes next in the above sequence?

(a)   (b)   (c)   (d)

2 Marks Questions

20. Find the correct alphabet that will replace the question mark(?).

| Z | A | Y | B | X | C | W | ? |

(a) W   (b) D   (c) E   (d) V

21. Observe the pattern on given LEDs and find out the missing number that will be displayed by the LED 6.

LED 1	LED 2	LED 3	LED 4	LED 5	LED 6
5	11	20	26	35	?

(a) 34   (b) 44   (c) 41   (d) 45

22. Observe the pattern given below

Using letters, this pattern can be shown by
(a) XYYXYYXYXY   (b) XYYXYXYYXY
(c) YXYXXYXXYX   (d) XYYYXYYYXY

23. Observe the pattern in the first four figures and calculate the number of dots in the sixth figure.

(a) 15   (b) 27
(c) 28   (d) 21

24. Study the pattern of numbers printed on the following piece of paper. How many numbers will there in Row 10?

Row	Numbers
1	4
2	5 6 7
3	8 9 10 11 12
4	13 14 15 16 17 18 19
5	20

(a) 10   (b) 22
(c) 9   (d) 18

25. Four different clocks are shown below. Observe the changes in each successive clock and find out the next clock.

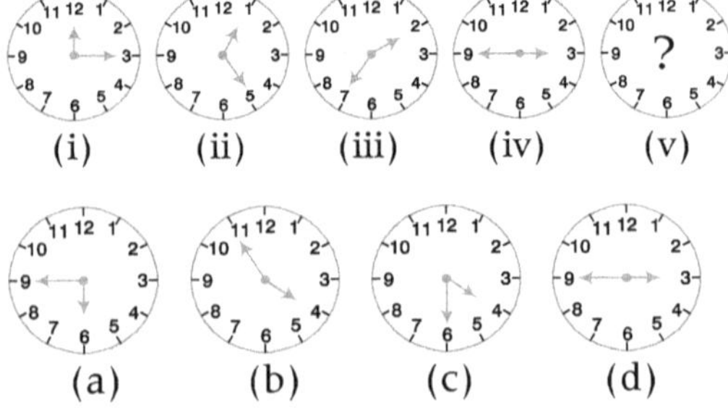

(i)   (ii)   (iii)   (iv)   (v)

(a)   (b)   (c)   (d)

Coding-Decoding

Consider the following example to understand the topic Coding-Decoding.

Some of the sports are coded as below

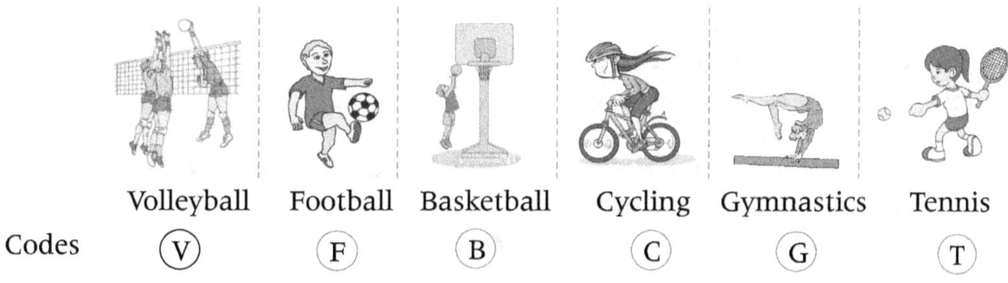

Volleyball	Football	Basketball	Cycling	Gymnastics	Tennis
Codes (V)	(F)	(B)	(C)	(G)	(T)

Now, from the above information, find the code for the SPORTS given below

(F)	(T)	(C)	(V)
Football	Tennis	Cycling	Volleyball

    (a) VCGT   (b) FTCV   (c) CBTF   (d) GTCF

Sol. *(b)* Let us find the code for each given sport.

Football ⟶ (F), Tennis ⟶ (T), Cycling ⟶ (C), Volleyball ⟶ (V)

So, the code for the given SPORTS is 'FTCV'.

Hence, option (b) is correct.

In Coding-Decoding, following types of questions are generally asked

EXAMPLE 1 Rahul asked to Daksh, "If HELLO is coded as OLLEH, then how could you write MAGIC in same code?"

    (a) CIGAM   (b) AMIGC   (c) MGAIC   (d) CMIAG

Sol. *(a)* The pattern is as follows

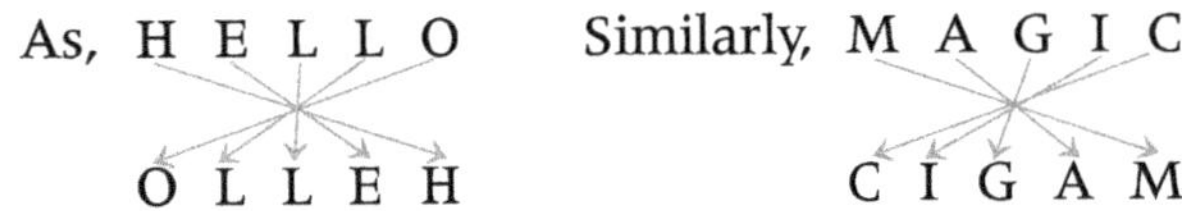

Hence, option (a) is correct.

EXAMPLE 2 If ○ is coded as △, △ is coded as □, □ is coded as □, □ is coded as ⬭ and ⬭ is coded as △, then area of which figure is (side × side)?

    (a)   (b)   (c)   (d)

Sol. (c) We know that, the area of square is (side × side). But here, square is coded as rectangle, so (side × side) is the area of rectangle.

Hence, option (c) is correct.

EXAMPLE 3 In a certain code language, 'it pit sit' means 'I am boy', 'it nit sit' means 'I am girl', which of the following means 'girl'?

    (a) it   (b) pit   (c) sit   (d) nit

Sol. *(d)* We have,

| it | pit | sit | → | I | am | boy |

| it | nit | sit | → | I | am | girl |

Here, 'it' and 'sit' are common in both the messages and 'I' and 'am' are common in both codes. Hence, code for 'girl' will be 'nit'.

Hence option (c) is correct.

EXAMPLE 4 Jack and Flora use the following table, consisting of the letters and their number codes for a coding-decoding game.

Letters	A	C	E	H	I	K	L	P	R	T
Number codes	0	3	1	2	5	8	7	9	6	4

They both make a word 'CAPITAL'. Find the code for this word.

    (a) 3068407   (b) 0375049   (c) 3095407   (d) 9540730

Sol. *(c)* Here, we will obtain the number code for each letter individually by using the given table.

C → 3, A → 0, P → 9, I → 5, T → 4, L → 7

So, the code for the word 'CAPITAL' will be '3095407'.

Hence, option (c) is correct.

⏰ Let's Practice

1 Mark Questions

1. The name of two cities are coded as below

Now, find the code for DELHI.
(a) IDLEH (b) IHLED
(c) EDHLI (d) IHDEL

2. In a certain language, RESULT is coded as SFTVMU. In that language, what will be the code for FIRST?
(a) STFIR (b) EJSTU
(c) GJSTU (d) GJTUV

3. If QVOJTI is written as PUNISH, then how will SFXBSE be written?
(a) RETARD (b) ROTARY
(c) REBUKE (d) REWARD

4. If in a certain code, SPORTS is written as RTSSPO, then how will FLOWER be written in the same code?
(a) WERFLO (b) REWOLF
(c) OLFREW (d) WOELFR

5. If the code of 85349 is 63127, then what will be the code for 6734?
(a) 7512 (b) 5623 (c) 8943 (d) 4512

6. If A = 1, ACE = 9, then ART = ?

(a) 10 (b) 39 (c) 29 (d) 38

7. In a certain code language, if MOTHER is coded as 920631 and LAND is coded as 4758, then NORTH will be coded as

72089 | 57163 | 52106 | 82160
(a) | (b) | (c) | (d)

8. If 836542 is coded for GARDEN, then what does 5436 stand for?
(a) RAGE (b) DEAR
(c) GEAR (d) NEAR

9. If F I N G E R $= 20 - 4 - 8 - 19 - 10 - 22$, then how is G I N G E R coded?
(a) $19 - 8 - 4 - 10 - 19 - 22$
(b) $22 - 20 - 19 - 10 - 4 - 8$
(c) $10 - 19 - 4 - 19 - 8 - 22$
(d) $19 - 4 - 8 - 19 - 10 - 22$

10. Rahul, Sunny and Rohit are the members of a cricket team. The jersey number of Rahul is 60 and of Sunny is 93. Find the jersey number of Rohit.

(a) 68 (b) 70 (c) 90 (d) 72

11. In a certain code, BRING is coded as \$!©@# and ROUND is coded as !%?@ + , then what is the code for BROOD?
(a) ©!%+% (b) \$%?+%
(c) \$!%%+ (d) ©!@@+

12. If 'Jelly' is called 'lotus', 'lotus' is called 'Cake', 'Cake' is called 'sweet' 'sweet' is called 'salt' then which will be the national flower of our country?
    (a) Sweet   (b) Lotus
    (c) Cake   (d) Jellly

13. If Mumbai is called Gujarat, Gujarat is called Kolkata, Kolkata is called Ranchi, Ranchi is called New Delhi and New Delhi is called Patna, then India gate is situated in?
    (a) Kolkata   (b) Ranchi
    (c) Patna   (d) Gujarat

14. If 'Delhi Daredevils' is called 'Sunrisers Hyderabad', 'Sunrisers Hyderabad' is called 'Mumbai Indians', 'Mumbai Indians' is called 'Chennai Super Kings' and 'Chennai Super Kings' is called 'Kolkata Knight Riders', then who won the IPL 2020?
    (a) Chennai Super Kings
    (b) Delhi Daredevils
    (c) Sunrisers Hyderabad
    (d) Kolkata Knight Riders

15. If 'air' means 'speed', 'speed' means 'slow', 'slow' means 'time', 'time' means 'fast' and 'fast' means 'water', then what is the formula of distance?
    (a) Air × Fast
    (b) Slow × Fast
    (c) Water × Time
    (d) Speed × Slow

16. In a certain code language, '123' means 'bright little boy', '145' means 'tall big boy' and '637' means 'beautiful little flower'. Which digit in that language means 'bright'?
    (a) 1   (b) 2
    (c) 3   (d) 4

2 Marks Questions

Directions (Q. Nos. 17 and 18) Following questions are to be answered by replacing the letters with numbers according to the following table.

Letters	A	B	D	H	I	J	R	N	E	T
Numbers	0	1	2	3	4	5	6	7	8	9

17. What is the code for BITE?
    (a) 2469   (b) 1489   (c) 3498   (d) 1498

18. What is the code for ARIHANT?
    (a) 0643089   (b) 0643079
    (c) 9681247   (d) 0581293

19. If '1' is coded as 'S', '5' is coded as '%', '6' is coded as '<<', '3' is coded as '+', '7' is coded as '#' and '4' is coded as '?'. What will be the correct code of the number 435671?
    (a) ?+%<<#S   (b) ?+%S#<<
    (c) ?+<<%#S   (d) S#<<%+?

Directions (Q. Nos. 20 and 21) Study the following information carefully and answer the given questions.

Numbers	0	1	2	3	4	5	6	7	8	9
Codes	A	R	I	H	N	T	B	O	K	S

Conditions
(i) If first number is odd, then it is to be coded as @.
(ii) If last number is even, then it is to be coded as ©.

20. What is the code for 2249?
    (a) ©INS   (b) ©©NS
    (c) IINS   (d) SNI©

21. What is the code for 6012?
    (a) ©IHN   (b) ©ARI
    (c) BAR©   (d) ARI©

Alphabet Test and Words Sequence Test

Alphabet Test

In Alphabet test, we will discuss the following topics.

  (i) Inserting a letter to complete the two words.

 (ii) Finding the word which can or cannot be formed from the letters of the given word.

(iii) Rearranging the letters to form a meaningful word.

(iv) Finding the number of letters from the given sequence of letters according to the question asked.

In 'Alphabet Test', following types of questions are generally asked

EXAMPLE 1 Analyse the following figure and identify the letter that will complete the given two words.

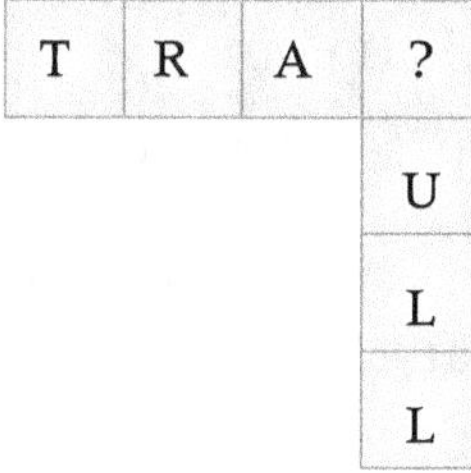

(a) T	(b) P
(c) M	(d) Z

Sol. *(b)* Here, the two words are given, i.e. TRA ? and ? ULL.

Now, if we put 'P' in place of question mark, we get TRAP and PULL.

Hence, option (b) is correct.

EXAMPLE 2 Choose the word which can be formed from the letters of the given word.

CONTRAST

(a) DAM   (b) RAT   (c) TAP   (d) TEN

Sol. *(b)* From the given alternatives, the only word 'RAT' can be formed because all the three letters are present in the word CONTRAST. Hence, option (b) is correct.

EXAMPLE 3 In the question, some letters are given which are numbered as 1, 2, 3, 4 and 5 followed by four alternatives containing combinations of these numbers. Find the combination of numbers so that letters arranged accordingly form a meaningful word.

R T E G A
1 2 3 4 5

(a) 4, 5, 1, 3, 2   (b) 1, 3, 2, 5, 4   (c) 4, 1, 3, 5, 2   (d) 5, 2, 3, 4, 1

Sol. *(c)* Arrange the letters one-by-one according to each option.

Option (a) , 4 5 1 3 2   Option (b), 1 3 2 5 4
            GARET   RETAG
Option (c), 4 1 3 5 2   Option (d), 5 2 3 4 1
         GREAT   ATEGR

Only the word GREAT formed from option (c) is a meaningful word. Hence, option (c) is correct.

EXAMPLE 4 How many meaningful English words can be made with the letters 'ERDU' using each letter only once in each word?

(a) None   (b) One   (c) Two   (d) Three

Sol. *(b)* Only one meaningful word 'RUDE' and can be formed by using the letters of 'ERDU'. Hence, option (b) is correct.

Words Sequence Test

In words sequence test the given words are arranged in a meaningful order or alphabetical order as they appear in dictionary.

In Words sequence test, following types of questions are generally asked.

EXAMPLE 1 Four words are given below. Arrange these words in a correct alphabetical order as they are arranged in dictionary.

1. Clue   2. Round   3. About   4. Dream

(a) 3, 4, 1, 2   (b) 3, 1, 4, 2   (c) 2, 3, 1, 4   (d) 4, 3, 1, 2

Sol. *(b)* As we know that, in a dictionary, the words are arranged according to English alphabetical order, i.e. A, B, C, D, …, Y, Z. Now, the given words can be arranged as

About …… 3,   Clue …… 1,   Dream …… 4,   Round …… 2

So, the correct sequence of words is 3, 1, 4, 2. Hence, option (b) is correct.

⏰ Let's Practice

1 Mark Questions

1. Select a letter from the given alternatives that will end the first word and start the second.

C L O U ⓘ A R K

(a) K   (b) T   (c) G   (d) D

2. Analyse the following figure and choose a letter that will complete both the given words.

R	E	W	?	R	D

			W		
			A		
			R		
			E		

(a) D   (b) A   (c) Z   (d) P

3. Choose the word which can be formed from the letters of given word INSTITUTION.

(a) INSTANT   (b) INTUTION
(c) TREATMENT   (d) NATION

4. Find the word which cannot be formed from the letters of given word UNIVERSITY.

(a) VERY   (b) RUSTY
(c) NEVER   (d) TINY

5. Select the word which can be formed from the letters of given word APOSTROPHE.

(a) TOMB   (b) SHOUT
(c) ORANGE   (d) PHOTO

6. Which word from the given alternatives cannot be formed from the letters of given word TREATMENT?

(a) EAT   (b) ENERGY
(c) TREAT   (d) NEAT

7. Choose the combination of two words, one from each group, which when joined together form a new word.

1	2	3	P	Q	R
Out	Care	Free	Tree	Taker	This

(a) 1P   (b) 2Q   (c) 3R   (d) 2P

8. How many meaningful English words can be made with 'EPRY' using each letter only once in each word?

(a) Two   (b) One   (c) Three   (d) Four

9. If in the word PARAMETERS, the first letter is interchanged with the last letter, the second letter is interchanged with the ninth letter and so on, which letter would come before the letter 'M' in the newly formed word?

(a) A   (b) E   (c) R   (d) P

10. How many P's are there in the following series which are immediately followed by W and immediately preceded by K?

K P C W K P W N K G P W W P H K V
P W Z P

(a) 0   (b) 1   (c) 2   (d) 3

11. The alphabet of English language is written in reverse order, what will be the third letter to the left of eleventh letter from the right?

(a) M   (b) N   (c) O   (d) P

12. How many such pairs of letters are there in the word 'JOURNEY' each of which has as many letters between them in the word (in both forward and backward directions) as they have between them in the English alphabetical order?

(a) None   (b) One   (c) Two   (d) Three

Directions (Q. Nos. 13 and 14) In each of the following questions, find out which of the letter-series follows the given rule.

13. Rule-Number of letters skipped in between the adjacent letters in the series is equal
    (a) SUXA   (b) RVZD
    (c) HKNS   (d) RVZH

14. Rule-Number of letters skipped in between the adjacent letters decreases in order.
    (a) SYDHK   (b) HNSWA
    (c) NSXCH   (d) AGMRV

15. Arrange the following words in alphabetical order.
    1. Heedful   2. Haste   3. Heart
    4. Horse   5. Hiemal
    (a) 2, 3, 1, 5, 4   (b) 2, 1, 3, 5, 4
    (c) 5, 4, 2, 3, 1   (d) 3, 2, 5, 4, 1

16. Which would be a meaningful order of the following?
    1. Consultation   2. Illness
    3. Doctor   4. Treatment
    5. Recovery
    (a) 4, 3, 1, 2, 5   (b) 2, 3, 4, 1, 5
    (c) 2, 3, 1, 4, 5   (d) 4, 1, 5, 3, 2

2 Marks Questions

17. Some letters are given which are numbered 1, 2, 3, 4, 5 and 6. Find the combination of numbers so that the letters are arranged accordingly to form a meaningful word.

    BMRNEU
    1 2 3 4 5 6

    (a) 4, 6, 5, 2, 1, 3   (b) 3, 6, 5, 2, 4, 1
    (c) 4, 6, 2, 1, 5, 3   (d) 6, 5, 2, 4, 1, 3

18. Choose the two words, one from each groups which when joined together form a new word.

1	2	3	P	Q	R
Paper	True	Be	Come	Easy	Pair

    (a) 1P   (b) 2Q   (c) 3R   (d) 3P

19. If a meaningful word be formed using the six letters 'COA I TN' each only once, then the third letter of that is?
    (a) A   (b) I   (c) T   (d) N

20. In the following letter sequence, how many D's are followed by F, but not preceded by E?
    X M N D F P R S T D D F O C E D F B T E D K
    (a) 1   (b) 2   (c) 3   (d) 4

21. How many such pairs of letters are there in the word 'CHANNEL', which has as many letters between them in the word as in the English alphabet?
    (a) None   (b) One   (c) Two   (d) Three

Directions (Q. Nos. 22 and 23) Answer the following questions on the basis of the following sequence of letters.

A B C D E F G H I J K L M
N O P Q R S T U V W X Y Z

22. Which letter is 8th to the right of 10th letter from the left?
    (a) P   (b) T   (c) R   (d) W

23. If 1st and 2nd letters interchange their positions and similarly 3rd and 4th letters, the 5th and 6th letters and so on, which will be 12th letter from the right end?
    (a) P   (b) O   (c) N   (d) Q

Ranking Test

In 'Ranking Test', the rank or position of a person/object either from left or right and top or bottom is determined.

Let us consider the following example to understand the concept of ranking test.

Eight friends are standing in a queue. Leena is fourth from the left end. What is her position from the right end?

(a) 4th   (b) 6th   (c) 5th   (d) 3rd

Sol. According to the question,

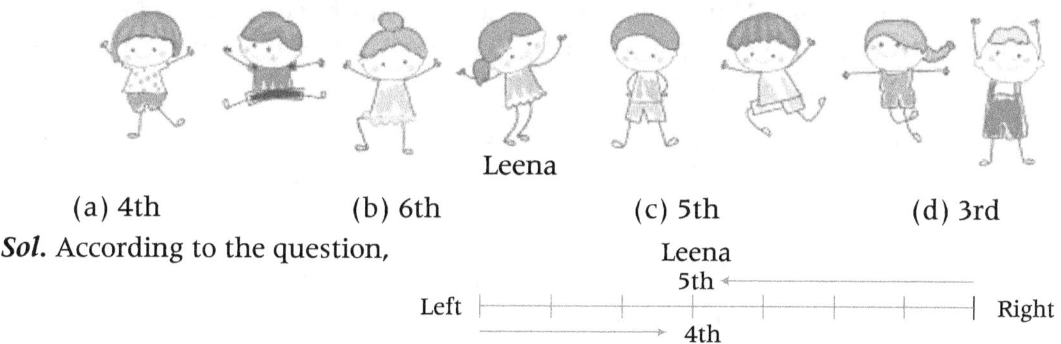

From the above diagram it is clear that, Leena is 5th from the right end.
Hence, option (c) is correct.

In 'Ranking Test', following types of questions are generally asked.

EXAMPLE 1 There are 15 girls in a class. The position of Tripti is 10th from the top. What is her position from the bottom.

(a) 6th   (b) 10th   (c) 8th   (d) 5th

Sol. *(a)* From the given figure, it is clear that, there are 9 girls above the Tripti and $15 - 10 = 5$ girls below the Tripti.

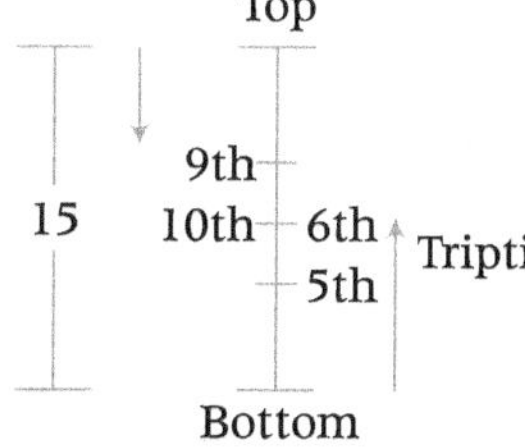

Thus, the rank of Tripti from the bottom $= 5 + 1 = 6$th. Hence, option (a) is correct.

EXAMPLE 2 Pawan is 12th from left and 15th from right end of a row. How many persons are there in the row?

(a) 25

(b) 27

(c) 30

(d) 26

Sol. (d) From the adjoining figure, it is clear that, 11 persons are to the left of Pawan and 14 persons are to the right of Pawan. So, the total number of persons in the row = 11 + Pawan + 14 = 11 + 1 + 14 = 26

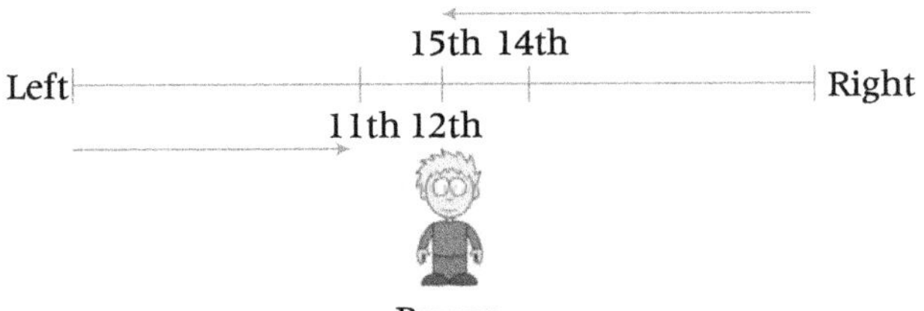

Hence, option (d) is correct.

EXAMPLE 3 Four friends Paul, Tim, Anna and Marie are standing on a weighing machine. While measuring the weights it is come to know that, Tim is heavier than Anna but lighter than Paul. Marie is heavier than Paul. Who is the heaviest?

(a) Paul

(b) Marie

(c) Tim

(d) Anna

Sol. (b) According to the question, Paul > Tim > Anna and Marie > Paul.

[here, we use'>' for heavier than and '<' for lighter than]

Now, we have Marie > Paul > Tim > Anna

Here, Marie is heavier than Paul, Paul is heavier than Tim and Tim is heavier than Anna. Thus, Marie is the heaviest. Hence, option (b) is correct.

⏰ Let's Practice

1 Mark Questions

1. Dinesh is standing on a ladder. He is standing on fourth rung from the bottom. Find the position of Dinesh from the top if there are 8 rungs in the ladder.

(a) 6th   (b) 4th   (c) 3rd   (d) 5th

2. A tree is 12th from both the ends of a row. How many trees are there in the row?

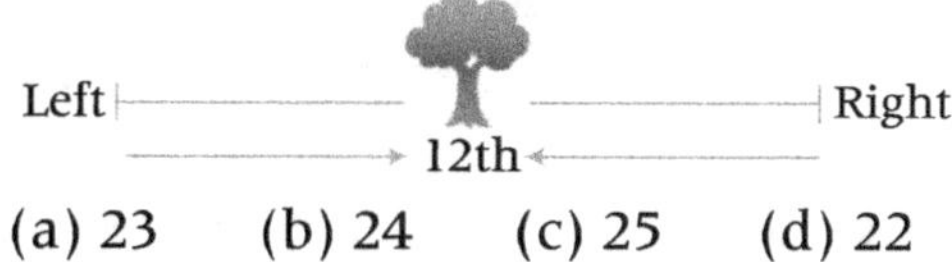

(a) 23   (b) 24   (c) 25   (d) 22

3. Eight friends are standing in a row. Ojas is third from the left. What is his position from the right?

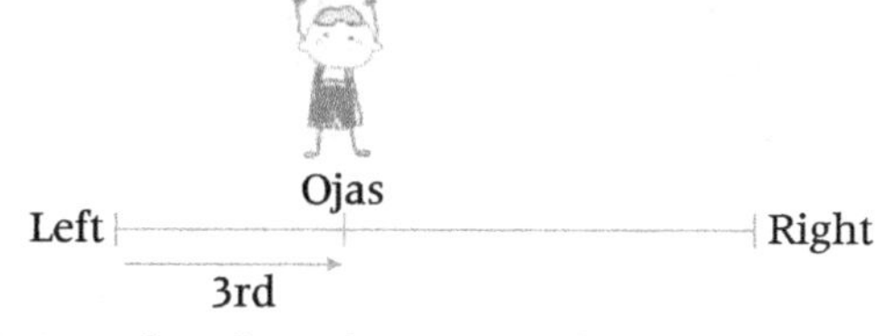

(a) 2nd   (b) 4th   (c) 6th   (d) 11th

4. 55 students participated in an Olympiad competition. Avni got 22nd rank from the top. What is her rank from the bottom?

(a) 33rd   (b) 35th
(c) 36th   (d) 34th

5. Hans arranged his toys in a row. A duck toy ranks sixteenth from the left and forty ninth from the right. How many toys did Hans has?

(a) 64   (b) 65
(c) 63   (d) 66

6. In a queue, John's position from the left is 13th and Joy's position from the right is 20th. If there are 4 boys between them. What is the total number of boys in the line?

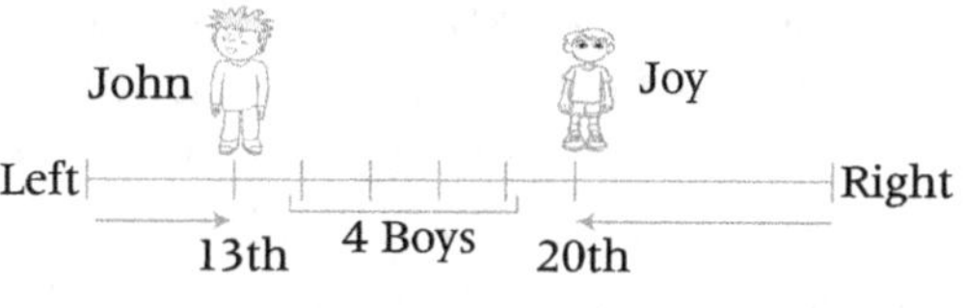

(a) 36   (b) 35
(c) 37   (d) 38

7. Komal is 8 ranks ahead of Pallavi in a class of 40. If Pallavi rank is twenty first from the last, what is Komal rank from the start?

(a) 12th   (b) 20th
(c) 22th   (d) 21th

8. Joy ranks twenty second in a class of 26. Dev is 8 ranks ahead of Joy. What is Dev rank from the last?

(a) 21st   (b) 22nd
(c) 13th   (d) 14th

9. There are 40 chairs in a row. A green colour chair is at 14th position from the front. A red colour chair is four positions behind the green colour chair. Find the position of red colour chair from the back.

(a) 23rd   (b) 21st
(c) 22nd   (d) 25th

10. There are 25 boys in a horizontal row. Sakshat was shifted by three places towards his right side and he occupied the middle position in the row. What was his original position from the left end of the row?

    (a) 15th   (b) 16th   (c) 12th   (d) 10th

11. If in a row, Raju is 10th from left and Mohan is 13th from right and there are four persons in between Raju and Mohan, then find the minimum number of persons in the row.

    (a) 18   (b) 17   (c) 15   (d) 19

12. Gori ranks sixth in a class. Ziba is ninth from the last. If Arjun is sixth after Gori and just in the middle of Gori and Ziba, then how many students are there in the class?

    (a) 26   (b) 27   (c) 25   (d) 28

13. Ankit is senior to David but not to Maya. Anil is junior to David but no one is senior to Joy. Who is the most junior?

    (a) Ankit (b) Joy   (c) David (d) Anil

14. Five boys took part in a race. Beena finished before Tiya but after Rahul. Diksha finished before Jay but after Tiya. Who won the race?

    (a) Diksha   (b) Beena
    (c) Tiya   (d) Rahul

2 Marks Questions

15. 16 members of a family are sitting on a bench to be photographed. Chandu is 7th from the right end. What is his position from the left end?

    (a) 9th   (b) 10th (c) 11th (d) 8th

16. Grace has a chain containing forty six hooks. A hook is twelfth from the top. What will be its position from the bottom?

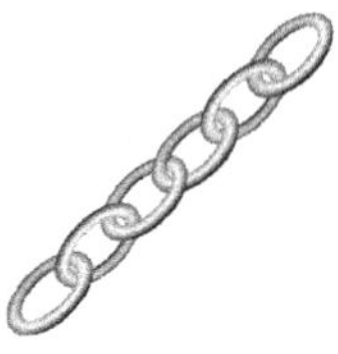

    (a) 34th   (b) 35th
    (c) 37th   (d) 3rd

17. In a row of 28 books, Maths and Reasoning books are ranked 18th and 19th, respectively from the left. What are their ranks from the right?

    (a) 10th and 11th   (b) 11th and 10th
    (c) 12th and 11th   (d) 13th and 14th

18. If Farah finds that she is 8th from the left end in a line of girls and 12th from the right end, then how many girls should be added to the line such that there are 30 girls in the line?

    (a) 11   (b) 10
    (c) 12   (d) 16

19. Divya lives at 14th floor from the top and Anjali lives at 18th floor from the bottom in a building of 40 floors. How many floors are there between Divya and Anjali floors?

    (a) 8   (b) 7   (c) 9   (d) 10

20. In a row of girls, Emily is ninth from the left and Hari is tenth from the right. When they interchange their positions, then Emily will be ninteenth from the left. What will be Hari position from the right?

    (a) 20th   (b) 19th
    (c) 18th   (d) 21st

Direction Sense Test

Main Directions and Sub-directions

The four main directions that we know are

(i) East   (ii) West   (iii) North   (iv) South

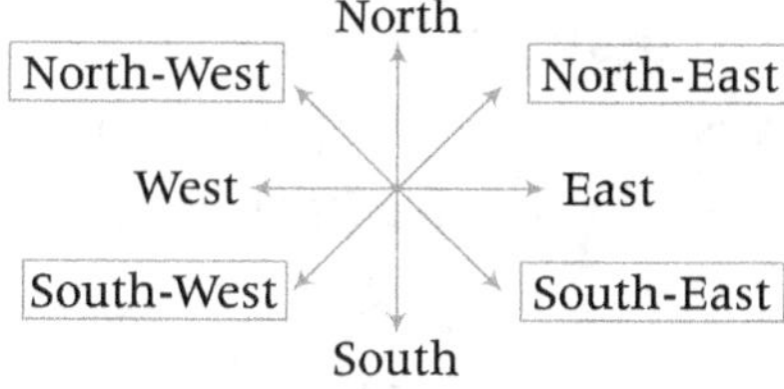

Apart from above four main directions, there are four sub-directions.

(i) North-East (NE)   (ii) North-West (NW)

(iii) South-East (SE)   (iv) South-West (SW)

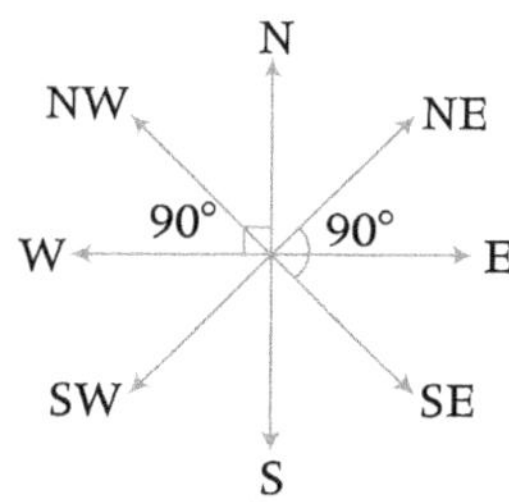

Concept of Angle

The angle between two consecutive main directions is 90° and between two consecutive sub-directions is also 90°.

The angle between a main and adjacent sub-direction is 45°.

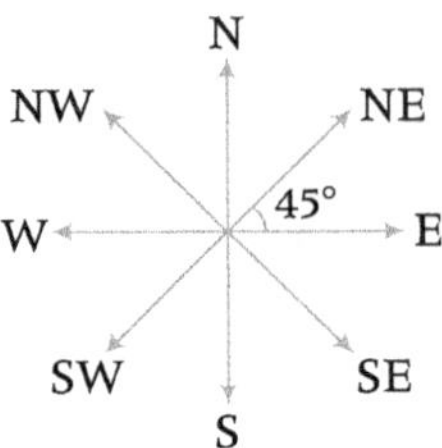

In 'Direction Sense Test', following types of questions are generally asked.

EXAMPLE 1 Four friends John, Leon, Martin and David are standing in four different directions as shown below

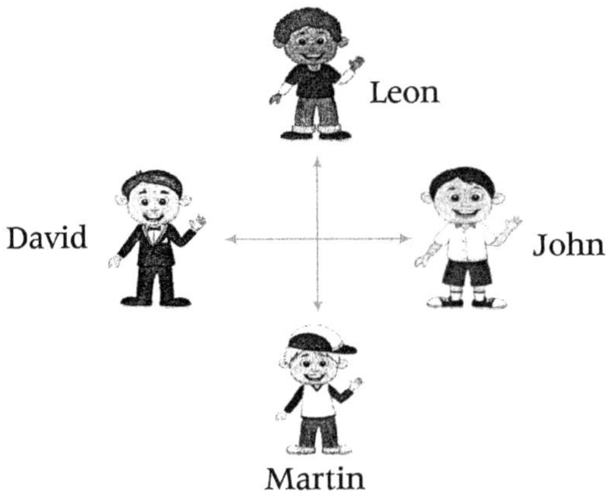

In which direction Leon is standing?

   (a) East   (b) West   (c) North   (d) South

Sol. (c) The positions of John, Leon, Martin and David can be represented as

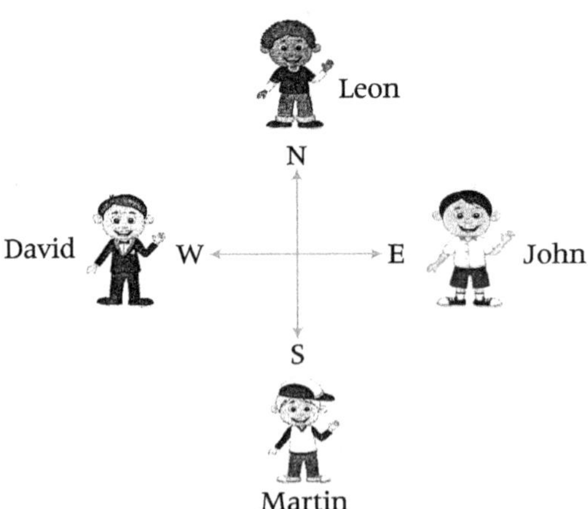

It is clearly shown in the above diagram that, Leon is standing in North direction.
Hence, option (c) is correct.

EXAMPLE 2 Study the following diagram carefully and find out which place is to the North-East of Noddy?

   (a) Cinema   (b) Park   (c) Home   (d) Airport

Sol. *(c)* The position of given places and Noddy can be represented with the help of direction diagram as

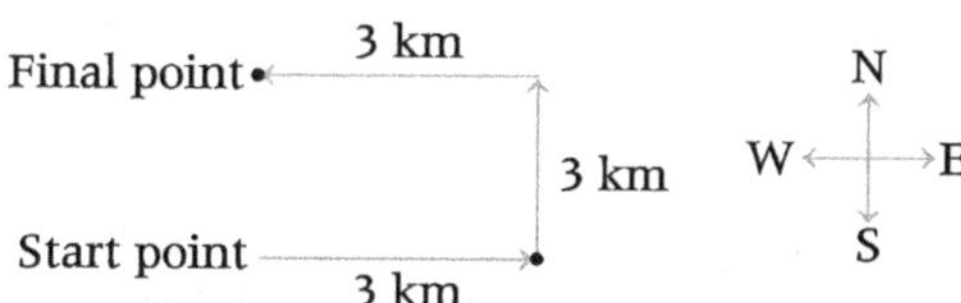

It is clear from the above diagram that, the home is in North-East direction of Noddy. Hence, option (c) is correct.

EXAMPLE 3 After starting from a point, Pihu walks 3 km towards East, then turning to her left she moves 3 km. After this, she again turns left and moves 3 km. In which direction now Pihu is from her starting point?

   (a) North   (b) East   (c) West   (d) South

Sol. *(a)* According to the question,

Thus, Pihu is in North direction from her starting point. Hence, option (a) is correct.

EXAMPLE 4 Pratyaksha starts from her house and travels 4 km in East direction, after that she turns towards left and moves 4km. Finally, she turns towards left and moves 4 km. At what distance she finally stands from her starting point?

   (a) 4 km   (b) 5 km   (c) 12 km   (d) 3 km

Sol. *(a)* According to the question,

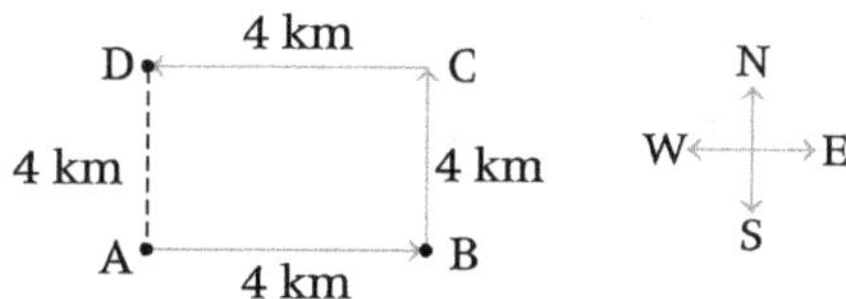

∴ Required distance, AD = CB = 4 km. Hence, option (a) is correct.

⏰ Let's Practice

1 Mark Questions

1. The bus is moving towards the hotel.

   In which direction is the bus moving?
   (a) South   (b) South-East
   (c) South-West   (d) East

2. Jack is facing South-East while James is facing exactly the opposite direction in which Jack is facing. Find the direction in which James is facing.
   (a) South   (b) South-East
   (c) North-West   (d) East

3. Study the following diagram carefully and find in which direction the garden is situated from Marie's present position.

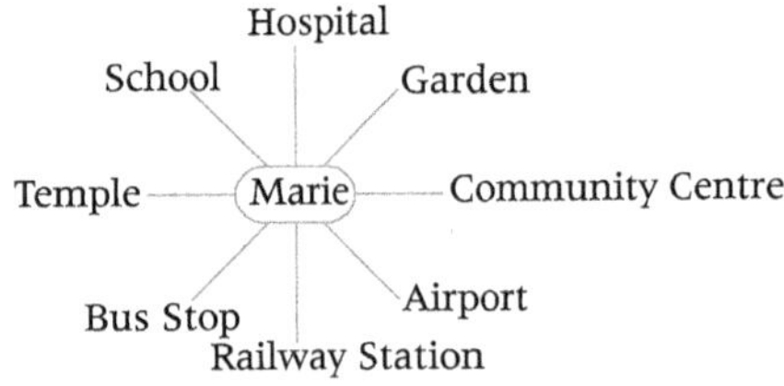

   (a) North   (b) North-West
   (c) South   (d) North-East

4. Edward is walking around this track. In which direction Edward will be moving, if he turns to his left?

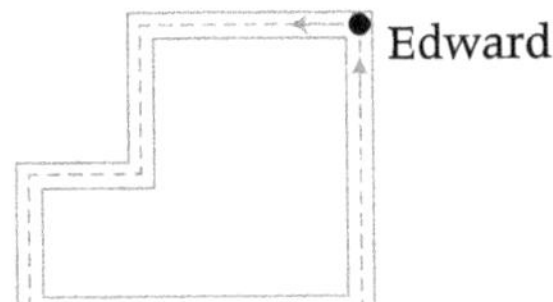

   (a) East   (b) West
   (c) North   (d) South

5. Adam is at point A. He wants to go at point B. So, in which direction will he have to move to reach at point B?

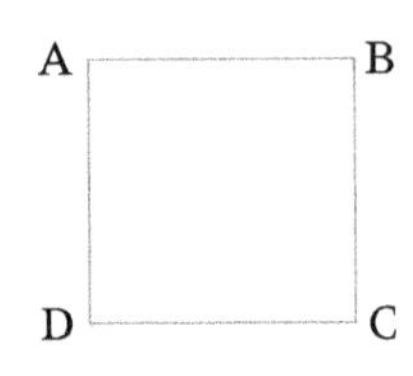

   (a) East   (b) West
   (c) North   (d) South

6. John is moving towards North. He takes right turn. After this, he takes another right turn. In which direction, he is moving now?
   (a) North   (b) East
   (c) West   (d) South

7. I am facing the school now. If I make 90° turn to the right I will be facing

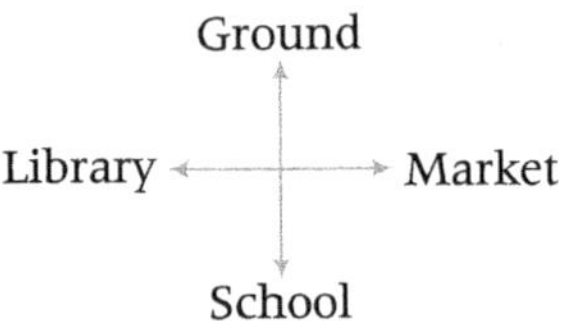

   (a) Ground   (b) Library
   (c) School   (d) Market

8. Paul was facing the airport at the beginning. He turned anti-clockwise to face the West. What angle did he turn through?

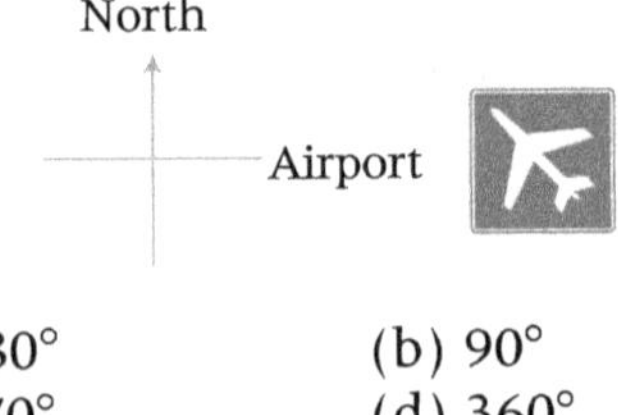

   (a) 180°   (b) 90°
   (c) 270°   (d) 360°

9. Study the following diagram carefully and answer the question given below

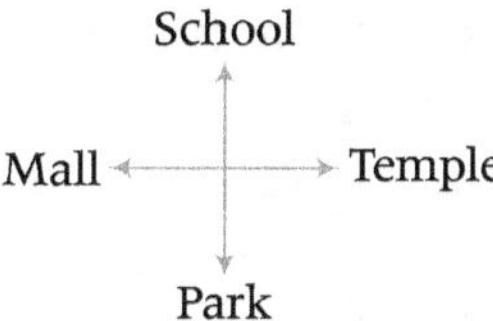

If the boy is facing park and turns 90° in anti-clockwise direction, then which place is he facing now?
(a) School   (b) Temple
(c) Mall   (d) Park

10. After starting from a point, a man walks 4 km towards West, then turning to his right he moves 4 km. After this, he again turns right and moves 4 km. Which choice given below indicates the correct direction in which he is from his starting point?
(a) North   (b) East
(c) South   (d) West

11. If South-East becomes North, North-East becomes West and so on. What will West become?
(a) North-East   (b) North-West
(c) South-East   (d) South-West

12. In the given clock, if the minute hand rotates 270° anti-clockwise, then in which direction will it point?

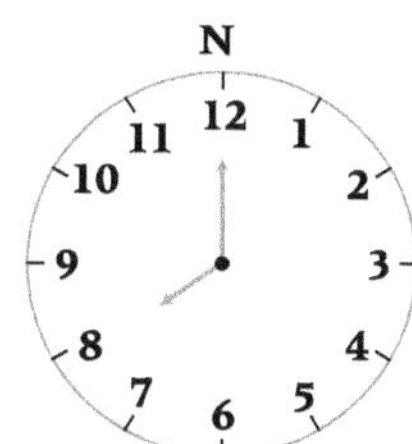

(a) North-East   (b) South-East
(c) East   (d) North-West

13. Arohi moves towards the East and then takes a left turn. After covering some distance in that direction she takes a right turn and finally, takes another right turn. In which direction she is facing now?
(a) East   (b) West
(c) North   (d) South

14. It is 6 : 15 in a clock. If the hour hand points West, in which direction the minute hand is?
(a) East   (b) West
(c) North   (d) South

15. A man turns his right thrice at an angle of 90° and then turns left at the angle of 90°. In how many rounds of such actions will he be in the original direction?
(a) 1   (b) 2   (c) 3   (d) 4

16. The picture shows a toy train on the track. The train starts from the position as shown and goes one-fourth of the way around the track in clockwise direction. It then stops.

Which point is closest to the train where it stops?

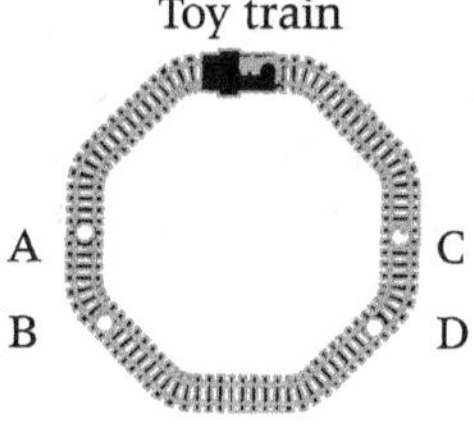

(a) A   (b) B   (c) C   (d) D

17. Ankit started walking towards North. After walking 30 m, he turned towards left and walked 40 m. Then, he turned left and walked 30 m. He again turned left and walked 50 m.

How far is he from his original position?

(a) 50 m   (b) 40 m
(c) 30 m   (d) None of these

2 Marks Questions

18. If P exchanges his position with R and S exchanges his position with Q, then the direction of R with respect to Q is

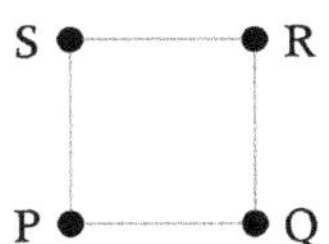

(a) North   (b) East
(c) South   (d) West

19. Study the following map carefully and find out which point is North-West of point O.

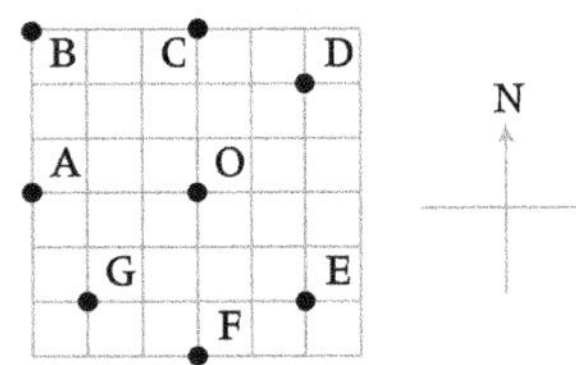

(a) D   (b) G   (c) E   (d) B

20. On the map, each side of square grid represents 1 kilometre. How much farther does Hina live from bus stand than Remo lives from the post office (considering the shortest distance)?

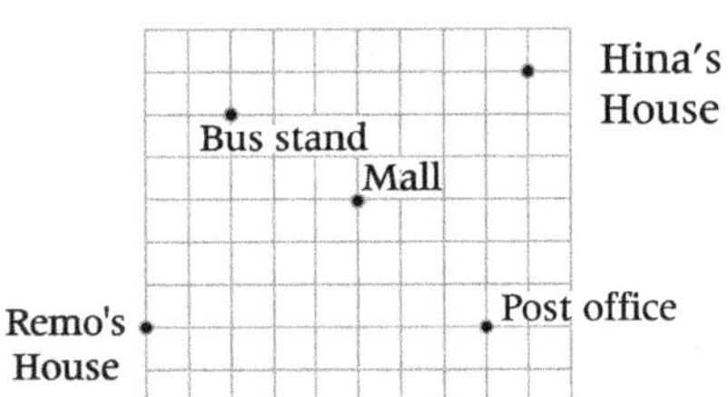

(a) Hina lives 1 km, farther than Remo.
(b) Remo lives 1 km, farther than Hina.

(c) Both are at the same distance.
(d) Cannot be determined

21. Jost is facing the playground. When he turns 2 right angles clockwise, then which place is he facing now?

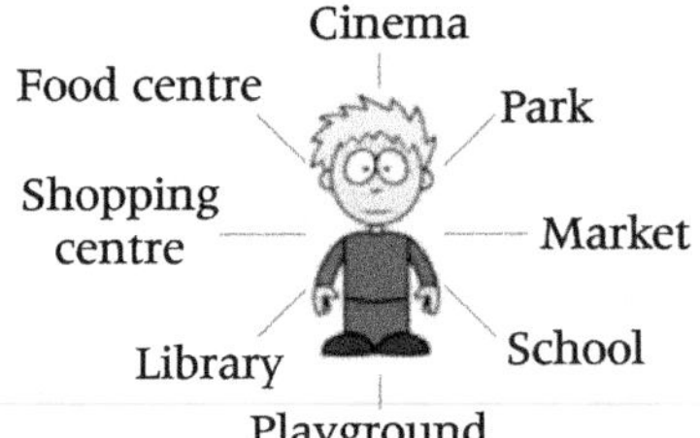

(a) Park   (b) Library
(c) Market   (d) Cinema

22. Pihu now faces North. She made a $\frac{1}{4}$ clockwise turn first followed by a $\frac{3}{4}$ anti-clockwise turn. In what direction was she facing in the end?

(a) North   (b) East
(c) South   (d) South-East

23. Shruti goes to 5 km in the North from her school. Now, turning to the left, she goes to 10 km and again turn to left and goes to 5 km. How far she is from her school and in which direction?

(a) 10 km, South   (b) 10 km, North
(c) 10 km, West   (d) 10 km, East

24. Study the diagram. If a person starts walking from point X and wants to reach point Y, in how many directions will that person have to walk?

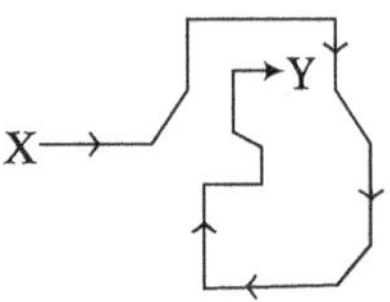

(a) 4   (b) 8   (c) 14   (d) 10

Chapter 08

Mathematical Operations

'Mathematical operations' are basically the simplification of an expression containing numbers and different mathematical symbols. To solve such questions we need to follow the VBODMAS rule for simplification of Mathematical operations.

V	B	O	D	M	A	S
Vinculum	Brackets	Of	Division	Multiplication	Addition	Subtraction
'−' or 'bar'	() {} []	×	÷	×	+	−
Do First						Do Last

EXAMPLE 1 If '×' means '−', '÷' means '+', '+' means '×', then $18 \times 5 \div 5 + 6$ is equal to

    (a) 58   (b) 49   (c) 43   (d) 33

Sol. (c) Change of symbols according to the question,

$$? = 18 \times 5 \div 5 + 6$$
$$\downarrow \quad \downarrow \quad \downarrow$$
$$- \quad + \quad \times$$
$$? = 18 - 5 + 5 \times 6 \qquad \text{(using VBODMAS rule)}$$
$$? = 18 - 5 + 30 \quad \Rightarrow \quad ? = 48 - 5 = 43$$

Hence, option (c) is correct.

EXAMPLE 2 Select the correct set of mathematical operations.

$$21 \_ 9 \_ 13 \_ 7 = 195$$

    (a) ×, −, ÷   (b) +, ÷, −   (c) +, −, ÷   (d) ×, +, −

Sol. (d) From option (d), we get,

$$21 \times 9 + 13 - 7 = 195$$

On applying VBODMAS,
$$189 + 13 - 7 = 195$$
$$202 - 7 = 195 \quad \Rightarrow \quad 195 = 195$$

Hence, option (d) is correct.

⏰ Let's Practice

1 Mark Questions

1. If '+' means '÷', '÷' means '−', '−' means '×' and '×' means '+' then
   $12 + 6 ÷ 3 − 2 × 8 = ?$
   (a) −2   (b) 4
   (c) 2   (d) 8

2. If '×' stand for '+', ÷ stands for '−', '−' stands for '×' and '+' stands for '÷', then find the value of following equation.
   $$54 ÷ 16 − 3 × 6 + 2 = ?$$
   (a) 9   (b) 12
   (c) 8   (d) 15

3. If '×' means subtraction, '+' means multiplication and '−' means addition, then find the value of following equation.
   $12 + (3 × 1) + 4 − 1 = ?$
   (a) 98   (b) 75
   (c) 85   (d) 97

4. If '−' denotes addition, '+' denotes subtraction, '×' denotes division and ÷ denotes multiplication, then
   $7 − 10 × 5 ÷ 6 + 4 = ?$
   (a) 3   (b) 12
   (c) 15   (d) 9

5. If '+' means 'minus', '−', means 'multiply', '÷' means 'plus' and '×' means 'divide', then
   $10 × 5 ÷ 3 − 2 + 3 = ?$
   (a) 5   (b) $\dfrac{53}{3}$
   (c) 21   (d) 36

6. If '÷' means addition and '×' means subtraction, then
   $(15 × 9) ÷ (12 × 4) × (4 ÷ 4)$ is equal to
   (a) 96   (b) 6
   (c) 3/128   (d) 143/8

7. If A means '+', B means '−', C means '×' and D means ÷, then
   $18 \ C \ 14 \ A \ 6 \ B \ 16 \ D \ 4 = ?$
   (a) 254   (b) 238
   (c) 188   (d) 258

8. If A means '×', B means '÷', C means '−' and D means '+', then
   $4 \ D \ 16 \ A \ 5 \ B \ 8 \ C \ 5 = ?$
   (a) 9   (b) 16
   (c) 13   (d) 7.5

9. If A means '−', B means '÷', C means '+' and D means '×', then
   $15 \ B \ 3 \ C \ 24 \ A \ 12 \ D \ 2 = ?$
   (a) 3   (b) 5
   (c) 7   (d) 9

10. $2 + 6 + 9 = 926, \ 1 + 8 + 2 = 218,$
    $4 + 3 + 1 = ?$
    (a) 314   (b) 341
    (c) 143   (d) 431

11. $7 − 4 − 1 = 714, \ 9 − 2 − 3 = 932,$
    $8 − 0 − 4 = ?$
    (a) 804   (b) 840
    (c) 408   (d) 480

12. $4 × 6 × 2 = 351, \ 3 × 9 × 8 = 287,$
    $9 × 5 × 6 = ?$
    (a) 270   (b) 845
    (c) 596   (d) 659

13. $5 \times 3 \times 9 = 395$, $9 \times 7 \times 5 = 759$,

    $7 \times 6 \times 4 = ?$
    (a) 676   (b) 476
    (c) 647   (d) 764

14. $4 \times 6 \times 9 = 694$, $5 \times 3 \times 2 = 325$,

    $7 \times 8 \times 2 = ?$
    (a) 729   (b) 872
    (c) 827   (d) 279

15. If $4 - 4 = 16$, $6 - 6 = 36$, $2 - 2 = 4$,

    $5 - 5 = ?$
    (a) 26   (b) 20
    (c) 25   (d) 24

2 Marks Questions

16. Select the correct set of mathematical operations.

    $64 \_ 4 \_ 5 \_ 8 = 88$
    (a) $\times, -, \div$ (b) $+, \div, -$
    (c) $+, -, \div$ (d) $\div, \times, +$

17. Choose the appropriate combination of signs to solve.

    $32 * 16 * 2 * 24$
    (a) $= - \div$ (b) $- \div =$
    (c) $\div - =$ (d) $\div = -$

18. In the following question, by using which mathematical operations will the expression become correct?

    70 ? 10 ? 20 ? 30 ? 8
    (a) $\div, +, =$ and $\times$ (b) $\times, \div, >$ and $\times$
    (c) $\div, \times, <$ and $\times$ (d) $\div, \times, <$ and $+$

19. If 'M' means '$\div$', 'R' means '$+$', 'T' means '$-$' and 'K' means '$\times$', then what will be the value of the following expression?

    40 R 32 K 10 M 20 T 16 = ?
    (a) 85   (b) 40   (c) 90   (d) 95

20. If 'A' stands for '$+$', 'B' stands for '$-$', 'C' stands for '$\times$', then what is the value of (20 C 8) A (8 C 8) B 12?
    (a) 218   (b) 215
    (c) 212   (d) 220

21. Which one of the four interchanges in signs and numbers would make the given equation correct?

    $3 + 5 - 2 = 4$
    (a) $+$ and $-$, 2 and 3
    (b) $+$ and $-$, 2 and 5
    (c) $+$ and $-$, 3 and 5
    (d) $-$ and $+$, 2 and 4

Inserting the Missing Character

'Inserting the Missing Character' means filling up the letter or number in the blank space given in a diagram.

In Inserting the Missing Character, following types of questions are generally asked.

EXAMPLE 1 Kate draws a number matrix as shown below in which a number is missing. Observe the pattern carefully and find the missing number.

7	2	14
3	4	12
5	9	

    (a) 15   (b) 45   (c) 25   (d) 35

Sol. (b) Here, in each row, the numbers in first and second blocks are multiplied to the get the number in third block.

In row I, $7 \times 2 = 14$ and in row II, $3 \times 4 = 12$. Similarly, in row III, $5 \times 9 = 45$

So, the missing number is 45. Hence, option (b) is correct.

EXAMPLE 2 Some alphabets are written in the following matrix. Observe the pattern and find out the missing alphabet.

A	D	H
F	I	M
K	N	

    (a) P   (b) Q   (c) R   (d) T

Sol. (c) Here, the letters in second and third rows are five steps ahead of those in the first and second rows, respectively.

i.e. $A \xrightarrow{+5} F \xrightarrow{+5} K, \quad D \xrightarrow{+5} I \xrightarrow{+5} N, \quad H \xrightarrow{+5} M \xrightarrow{+5} R$

So, R is the missing alphabet. Hence, option (c) is correct.

EXAMPLE 3 Choose the pair of a number and letter that will replace the question mark (?).

2P	6R	12Q
3R	1Q	3P
8Q		24R

(a) 2P   (b) 3Q   (c) 4P   (d) 3P

Sol. (d) Here, in each row and column, letters P,Q and R must appear once.

So, the missing letter is P. Also, the numbers follow below pattern rowwise,

In row I, $2 \times 6 = 12$

In row II, $3 \times 1 = 3$

In row III, $8 \times ? = 24$

$\Rightarrow$ $? = \dfrac{24}{8} = 3$

So, the missing pair will be 3P.
Hence, option (d) is correct.

EXAMPLE 4 Find the value of X and Y respectively, if each number is the sum of the two numbers directly below it.

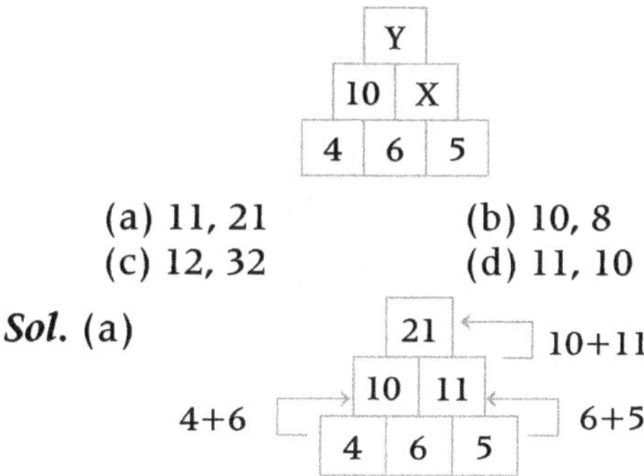

(a) 11, 21   (b) 10, 8
(c) 12, 32   (d) 11, 10

Sol. (a)

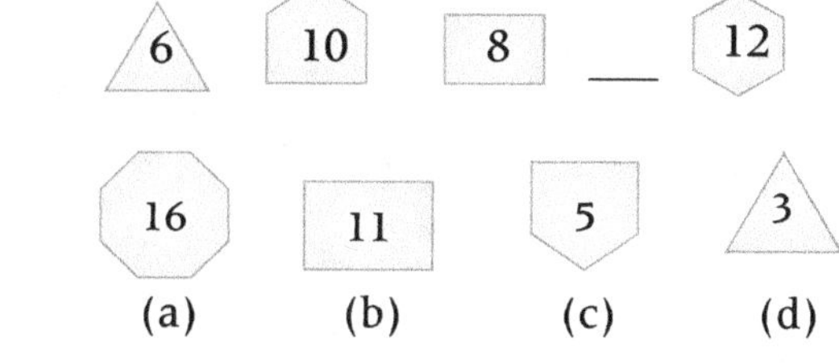

$\therefore$ X = 11 and Y = 21.
Hence, option (a) is correct.

EXAMPLE 5 Find the number which will come in place of question mark in the multiplication table given below.

X	5	6	7
		36	42
5	25	?	

(a) 30   (b) 40
(c) 50   (d) 35

Sol. (a)

X	5	6	7
6	30	36	42
5	25	30	35

$\therefore$ $? = 30$

Hence, option (a) is correct.

EXAMPLE 6 .... will replace the question mark (?) to complete the given pattern.

6	10	8	__	12

16	11	5	3
(a)	(b)	(c)	(d)

Sol. (a) As, $\triangle$ = 3 sides

$\Rightarrow 3 \times 2 = 6$

and $\square$ = 5 sides

$\Rightarrow 5 \times 2 = 10$

Similarly, $\hexagon$ = 8 sides

$\therefore$ $8 \times 2 = 16$

Hence, option (a) is correct.

⏰ Let's Practice

1 Mark Questions

Directions (Q. Nos. 1-11) In each of the following questions find the number/letter that will replace the question mark(?).

1.

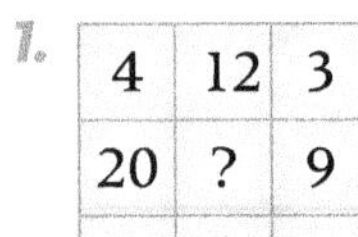

4	12	3
20	?	9
5	15	3

(a) 200   (b) 180   (c) 120   (d) 29

2.

8	6	2
20	7	9
2	9	11
30	?	22

(a) 22   (b) 35   (c) 20   (d) 18

3.

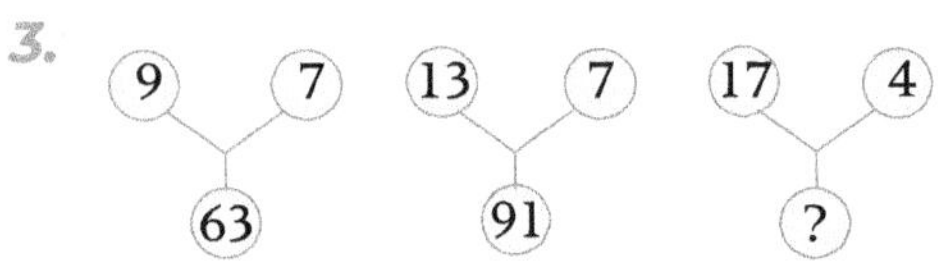

(a) 21   (b) 85
(c) 41   (d) 68

4.

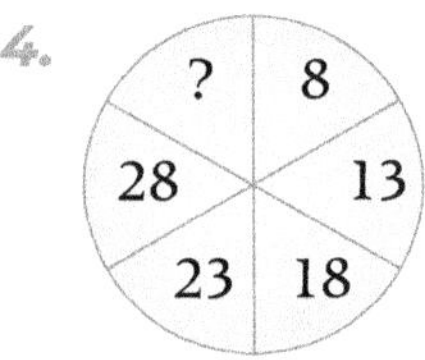

(a) 38   (b) 30
(c) 32   (d) 33

5.

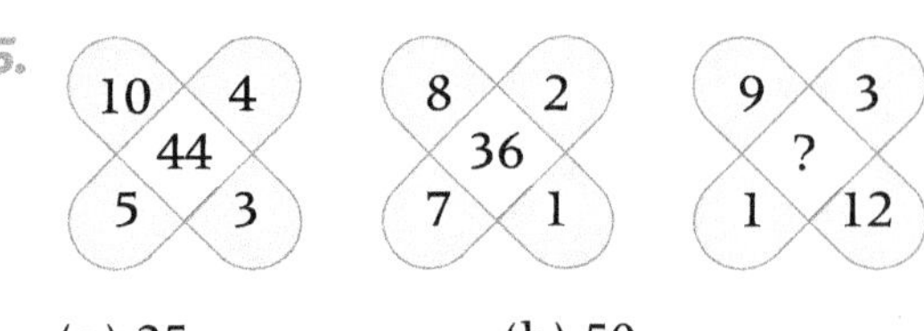

(a) 25   (b) 50
(c) 42   (d) 52

6.

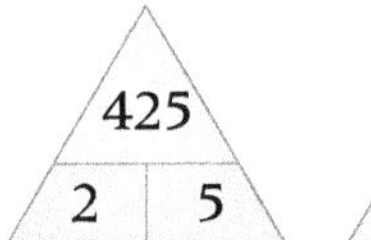

(a) 189   (b) 168
(c) 389   (d) 981

7.

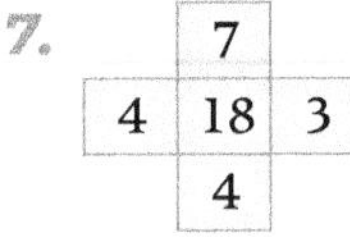

(a) 28   (b) 46
(c) 32   (d) 59

8.

6	52	4
7	?	1
4	97	9

(a) 64   (b) 50
(c) 48   (d) 90

9.

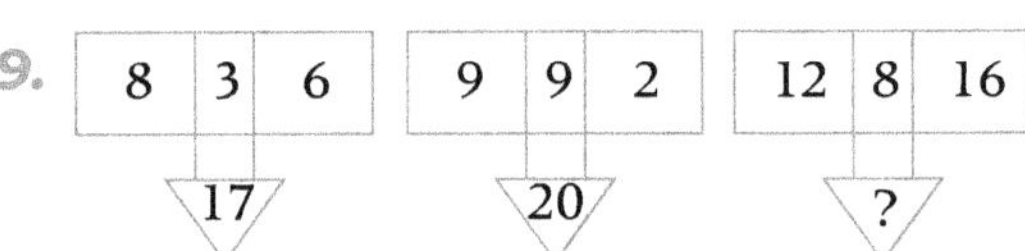

(a) 36   (b) 41
(c) 47   (d) 49

10.

B	D	F
D	F	H
F	H	?

(a) K   (b) I
(c) J   (d) G

11.

	V	A	
S			D
?			G
	M	J	

(a) P   (b) N
(c) O   (d) Q

12. Which letter will replace the question mark(?) ?

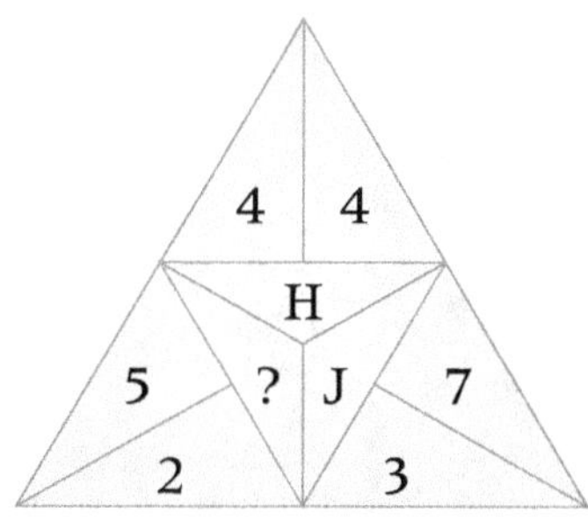

(a) G   (b) I
(c) C   (d) B

13. Find the value of P and Q respectively, if each number is the sum of the two numbers directly below it.

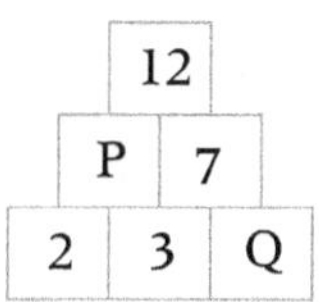

(a) 5, 4   (b) 6, 7
(c) 4, 2   (d) 5, 6

14. Find the number which will come in place of question mark (?) in the multiplication table below.

X	6	4	8
		12	24
4	24	?	

(a) 3   (b) 2
(c) 8   (d) 16

15. _______ will replace question mark (?) to complete the given pattern.

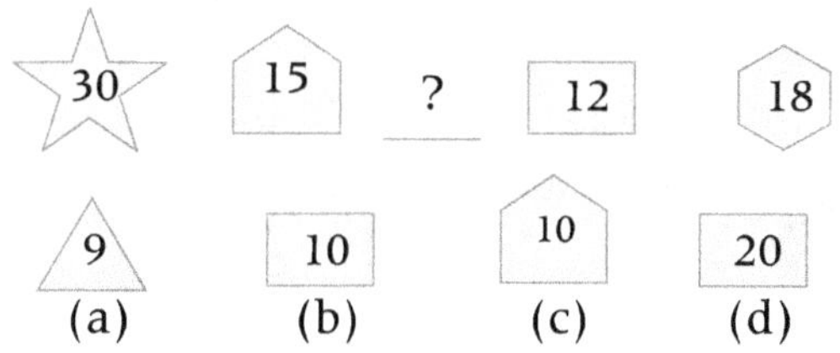

(a)   (b)   (c)   (d)

2 Marks Questions

16. Identify the number which will replace the question mark (?).

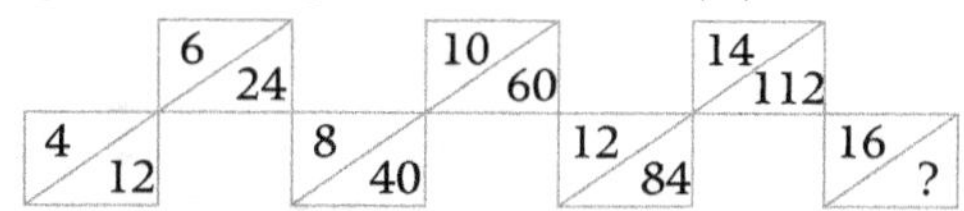

(a) 160   (b) 128   (c) 112   (d) 144

17. Find the missing character which will replace the question mark(?).

3	H16	5
2	K22	9
4	?	1

(a) F12   (b) E10
(c) C9   (d) I18

18. Find the pair of a number and letter which replace the question mark (?) in the following grid.

2C	7A	8B
12A	63B	?
6B	9C	4A

(a) 36C   (b) 12B   (c) 38A   (d) 32C

19. Find the value of P and Q respectively, if each number is the sum of the two numbers directly below it.

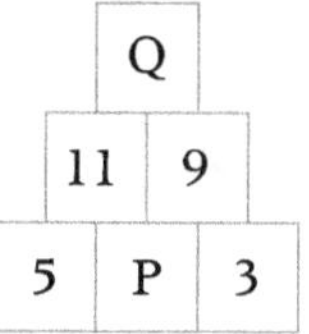

(a) 6, 22   (b) 6, 20   (c) 7, 9   (d) 8, 20

20. Find the number which will come in place of question mark in the multiplication table below.

X	10	8	12
?		64	
4	40		48

(a) 8   (b) 80   (c) 32   (d) 48

Hidden Figures

'Hidden Figures' can be understood with the help of the following example.

David draws four different pictures and asks Joy to find out the figure in which the figure (X) is hidden.

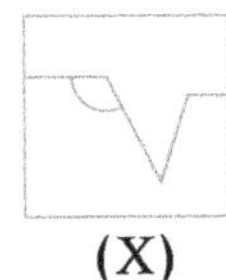 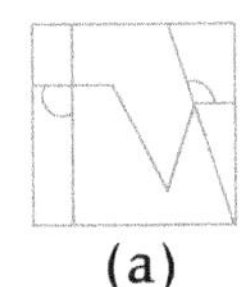 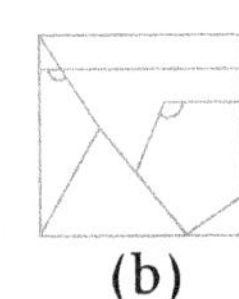  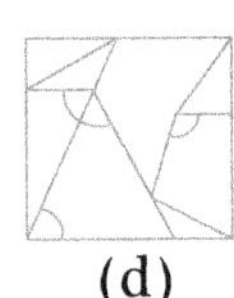

   (X)   (a)   (b)   (c)   (d)

Sol. *(d)* Given figure (X) is hidden in option (d) figure as shown in given figure, hence option (d) is correct.

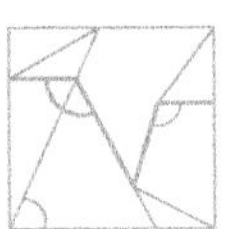

In 'Hidden Figures', following types of questions are generally asked.

EXAMPLE 1 Amongst the given alternatives choose the shape which is hidden in the given figure (X)?

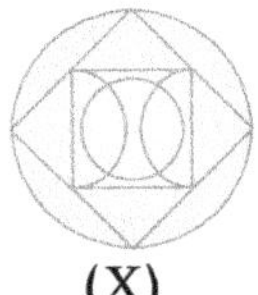 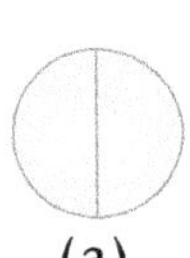   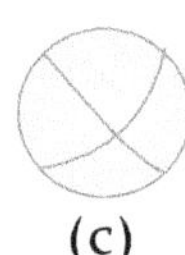   

   (X)   (a)   (b)   (c)   (d)

Sol. *(b)* The option figure (b) is hidden in the given figure (X) as shown in adjoining figure. Hence, option (b) is correct.

EXAMPLE 2 A teacher draws four different pictures on blackboard. He asks Mike to find out the figure in which the figure (X) is hidden?

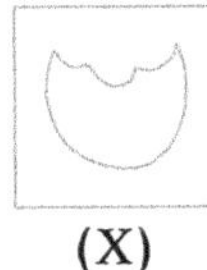    

   (X)   (a)   (b)   (c)   (d)

Sol. *(d)* The given figure (X) is hidden in option figure (d) as shown in adjacent figure. Hence, option (d) is correct.

⏰ Let's Practice

1 Mark Questions

1. An alphabet is given below in figure (X).
Choose the figure from the alternatives in which the given alphabet is hidden.

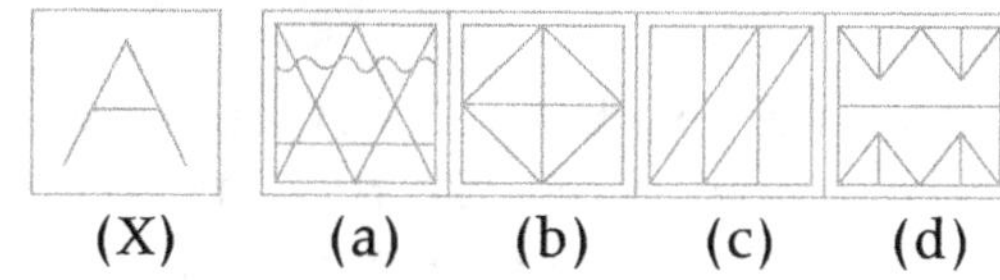

(X)   (a)   (b)   (c)   (d)

2. In which option figure, is the shape (X) hidden?

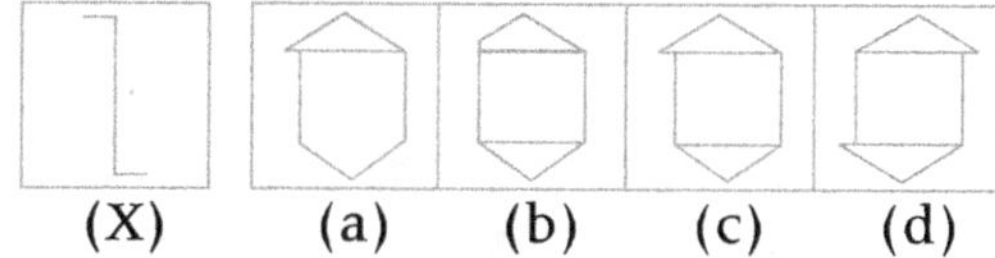

(X)   (a)   (b)   (c)   (d)

3. Samy draws four different pictures. He asks Sandy to find out the figure in which the figure (X) is hidden?

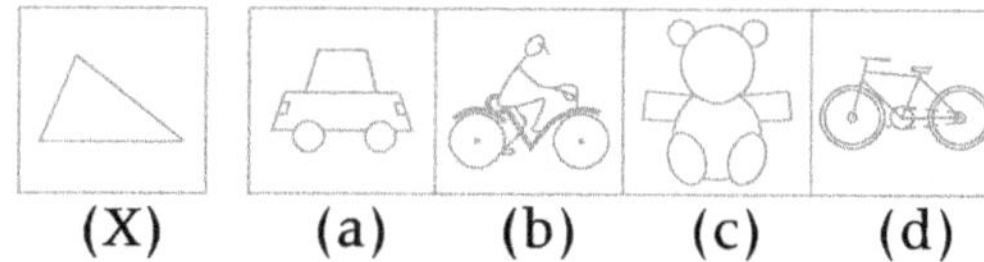

(X)   (a)   (b)   (c)   (d)

4. In which larger shape, is the smaller shape (X) hidden?

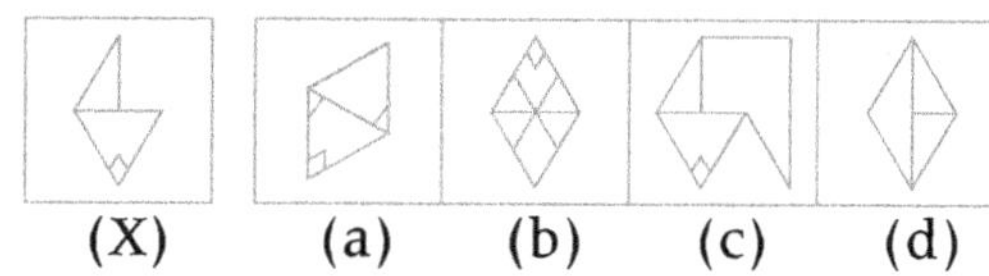

(X)   (a)   (b)   (c)   (d)

5. An alphabet is given in figure (X). Choose the figure from the alternatives in which the given figure (X) is hidden.

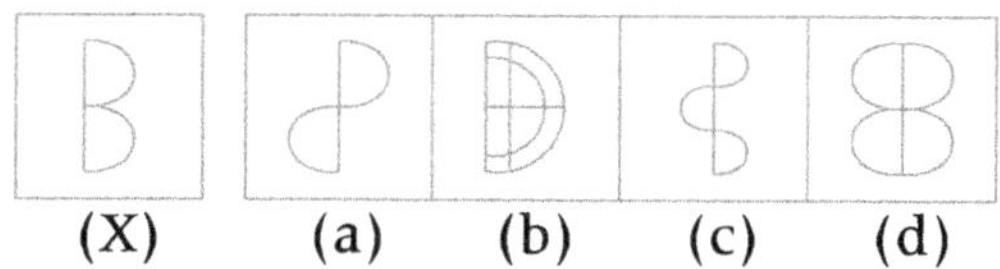

(X)   (a)   (b)   (c)   (d)

6. Paul is playing with four toys. At the time of playing, he broke a part of one toy. Find the toy from which the below part (X) is broken.

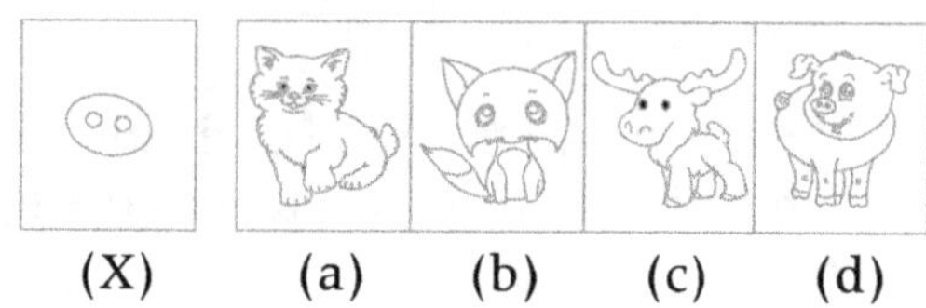

(X)   (a)   (b)   (c)   (d)

7. Find out the alternate figure which contains figure (X) as its part.

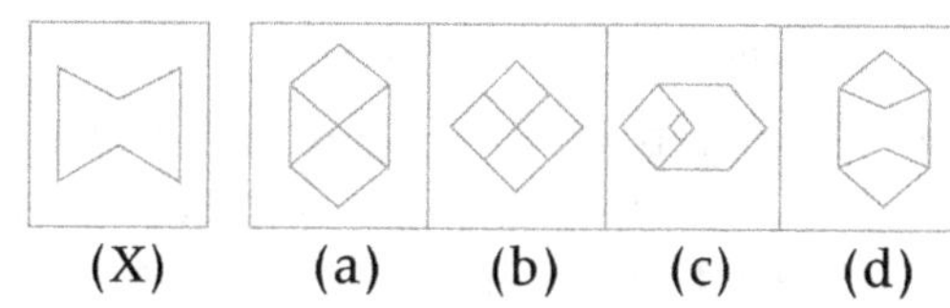

(X)   (a)   (b)   (c)   (d)

8. Liza draws the following figures for her brother Bryan. Help Bryan to find out the figure in which the smaller figure (X) is hidden.

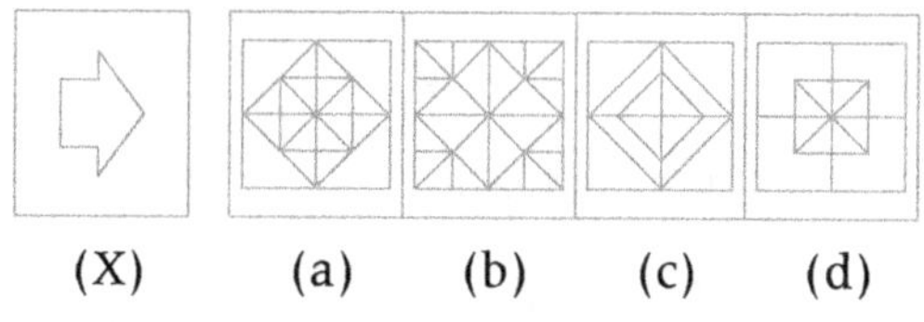

(X)   (a)   (b)   (c)   (d)

9. Choose the figure from the given alternatives which is exactly embedded in figure (X).

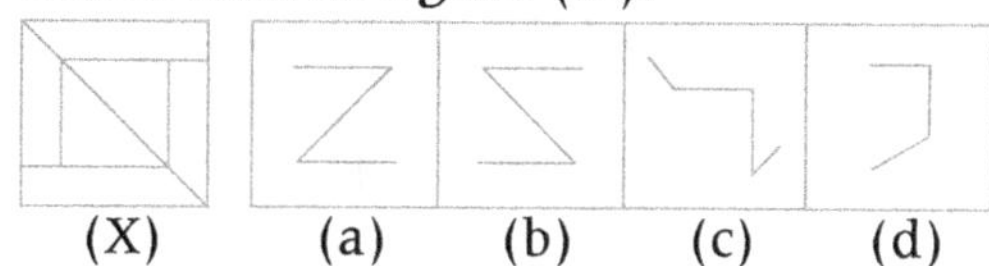

(X)   (a)   (b)   (c)   (d)

10. Amongst the given alternatives, choose the figure which is hidden in the given figure (X).

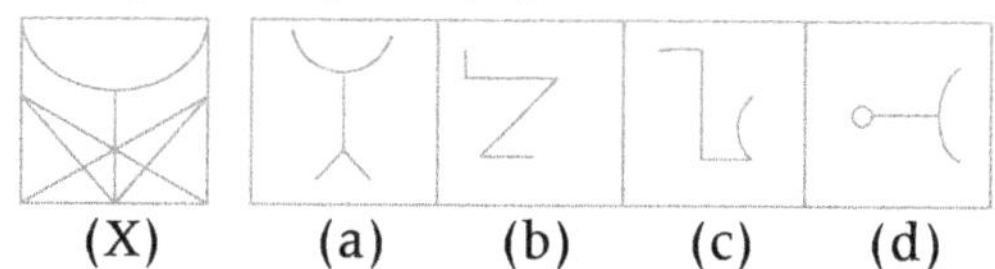

(X)   (a)   (b)   (c)   (d)

2 Marks Questions

11. Amongst the given alternatives, choose the figure which is hidden in the given figure (X).

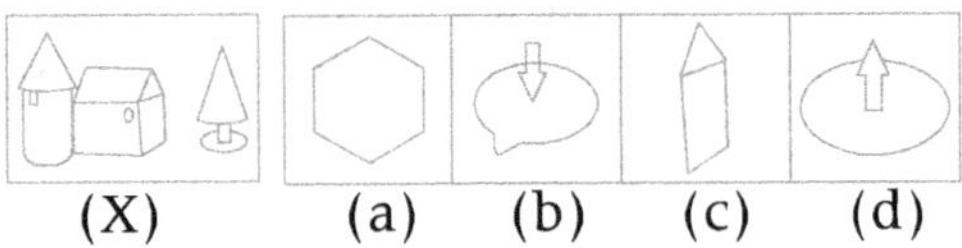

(X)   (a)   (b)   (c)   (d)

12. Choose figure from the given alternatives which is exactly embedded in the figure (X).

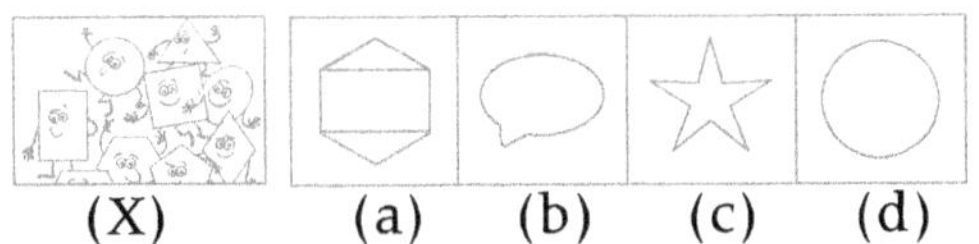

(X)   (a)   (b)   (c)   (d)

13. Amongst the given alternatives, choose the figure which is hidden in the given figure (X).

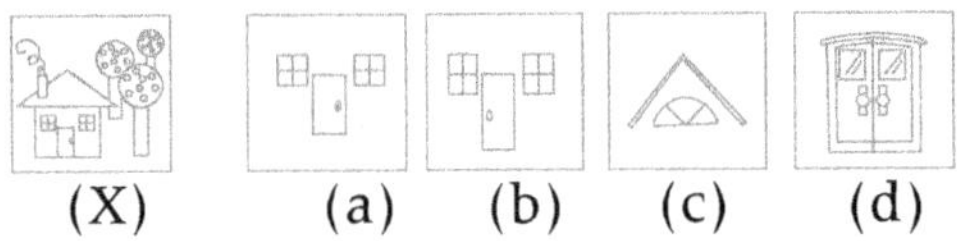

(X)   (a)   (b)   (c)   (d)

14. A teacher drew some shapes on the board and asked the students to find the figure in which figure (X) is hidden.

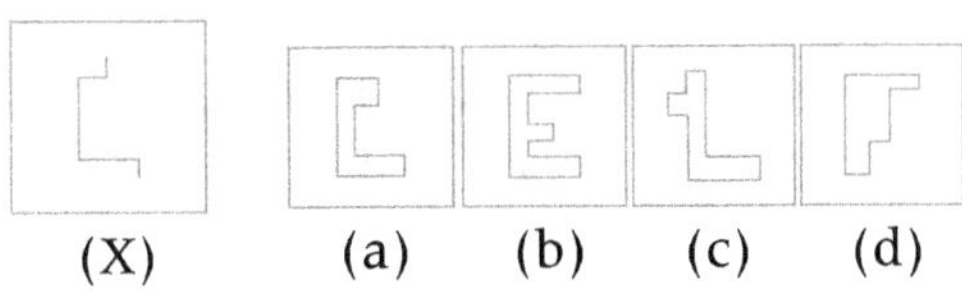

(X)   (a)   (b)   (c)   (d)

15. Ankit is playing with four different penguine toys. At the time of playing, he broke a part of one toy. Find the toy from which the below part (X) is broken.

(X)   (a)   (b)   (c)   (d)

Mirror Images

Look at the following example to understand the concept of 'Mirror and Water Images'. Observe the figure of Micky mouse.

The mirror image of Micky mouse is as shown in following figure. If we carefully observe these images, we see that the right half of the body of Micky mouse becomes the left half in mirror image and *vice-versa*.

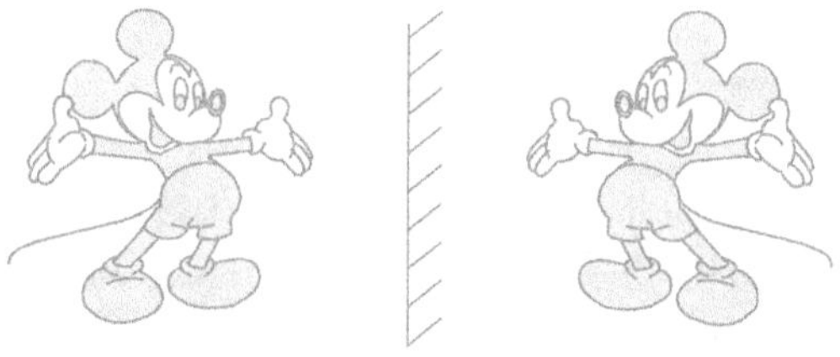

Original image   Mirror   Mirror image

So, the image of an object as seen in the plane mirror is called 'mirror image'. Here, the right half of the object becomes the left half in mirror image and *vice-versa*.

Let us observe the mirror images of numbers and capital letters.

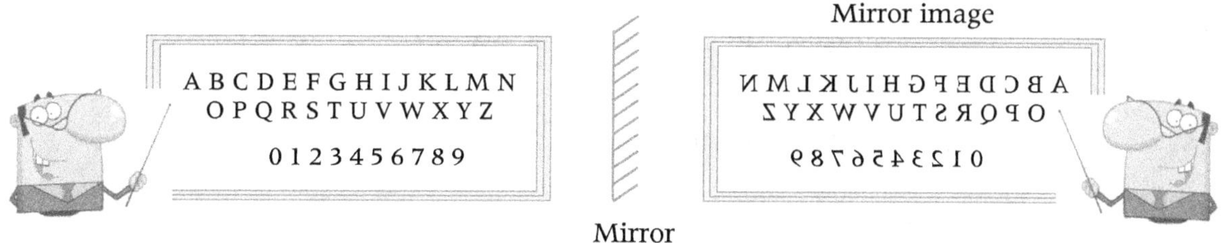

Mirror

In 'mirror images', following types of questions are generally asked.

EXAMPLE 1 Find the correct mirror image of the given figure (X).

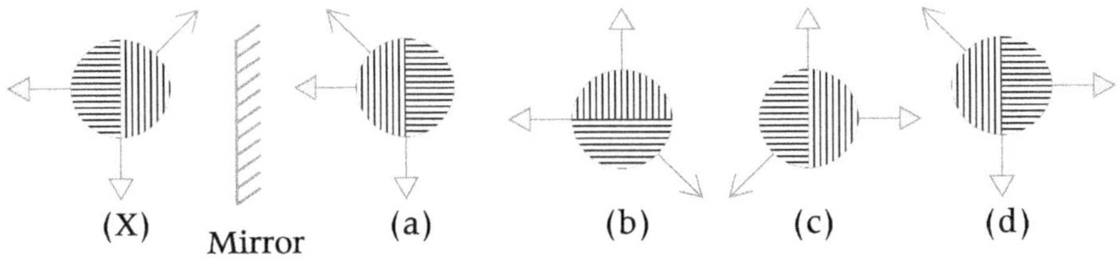
(X)
Mirror
(a)
(b)
(c)
(d)

Sol. (d) The correct mirror image is shown in figure below.

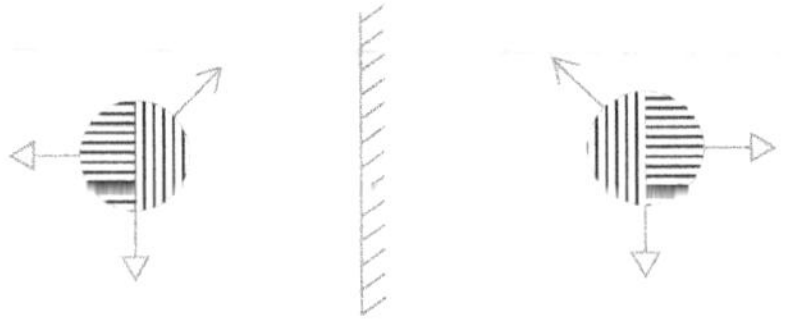

Figure (X) Mirror Mirror image

Hence, option (d) is correct.

EXAMPLE 2 Remo writes a word on a board which is placed exactly to the right of the mirror, then find the correct mirror image of the word.

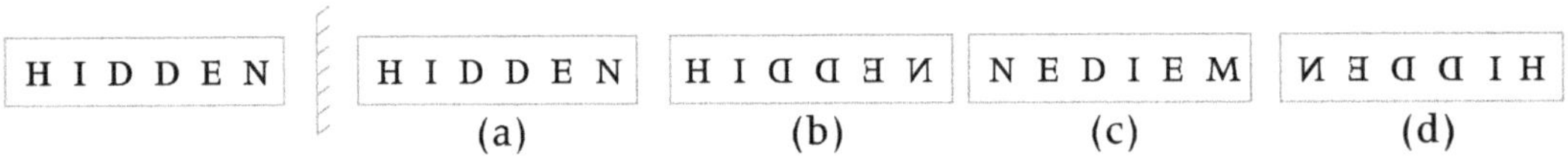
H I D D E N
H I D D E N
N E D I E M
(a)
(b)
(c)
(d)

Sol. (d) The correct mirror image of the given words is as shown in figure below.

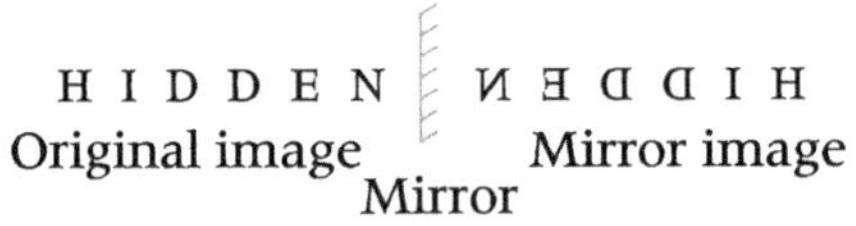
H I D D E N
Original image
Mirror
Mirror image

Hence, option (d) is correct.

EXAMPLE 3 Find the correct mirror image of the following number.

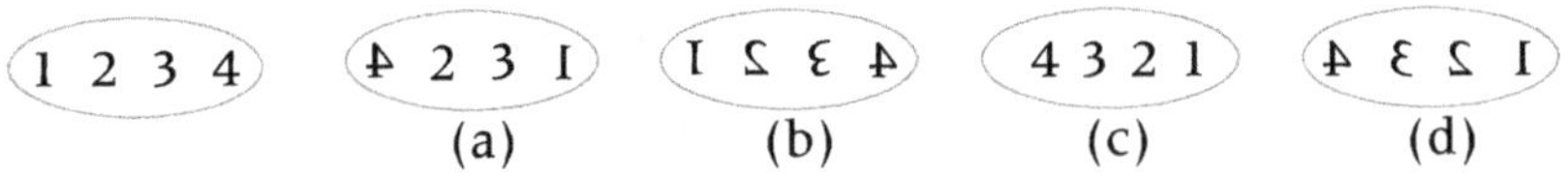
1 2 3 4
4 3 2 1
(a)
(b)
(c)
(d)

Sol. (d) The correct mirror image of the given number is as shown in adjacent figure below.

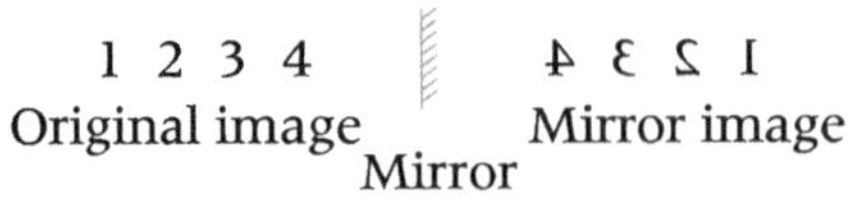
1 2 3 4
Original image
Mirror
Mirror image

Hence, option (d) is correct.

NOTE If not mentioned, the mirror is assumed to be placed to the vertically right of the object.

⏰ Let's Practice

1 Mark Questions

1. Choose the correct mirror image of figure (X) if mirror is placed along MN.

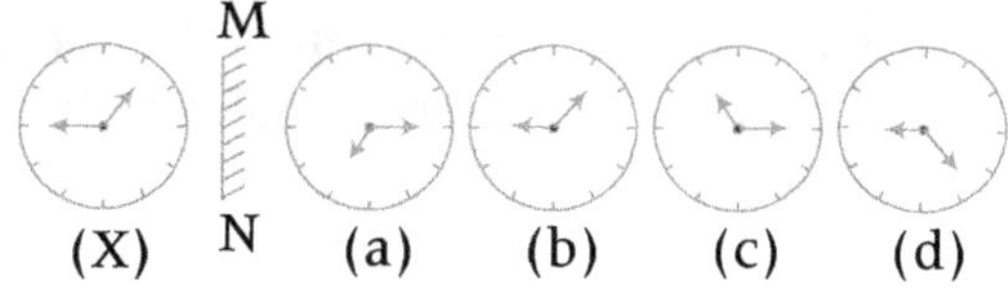

2. Jerry is standing in front of the mirror. He holds a piece of cheese. Choose the image which will be shown in the mirror.

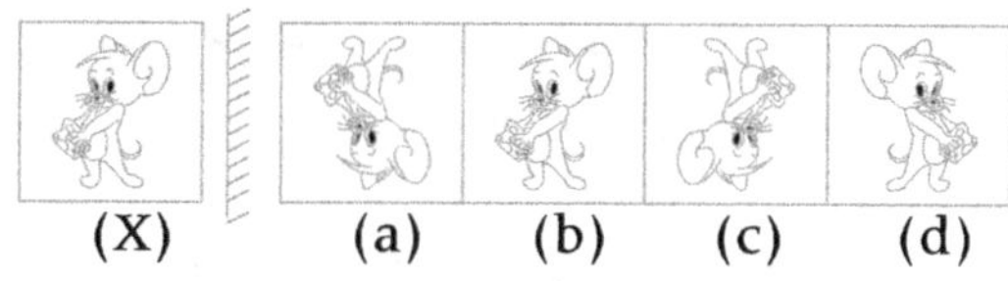

3. Amongst the given alternatives, choose the shape which is the reflection of the given shape (X) in a plane mirror.

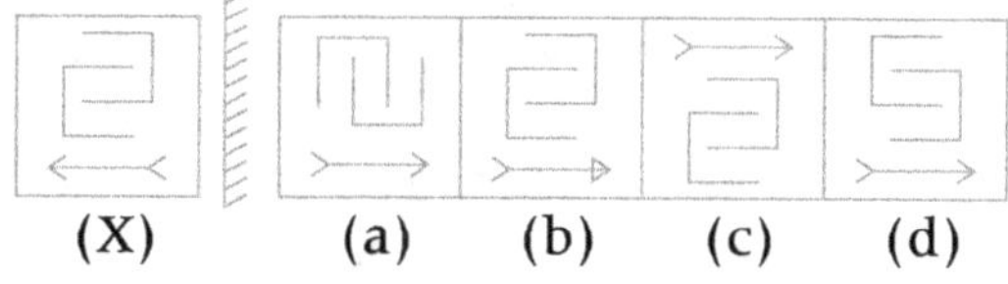

4. Choose the correct mirror image of the given figure (X)

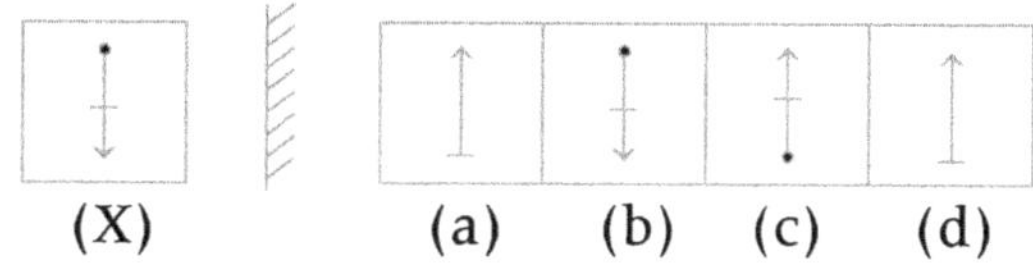

5. Find the mirror image of the figure (X) given below.

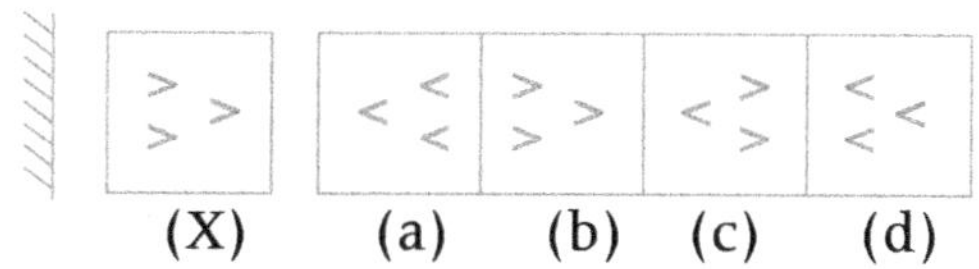

6. An image (X) is drawn below. Find the reflection of the image (X) when the mirror is placed vertically left of the image.

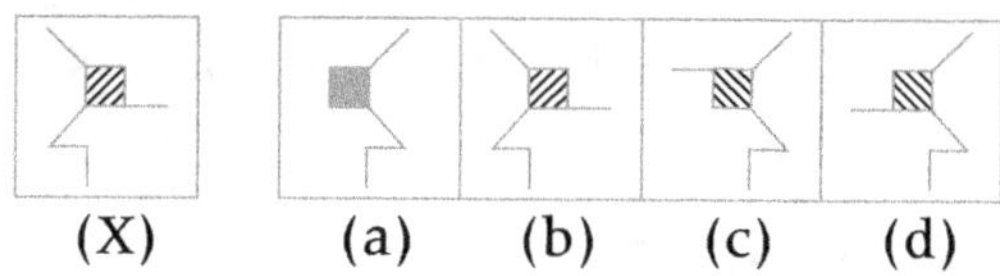

7. Choose the correct mirror image of the following word.

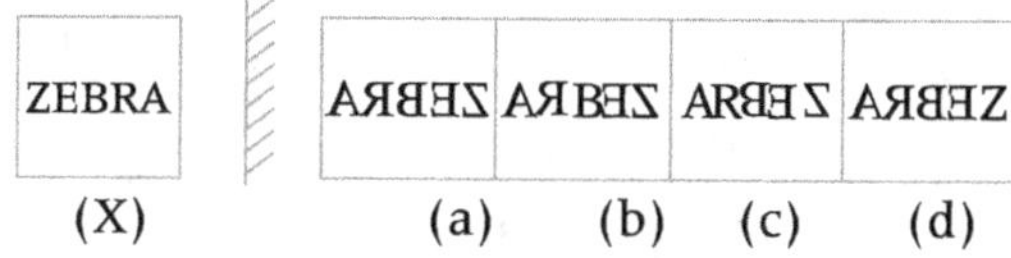

8. Which of the following is the correct mirror image of given word, if the mirror is placed vertically left?

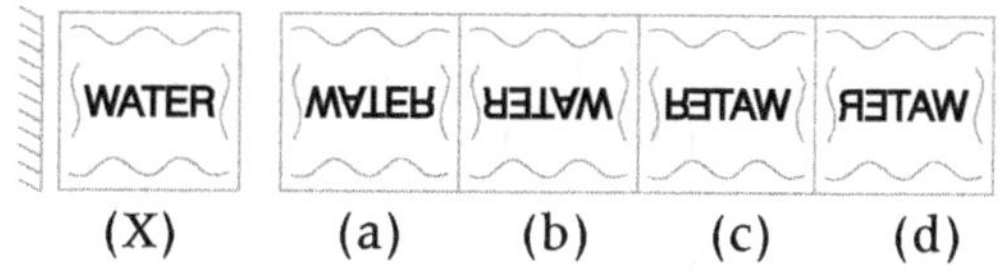

9. Choose the correct mirror image of the given number.

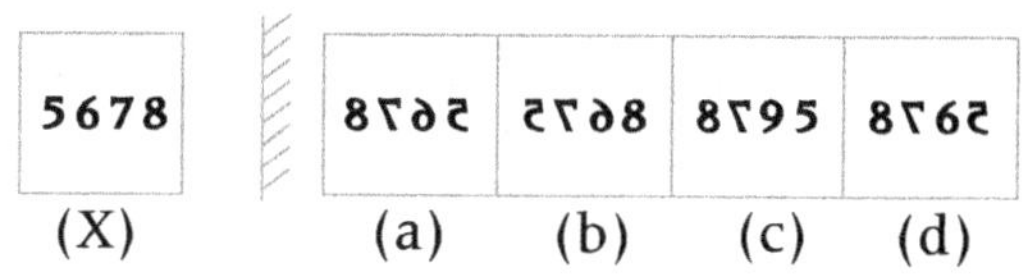

10. A number is written on an umbrella. How will it appear in a plane mirror?

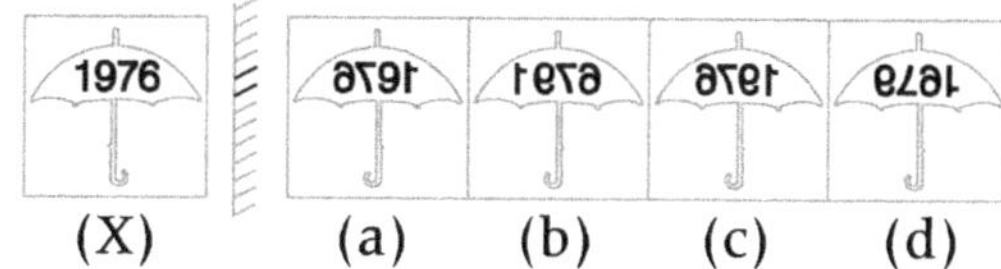

11. A combination of alphabet and numbers is given below. Find out its mirror image.

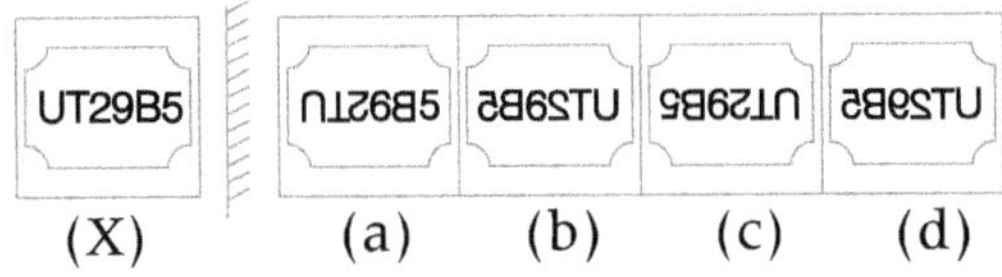

(X)   (a)   (b)   (c)   (d)

12. A digital clock shows 07:50 AM. If a mirror is placed in front of this clock the image will be

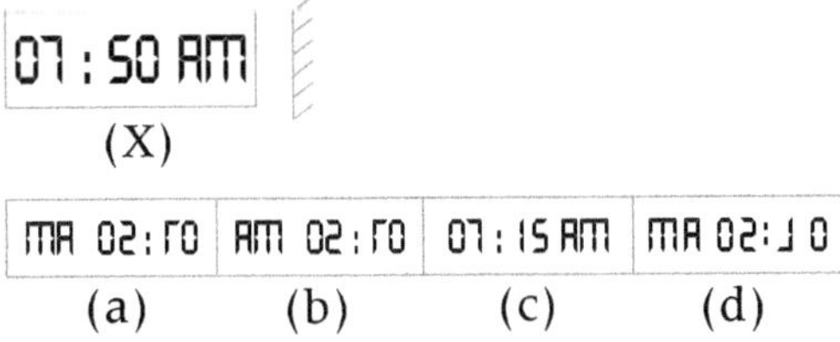

(X)

(a)   (b)   (c)   (d)

13. Find the correct mirror image of the following figure.

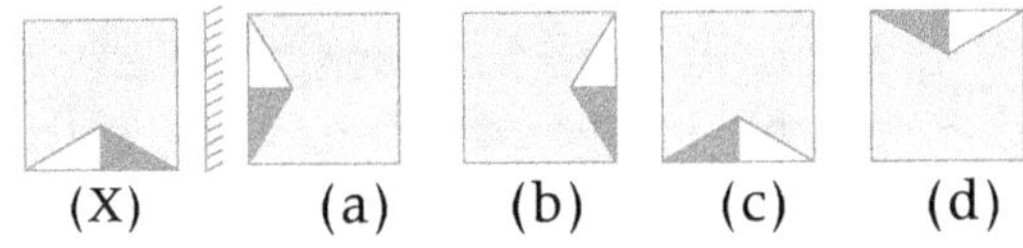

(X)   (a)   (b)   (c)   (d)

14. Find the correct mirror image of the following figure.

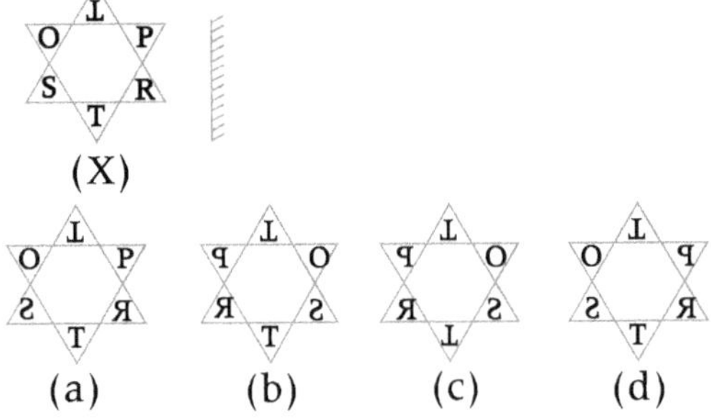

(X)

(a)   (b)   (c)   (d)

15. Find the correct mirror image of the following figure.

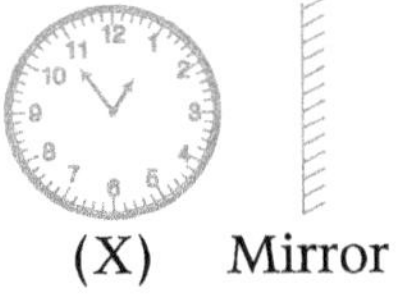

(X)   Mirror

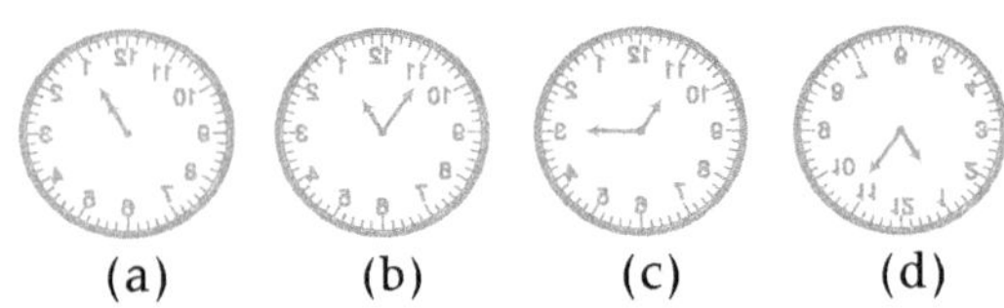

(a)   (b)   (c)   (d)

2 Marks Questions

16. Choose the correct mirror image of figure (X) if mirror is placed along MN.

(X) N   (a)   (b)   (c)   (d)

17. Choose the correct mirror image of the given word.

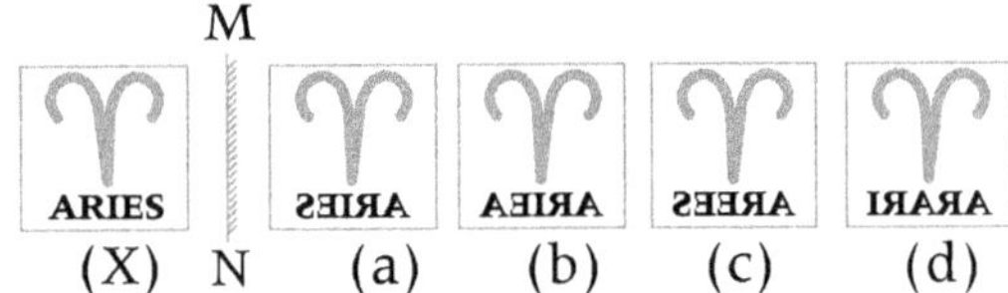

(X) N   (a)   (b)   (c)   (d)

18. Rakhi is playing with dice infront of the mirror. She holds some dice. Choose the image which will be shown in the mirror.

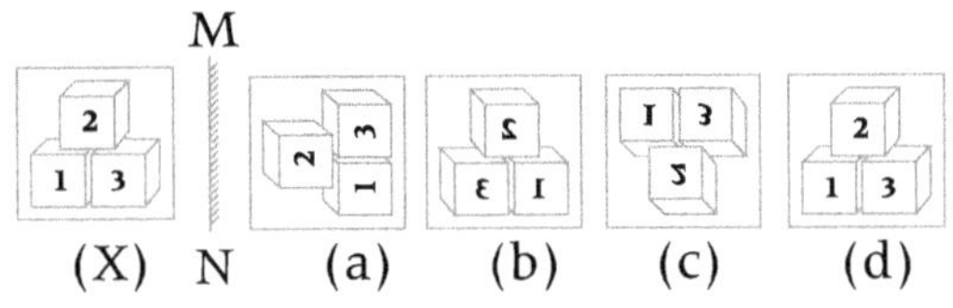

(X) N   (a)   (b)   (c)   (d)

19. Find the mirror image of the figure (X) given below.

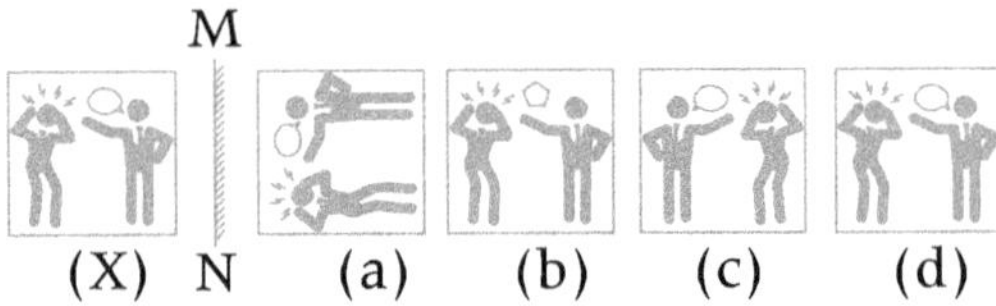

(X) N   (a)   (b)   (c)   (d)

Water Images

Look at the following example to understand the concept of ' Water Images'.

Observe the figure of Micky mouse 

The water image of Micky mouse is as shown in adjoining figure. If we carefully observe the adjoining images, we see that the lower half part of the body of Micky mouse becomes the upper half part in water image and *vice-versa*.

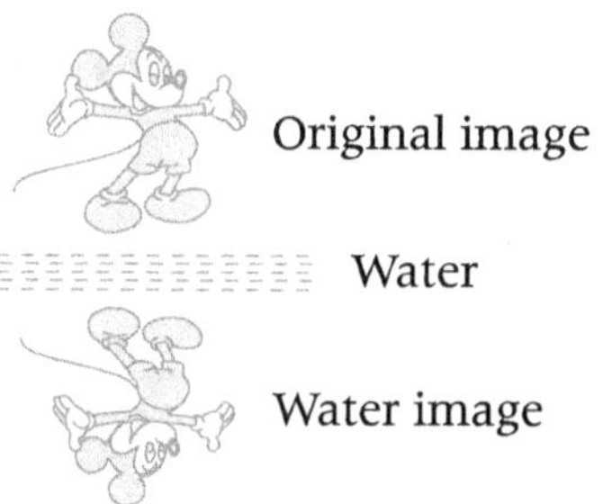

Original image

Water

Water image

So, the image of an object as seen in water is called "water image". Here, the upper half of the object becomes the lower half of the water image and *vice-versa*.

Let us observe the water images of numbers and capital letters.

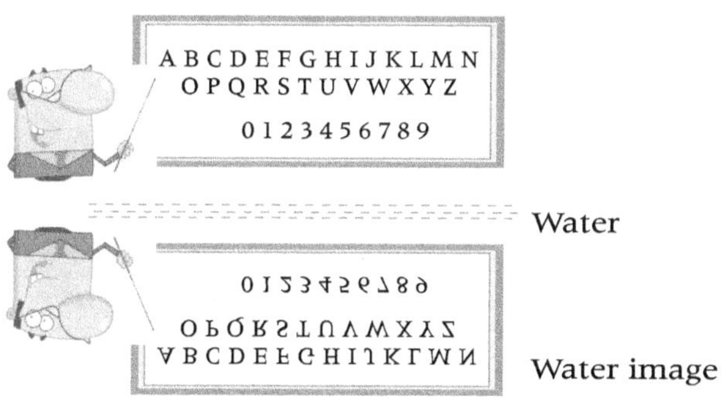

Water

Water image

In 'water images', following types of questions are generally asked.

EXAMPLE 1 Choose the correct water image of the given figure (X).

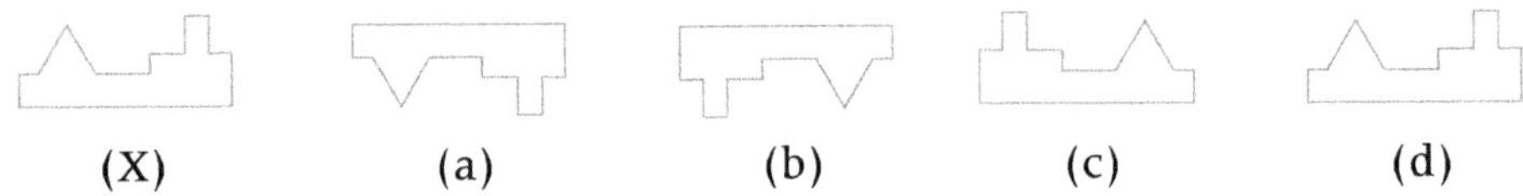

(X)   (a)   (b)   (c)   (d)

Sol. (a) The correct water images is

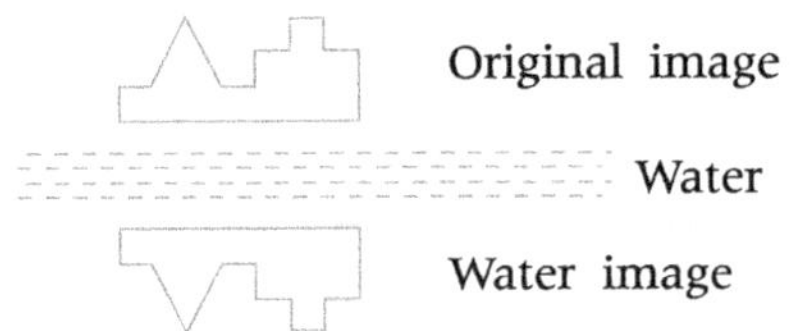

Original image

Water

Water image

Hence, option (a) is correct.

EXAMPLE 2 Choose the correct water image of given word.

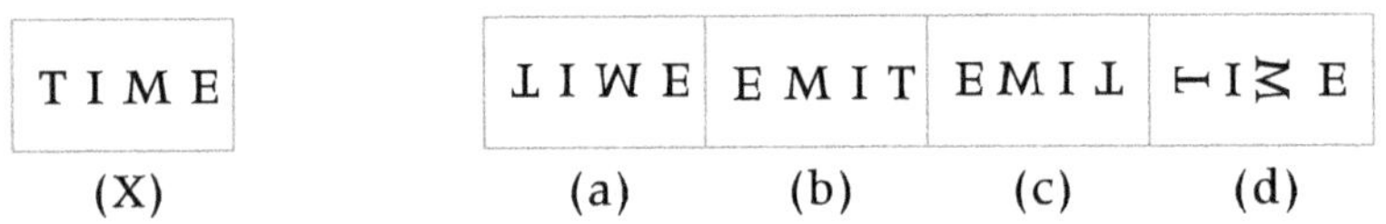

(X)   (a)   (b)   (c)   (d)

Sol. (a) The correct water image of the given word is as shown in figure below.

TIME
Water
⅃IWE

Hence, option (a) is correct.

EXAMPLE 3 Find the correct water image of given number.

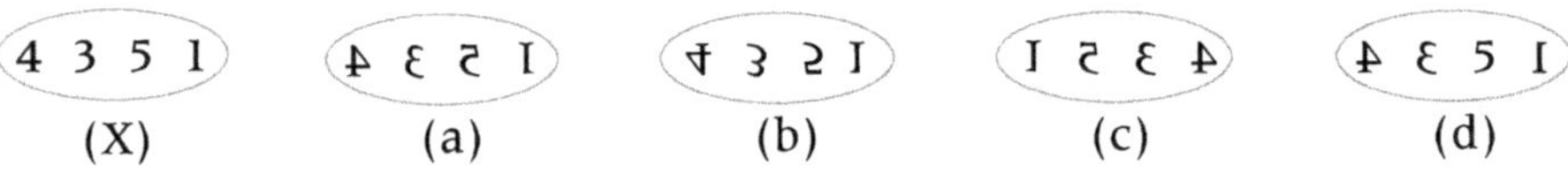

(X)   (a)   (b)   (c)   (d)

Sol. (b) The correct water image of the given number is as shown in adjacent figure.

4 3 5 1
Water
բ 3 ਟ I

Hence, option (b) is correct.

⏰ Let's Practice

1 Mark Questions

1. Find the correct water image of the following animal.

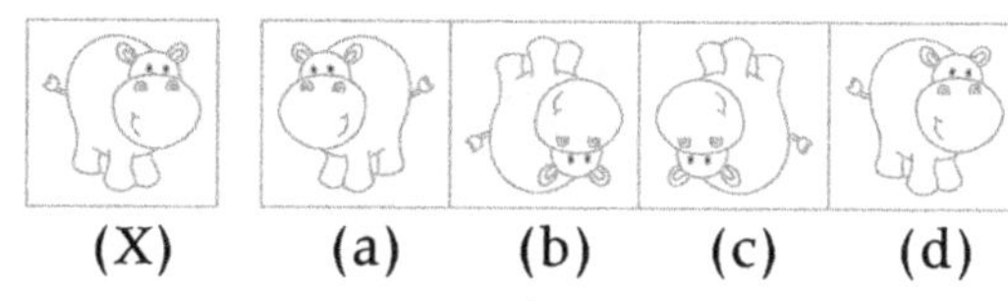

(X)   (a)   (b)   (c)   (d)

2. Choose the correct water image of the below figure (X).

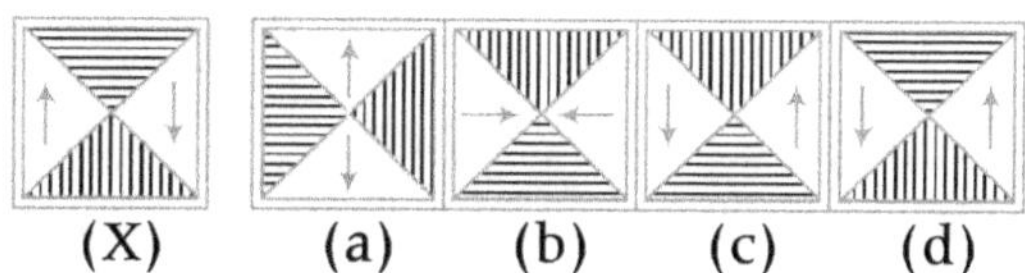

(X)   (a)   (b)   (c)   (d)

3. Choose the correct water image of the given figure (X).

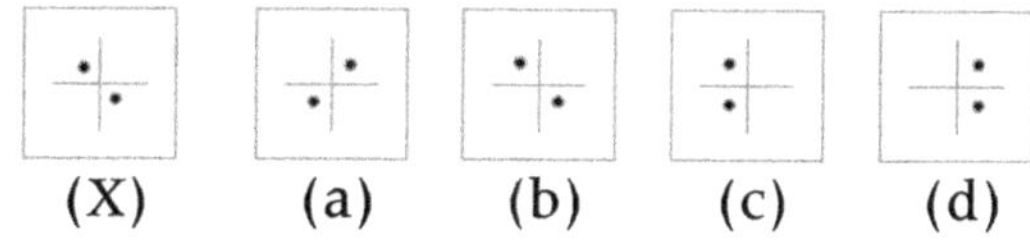

(X)   (a)   (b)   (c)   (d)

4. Find the correct water image of the given figure (X).

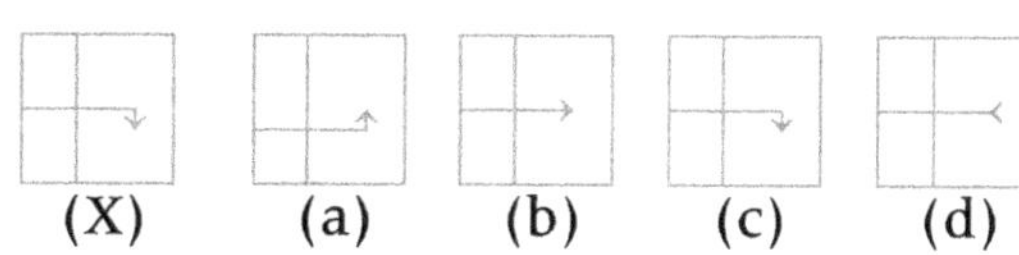

(X)   (a)   (b)   (c)   (d)

5. Choose the correct water image of the given figure (X).

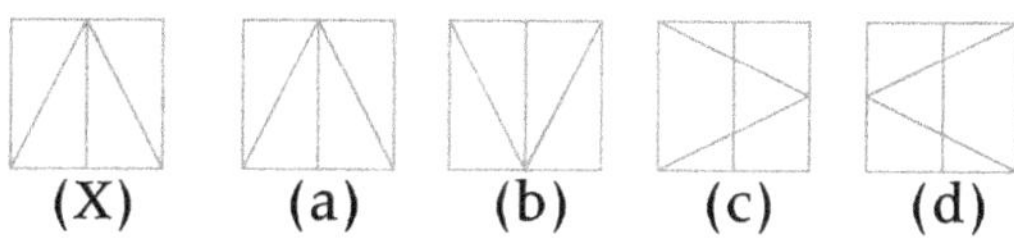

(X)   (a)   (b)   (c)   (d)

6. Find the correct water image of the given figure (X).

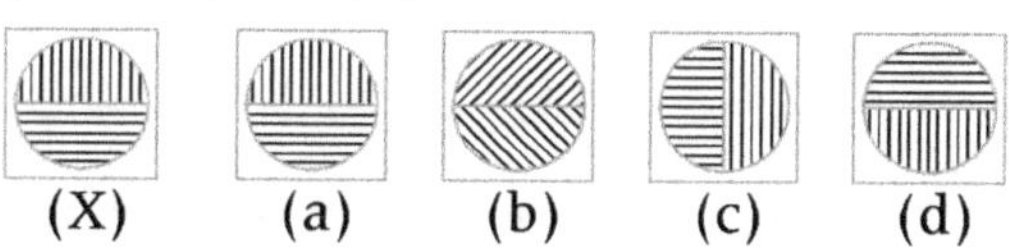

(X)   (a)   (b)   (c)   (d)

7. Find the correct water image of the given word.

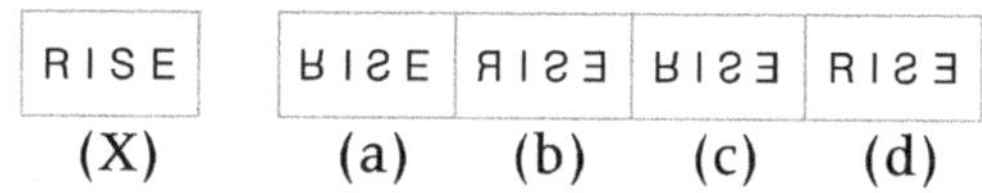

(X)   (a)   (b)   (c)   (d)

8. A flag having a word written on it is given below. There is a pond in front of the flag. Find the image of the flag that will be formed in the pond.

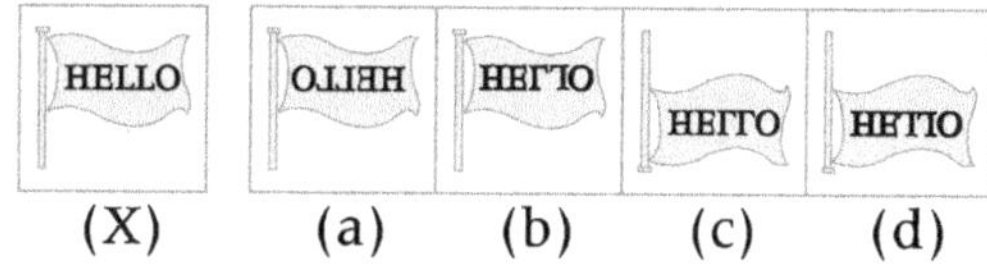

(X)   (a)   (b)   (c)   (d)

9. Choose the correct water image of the given number.

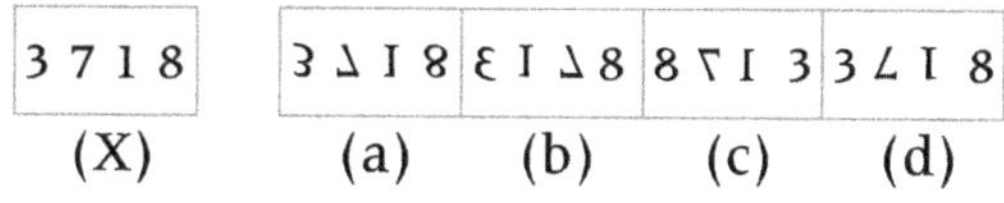

(X)   (a)   (b)   (c)   (d)

10. A number is written on an arrow. Find the correct water image of this arrow.

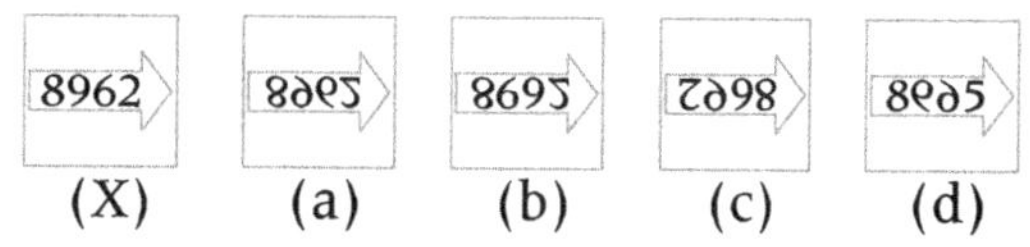

(X)   (a)   (b)   (c)   (d)

2 Marks Questions

11. Choose the correct water image of the following figure (X).

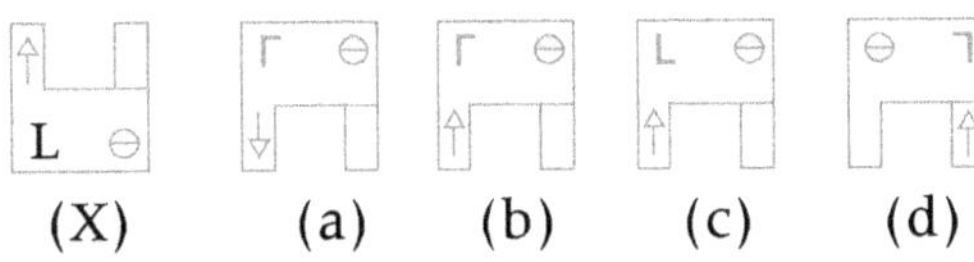

  (X)   (a)   (b)   (c)   (d)

12. Find the correct water image of the following figure (X).

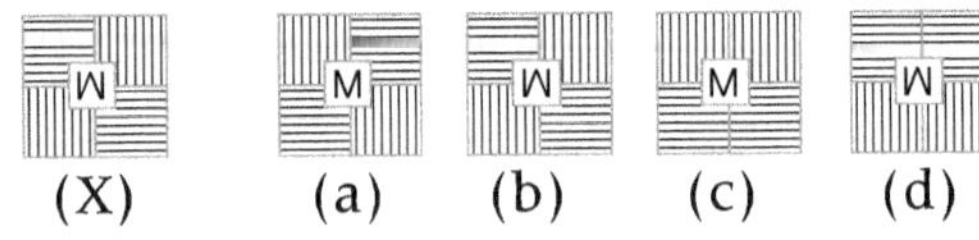

  (X)   (a)   (b)   (c)   (d)

13. Choose the correct water image of below figure (X).

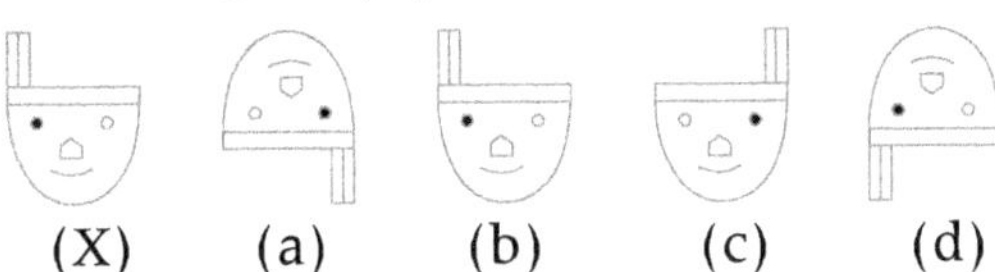

  (X)   (a)   (b)   (c)   (d)

14. Choose the correct water image of figure (X).

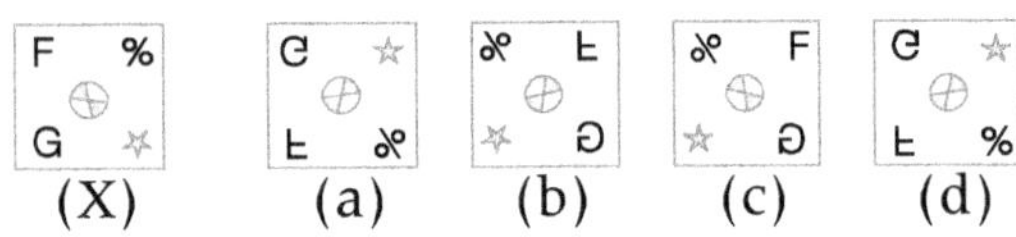

  (X)   (a)   (b)   (c)   (d)

15. Choose the correct water image of the following figure (X).

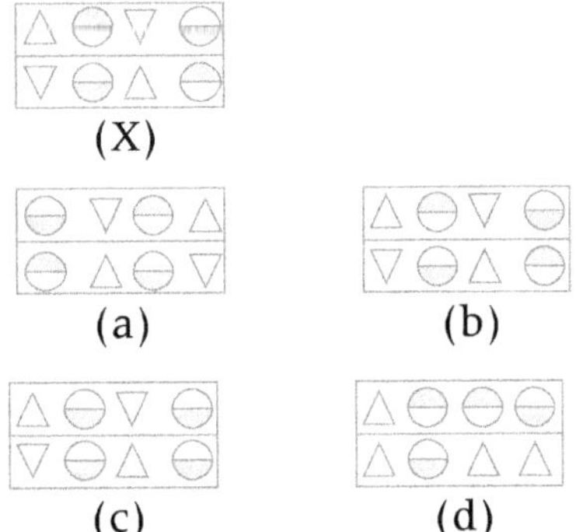

Counting of Figures

Counting of Figure means to count the total number of figures given in a particular image. The figures which are asked for counting can be a straight line, triangle, square, rectangle, circle etc. Let us consider the following example to understand this topic.

EXAMPLE 1 How many squares are there in the following figure?

    (a) 4   (b) 5   (c) 2   (d) 6

Sol. (b) The given figure can be represented as in adjoining figure.
The number of small squares are 4, i.e. ☐ ABIH, ☐ BCDI, ☐ IDEF and ☐ HIFG.
The number of large square is 1, i.e. ☐ ACEG.
∴ Total number of squares $= 4 + 1 = 5$. Hence, option (b) is correct.

In 'geometrical shapes', following types of questions are generally asked

EXAMPLE 2 Jack draws a figure having certain number of straight lines. Count the number of lines.

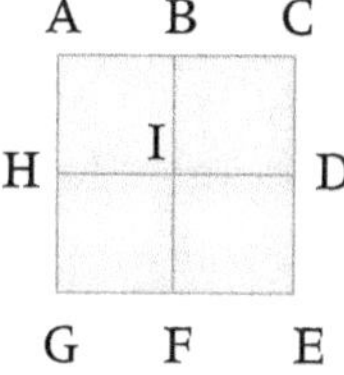

    (a) 10   (b) 12   (c) 18   (d) 22

Sol. (b) We can label the given figure as shown below

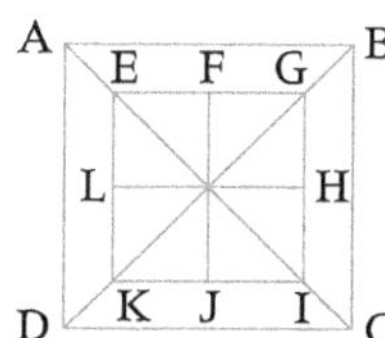

Straight lines are AB, BC, CD, DA, EG, GI, IK, KE, LH, FJ, AC and BD $= 12$.
Hence, option (b) is correct.

EXAMPLE 3 Count the number of circles in the given figure.

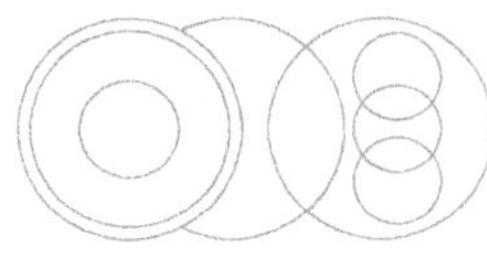

    (a) 10   (b) 8   (c) 7   (d) 12

Sol. (c) The circles can be labelled as shown in adjoining figure.
So, there are 7 circles in the given figure. Hence, option (c) is correct.

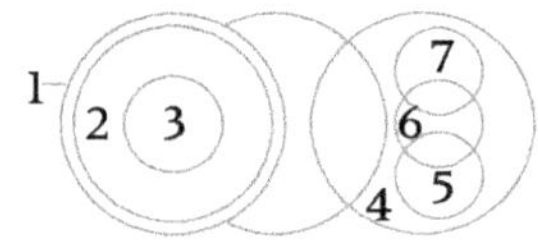

EXAMPLE 4 Count the number of triangles in the figure below.

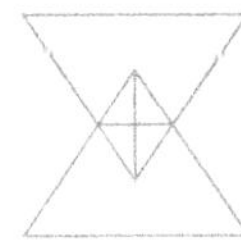

    (a) 10   (b) 12   (c) 8   (d) 15

Sol. (a) The given figure may be labelled as shown in adjoining figure.

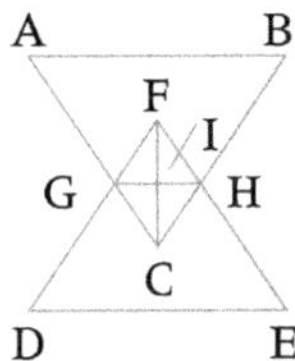

Unit triangles are $\triangle GFI$, $\triangle FHI$, $\triangle HCI$ and $\triangle CGI = 4$
Triangles formed from two units are $\triangle FGH$, $\triangle GCH$, $\triangle FGC$ and $\triangle FHC = 4$
Triangles formed from five units are $\triangle ABC$ and $\triangle DEF = 2$
$\therefore$ Total number of triangles $= 4 + 4 + 2 = 10$. Hence, option (a) is correct.

EXAMPLE 5 Count the number of cubes in the following figure.

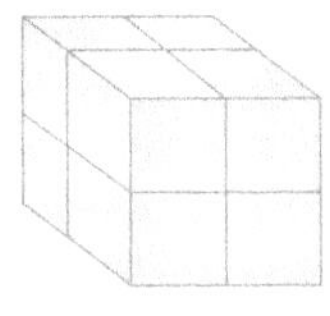

    (a) 8   (b) 4   (c) 16   (d) 10

Sol. (a)

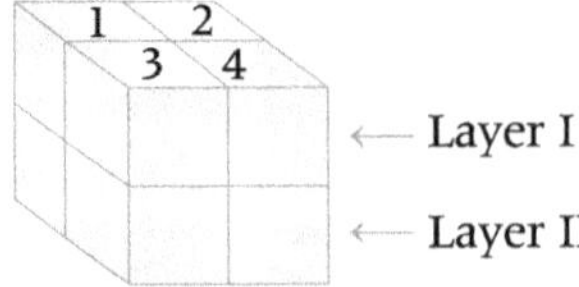

There are 4 cubes each in layer I and layer II.
$\therefore$ Total number of cubes $= 4 + 4 = 8$. Hence, option (a) is correct.

1 Mark Questions

1. Count the number of straight lines in the following figure.

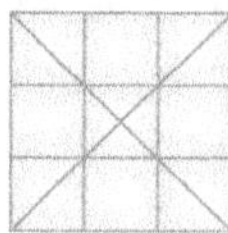

(a) 8   (b) 10   (c) 12   (d) 13

2. How many circles are there in the following figure?

(a) 6   (b) 8   (c) 4   (d) 5

3. How many squares are there in the following figure?

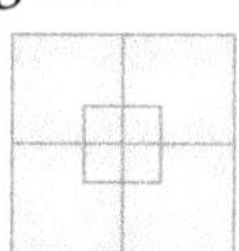

(a) 10   (b) 9   (c) 12   (d) 8

4. How many squares are there in the following figure?

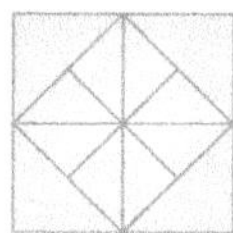

(a) 20   (b) 10
(c) 12   (d) 28

5. How many triangles are there in the following figure?

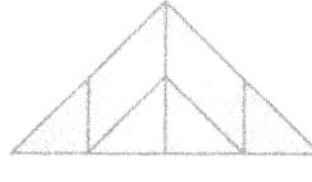

(a) 8   (b) 10
(c) 6   (d) 9

6. Marie draws a following shape. Count the number of rectangles in this shape.

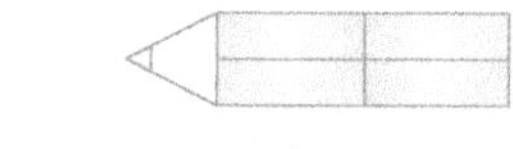

(a) 8   (b) 10
(c) 12   (d) 9

7. Count the number of straight lines in figure given below.

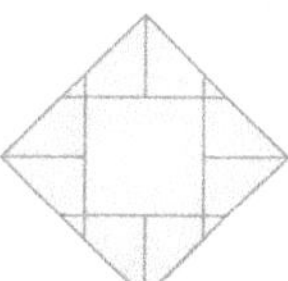

(a) 12   (b) 10   (c) 14   (d) 8

8. How many triangles are there in below figure?

(a) 10   (b) 16   (c) 14   (d) 12

9. Tim draws 5 dots below. How many triangles can be drawn using any three dots?

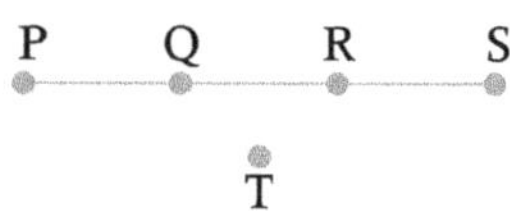

(a) 6   (b) 8   (c) 4   (d) 3

10. How many circles are there in the following figure?

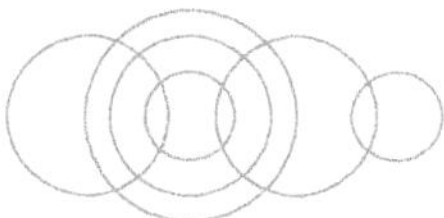

(a) 6   (b) 7
(c) 10   (d) 8

2 Marks Questions

11. Count the number of straight lines in the below figure.

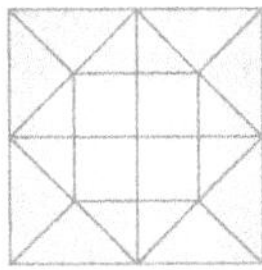

(a) 9   (b) 18
(c) 11   (d) 17

12. How many circles are there in the following figure?

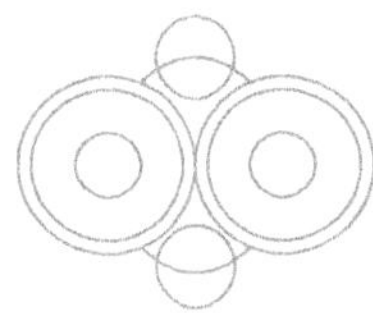

(a) 12
(b) 8
(c) 11
(d) 16

Directions (Q. Nos. 13 and 14) Following questions are based on figure given below.

13. How many straight lines are there in the following figure?
(a) 16   (b) 12   (c) 18   (d) 13

14. How many squares are there in the following figure?
(a) 3   (b) 4   (c) 5   (d) 6

15. Count the number of cubes in following figure.

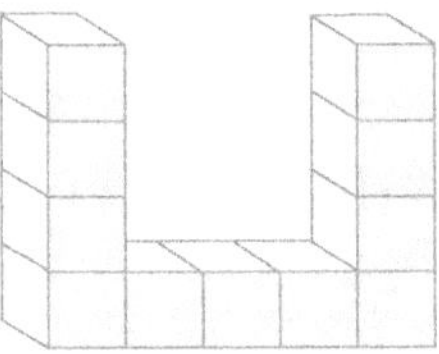

(a) 7   (b) 8   (c) 10   (d) 11

PRACTICE SET  01

1 Mark Questions

1. Identify the letter that will end the first word and start the second.

RUS?OP

(a) P   (b) A   (c) S   (d) T

2. Which shape or pattern completes the second pair in the same way as the first pair?

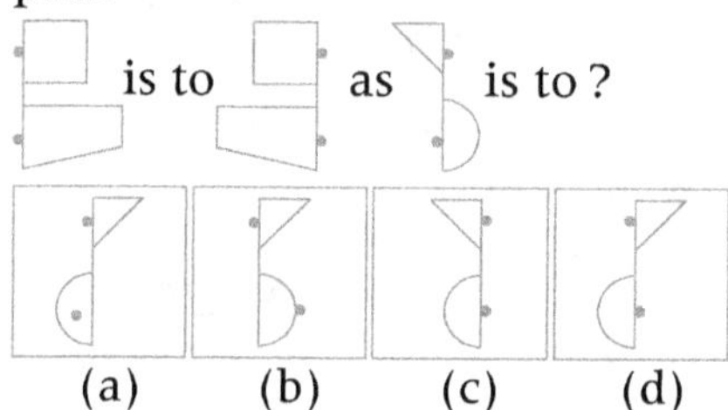

(a)   (b)   (c)   (d)

3. A Car parking lot is shown below. Find the number of parking spot on which a car is standing.

2	5	9	14		27

(a) 19   (b) 18   (c) 20   (d) 21

4. James draws four figures on a paper. In these four figures, three are similar in a certain way. Choose the figure which is different from others.

(a)   (b)   (c)   (d)

5. If 'apple' is called 'jelly', jelly is called 'banana', 'banana' is called 'green', 'green' is called 'carrot' and 'carrot' is called 'mango', then what is the colour of leaf?

(a) Green   (b) Carrot   (c) Banana   (d) Apple

6. Julia is facing the university. Where will she be facing, if she turns 180° clockwise?

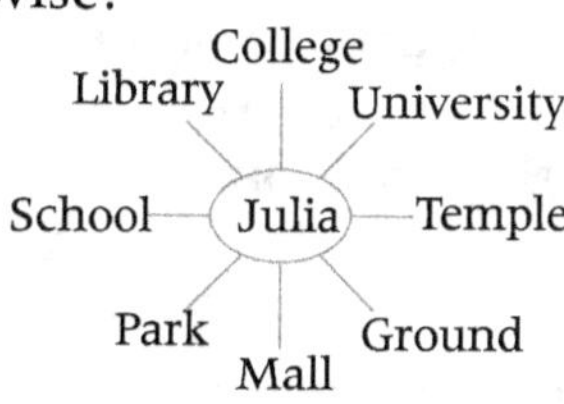

(a) School   (b) Mall

(c) Library   (d) Park

7. Which word can be formed from the letters of the given word?

CORPORATION

(a) ROTATION   (b) PRINT

(c) REPEAT   (d) CARPET

8. Danny is 16th rrom the left end in a row of 35 boys. What is has position form the right end?

(a) 20th   (b) 19th   (c) 18th   (d) 21st

9. Identify in which of the following figures the given shape (X) is exactly embedded?

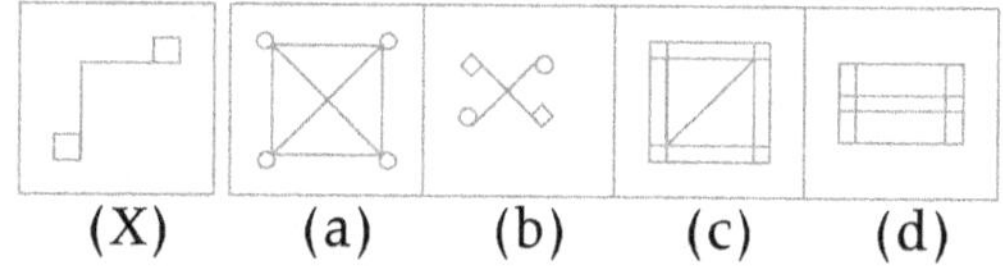

(X)   (a)   (b)   (c)   (d)

10. Find the number that will replace the question mark(?).

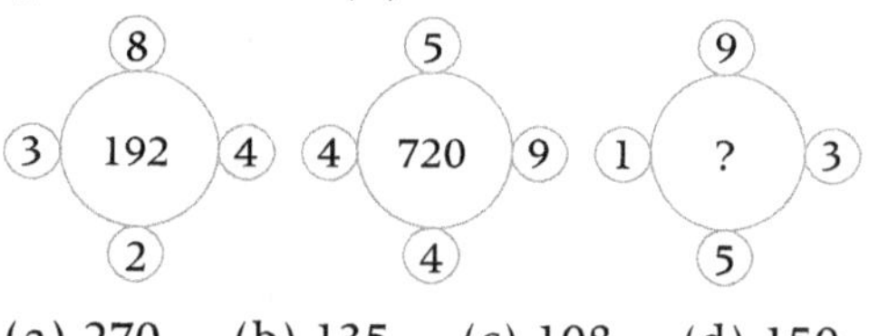

(a) 270   (b) 135   (c) 108   (d) 150

11. Which of the following is the correct mirror image of given combination of letters and numbers?

    UK26IC

    (a) CI∂2ꓘU   (b) ƆI∂2ꓘU

    (c) ƆI∂2ꓘU   (d) CI∂2KU

12. Arrange the following animals according to their size in increasing order.

    1. Dog   2. Horse   3. Ant
    4. Giraffe   5. Mouse
    (a) 3, 1, 5, 2, 4   (b) 3, 5, 1, 4, 2
    (c) 3, 5, 1, 2, 4   (d) 3, 5, 2, 4, 1

13. How many squares are there in the following figure?

    (a) 8   (b) 7   (c) 6   (d) 5

14. Lina and Anna like burger. Kari and Paul like ice-cream. Lina and Kari like pizza. Paul does not like pizza. Who likes pizza and ice-cream?
    (a) Lina   (b) Kari   (c) Anna   (d) Paul

15. 'Lawyer' is related to 'Court', in the same way 'Scientist' is related to?
    (a) School   (b) College
    (c) Laboratory   (d) Hospital

16. Choose odd one out.
    (a) O S T W   (b) M O P S
    (c) G K L O   (d) D H I L

17. As D 23 F 21 H 19 is related to E 22 G 20 I 18, then P 11 R 9 T 7 is related to
    (a) Q11S12U7   (b) Q10S9U5
    (c) Q10S5U9   (d) Q10S8U6

18. Which word does not belong to the group?
    (a) Monday   (b) Calender
    (c) Date   (d) Birth

19. Which group does not belong the group?
    (a) MN14NO   (b) PQ17QR
    (c) AB3BC   (d) TU21UV

20. Four fishes are labelled with five different price tags. These tags shows different numbers. One new fish joins the group. Find the price of fifth fish.

    ₹25   ₹35   ₹45   ₹55   ?

    (a) ₹ 50   (b) ₹ 60   (c) ₹ 65   (d) ₹ 75

21. If the code of 78549 is 56327, then what will be the code for 35926?
    (a) 23704   (b) 37104   (c) 01347   (d) 13704

22. Choose the word which can be formed from the letters of given word 'MANAGEMENT'.
    (a) GAP   (b) ANGER
    (c) MINT   (d) MAGNET

23. If in certain code, FOOTBALL is written as TOOFLLAB, then how will UNSHADED be written in the same code?
    (a) HNUSDEDA   (b) HSNUDEDA
    (c) HUNSDEDA   (d) HSNUDDEA

24. In the following letter sequence, how many D's are followed by 'X', but not preceded by 'E'?
    Y M N D X P R S T D D X O C E D X B T E D K
    (a) 1   (b) 2   (c) 3   (d) 4

25. Identify the relationship of the first pair and then find the missing term in the second pair.

    DFH : GIK : : MPT : ?
    (a) NPW   (b) QSW   (c) PSW   (d) OSX

26. Jiya writes some names choose the one which is different from others.

    Rose   Lily   Lotus   Orange
    (a)   (b)   (c)   (d)

27. What is the missing term in the series given below?

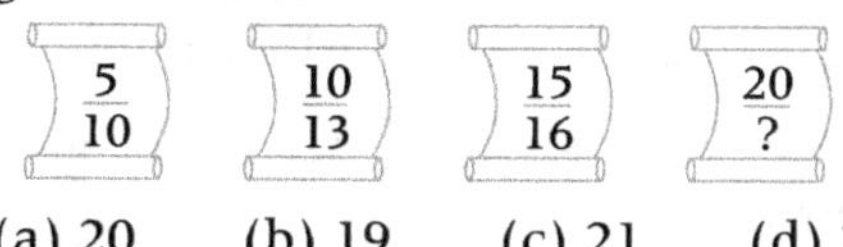

(a) 20   (b) 19   (c) 21   (d) 23

28. Analyse the following figure and identify the letter that will complete the given two words.

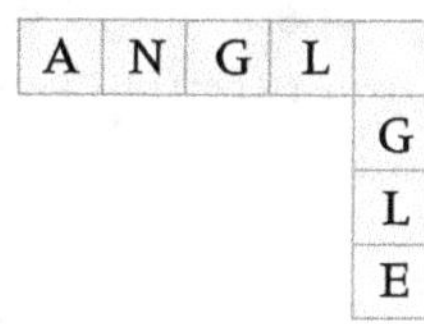

(a) C   (b) S   (c) E   (d) M

29. Find the number that will replace the question mark(?).
8 is to 64 as 19 is to?
(a) 150   (b) 152   (c) 133   (d) 130

30. Find the number which is different from others.

(a) 81   (b) 18   (c) 35   (d) 72

31. Gyani ranked 8th from the top in a class of 50 students. What is her rank from the bottom in the class?
(a) 42nd   (b) 43rd   (c) 44th   (d) 45th

32. If $5 \times 7 \times 4 = 745$ and $9 \times 6 \times 2 = 629$, then $3 \times 5 \times 8 = ?$
(a) 835   (b) 385   (c) 583   (d) 538

33. If EGYPT is coded as 93456 and GREEN is coded as 38991, then how will TREE coded as?
(a) 8699   (b) 9868   (c) 6899   (d) 4899

34. Among PQ, RS, TU and VW, RS is heavier than PQ and TU. TU is not as heavy as PQ. VW is heavier than RS. Who is the heaviest?
(a) PQ   (b) RS   (c) TU   (d) VW

35. If Paras exchanges his position with Rajan and Sweety exchanges her position with Anjana, then the direction of Rajan with respect Anjana is

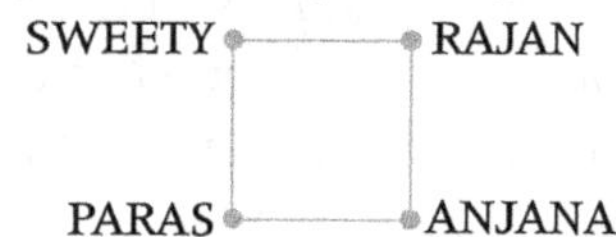

(a) North   (b) East   (c) South   (d) West

36. If '$\times$' means '$-$', '$\div$' means '$+$', '$+$' means '$\times$', then $36 \times 10 \div 10 + 12$ is equal to?
(a) 142   (b) 150   (c) 146   (d) 155

37. Choose the pair of a number and letter that will replace the question mark.

T3	P4	J12
P7	J2	T14
J9	?	P27

(a) P3   (b) T3   (c) P4   (d) T5

38. Amongst the given alternatives choose the shape which is hidden in the given figure (X).

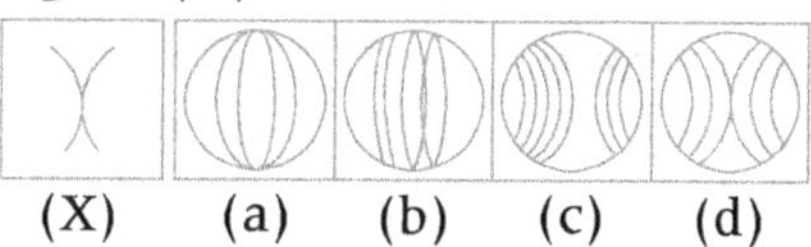

(X)   (a)   (b)   (c)   (d)

39. Find the value of A and B respectively. If each number is the sum of the two numbers directly below it.

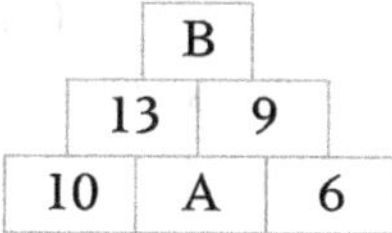

(a) 16,22   (b) 4,24   (c) 3,22   (d) 22,15

40. Amongst the given alternatives, choose the shape which is hidden in the given figure (X).

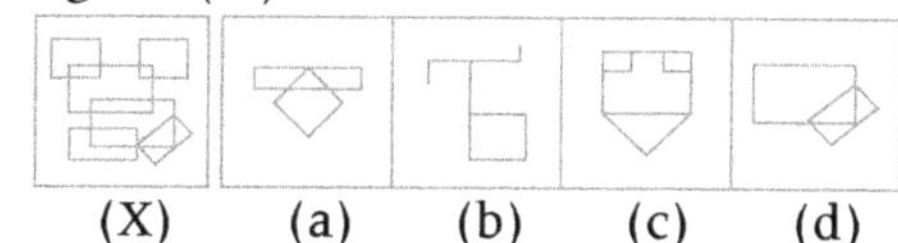

(X)   (a)   (b)   (c)   (d)

2 Marks Questions

Directions (Q. Nos. 41 and 42) In a certain code language

    'pot dot not' means 'you are good'
    'dot tot qot' means 'good and bad'
    'tot not sot' means 'they are bad'

41. In that language, which code stands for 'they'?
(a) not   (b) tot   (c) sot   (d) pot

42. Find the code for the word 'bad'?
(a) tot   (b) not   (c) sot   (d) dot

Directions (Q. Nos. 43 and 44) Study the following sequence carefully and answer the given questions.

F J M P O W E R E N T E M P E R A C E U P M

43. Which letter is third to the right of sixteenth letter from the left corner?
(a) M   (b) E
(c) C   (d) U

44. How many E's are there in the following sequence which are immediately followed by a consonant?
(a) One   (b) Two
(c) Three   (d) Four

Directions (Q. Nos. 45 and 46) Study the following information carefully and answer the given questions.

Seven huts A, B, C, D, E, F and G are situated as follows

    E is 2 km to the West of B.
    C is 1 km to the West of A.
    G is 2 km to the East of C.
    F is 2 km to the North of A.
    D is 2 km to the South of G.
    D is exactly in the middle of B and E.

45. A is in the middle of
(a) E and C   (b) E and G
(c) F and G   (d) G and C

46. How far is E from F (in km) as the crow flies?
(a) 4 km   (b) $\sqrt{20}$ km
(c) 5 km   (d) $\sqrt{26}$ km

Directions (Q. Nos. 47 and 48) Study the following picture and answer the given question.

47. Find the total number of triangles present in the given picture.
(a) 10   (b) 11   (c) 12   (d) 13

48. Find the total number of circles present in the given picture.
(a) 1   (b) 2   (c) 3   (d) 4

Directions (Q. Nos. 49 and 50) Observe the following figures given below and answer the following questions.

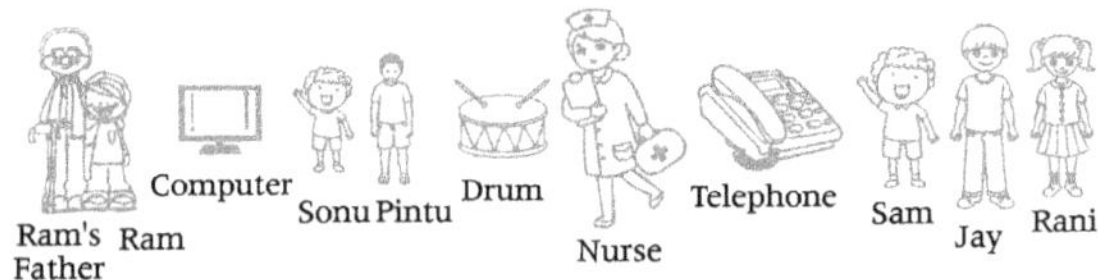

49. ______ is fourth to the right of fifth object/person from the left end.
(a) Rani   (b) Jay   (c) Sam   (d) Ram

50. If telephone interchange its position from computer then, write the name of the person who is third to the left of computer?
(a) Sonu   (b) Pintu
(c) Sam   (d) Jay

PRACTICE SET 02

1 Mark Questions

1. Complete the second pair in the same way as first pair.

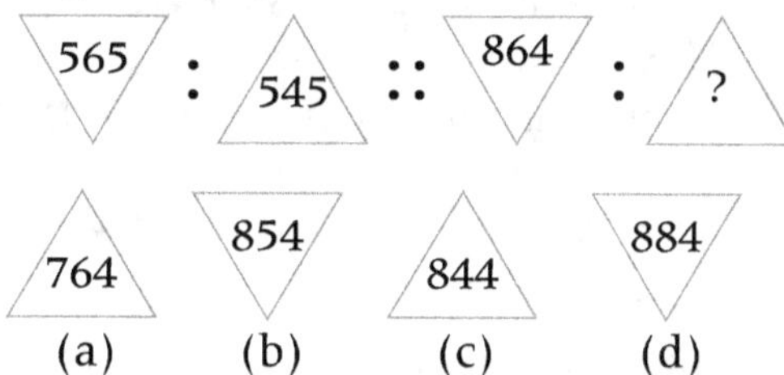

(a)   (b)   (c)   (d)

2. Which figure will replace the question mark(?) in the figure pattern below?

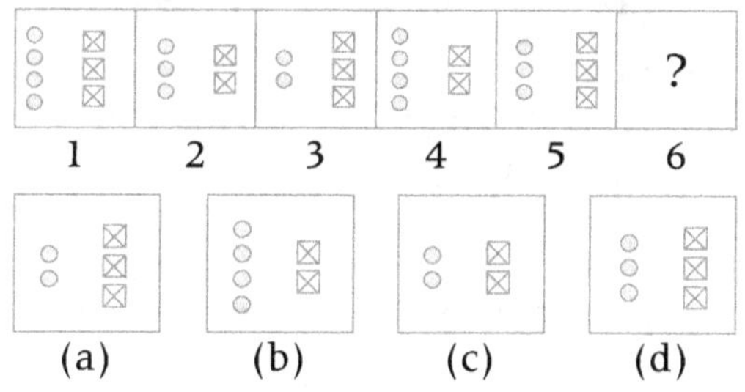

(a)   (b)   (c)   (d)

3. Lee writes four different organs name. Out of these four, three are similar in a certain way.

Choose the one which is different from others.

(a) Ears   (b) Tongue
(c) Kidneys   (d) Lungs

4. In a certain code language. 'WATCH' is coded as '72453' and 'TEACHER' is coded as '4625369', then how will 'ETCHER' be coded?

(a) 463596   (b) 645369
(c) 946356   (d) 564963

5. In the following question, some letters are given which are numbered 1, 2, 3, 4 and 5 followed by four alternatives containing combinations of these numbers. Find the combination of numbers so that letters arranged accordingly form a meaningful word.

O C U T H
1 2 3 4 5

(a) 3, 1, 2, 5, 4   (b) 5, 1, 2, 3, 4
(c) 4, 2, 1, 3, 5   (d) 4, 1, 3, 2, 5

6. In the following list of letters, how many Q's are followed by P and preceded by R?

P R Q P R P Q P R Q P Q Q P R Q R P Q
(a) One   (b) Two   (c) Three   (d) Four

7. In a group of four friends. Tim is second in height. Brane is taller than Rafle. Tim is shorter than Joy. Who is the shortest?

(a) Tim   (b) Brane   (c) Rafle   (d) Joy

8. Arrange the given words as they are arranged in dictionary.

1. Tabard   2. Pain
3. Peach   4. Temple
5. Nubbin

(a) 5, 2, 3, 1, 4   (b) 5, 3, 2, 4, 1
(c) 2, 4, 3, 5, 1   (d) 3, 2, 4, 1, 5

9. Casper is facing the South moves some distance straight. He then turns left, then turns right and then turns right again. Now, in which direction is he facing?

(a) East   (b) West   (c) North   (d) South

10. Find the number that will replace the question mark(?).

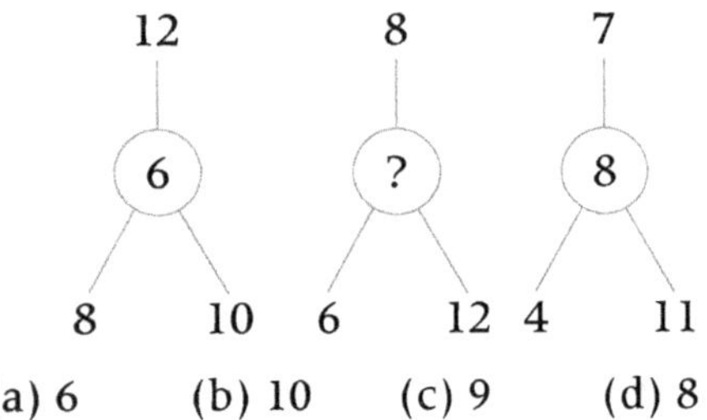

(a) 6   (b) 10   (c) 9   (d) 8

11. Choose the correct mirror image of the figure given below?

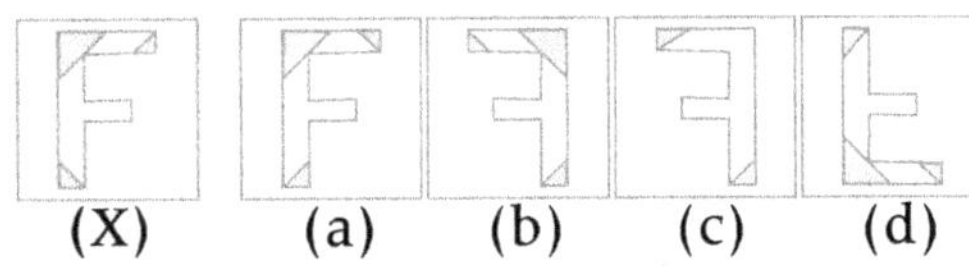

(X)   (a)   (b)   (c)   (d)

12. Identify in which of the following figures the given shape (X) is hidden.

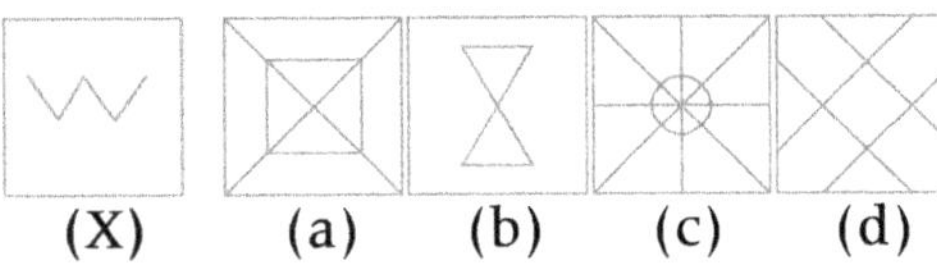

(X)   (a)   (b)   (c)   (d)

13. Count the number of straight lines in the following figure.

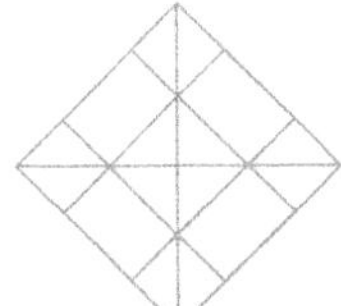

(a) 6   (b) 8   (c) 10   (d) 12

14. Choose the missing word in place of question mark (?) on the basis of the relationship between the words given on the left/right hand side of the sign of analogy.

Radio : Listener : : Drama : ?
(a) Producer   (b) Director
(c) Actor   (d) Viewer

15. Choose the figure which is different from the rest.

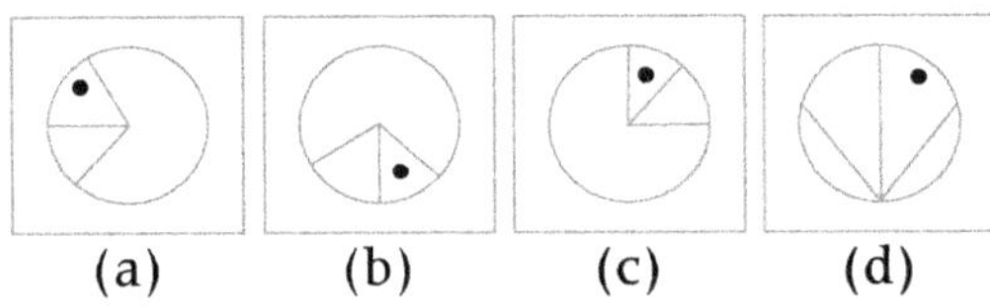

(a)   (b)   (c)   (d)

16. In a certain code, DUMP is coded as $!©@ and ROLLUP is coded as %#**!@.

Then what will be the code for DOLL?
(a) $ * * @   (b) $ # * *
(c) © # * *   (d) ! @ * #

17. Arrange the following words in alphabetical order as in a dictionary.
1. Sport   2. Spouse
3. Squash   4. Sporadic
(a) 4231   (b) 3214   (c) 1234   (d) 4123

18. Identify the relationship of the first pair and then find the missing term in the second pair.
GRIP : 718932 :: LPDT : ?
(a) 1316440   (b) 1516840
(c) 1216840   (d) 1216440

19. Choose odd one out.
(a) Day   (b) Fortnight
(c) Week   (d) Month

20. Find the correct mirror image of the given word.

QUALITY

(a) YITLAUႶ   (b) YTILAႶQ
(c) YTIႩAUႶ   (d) YTIႩVUႶ

21. Find the correct water image of the combination of numbers and letters.

M h R 1 S 2

(a) WႥʁI2ꝛ   (b) WႥR12ꝛ
(c) WႸʁI22   (d) WႥʁI2ꝛ

22. Choose the set of number from the four alternative sets, which is similar to the given set.

    (16, 25, 100)

    (a) (36, 85, 10)   (b) (8, 16, 9)
    (c) (81, 64, 36)   (d) (100, 90, 81)

23. If '2' is coded as '&', '5' is coded as '%', '7' is coded as '@', '9' is coded as '#' '4' is coded as '*' and '3' is coded as '!'. Then, what will be the correct code for the number '4593'?

    (a) * % # !   (b) & % # !
    (c) * % @ !   (d) ! # % &

24. Find the missing successive time in the clock given below.

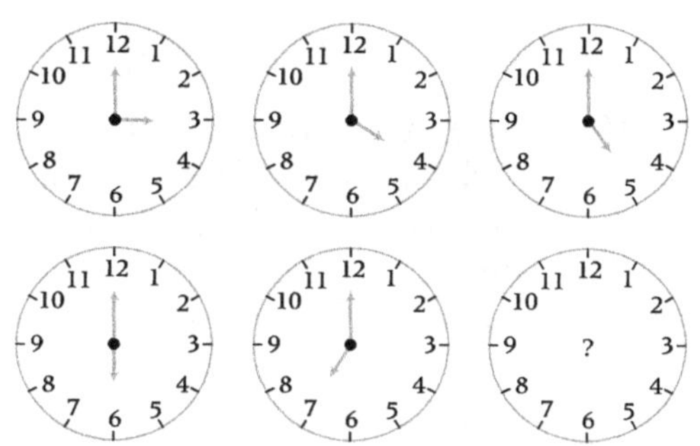

    (a) 8 : 00   (b) 9 : 00   (c) 11 : 00   (d) 2 : 00

25. Shyam asked his friend, "If LOGIC is coded as OLGCI, then how could you write 'TYPES' in same code?

    (a) SEPYT   (b) YTPSE
    (c) YTESP   (d) PESTY

26. Amongst the following, which figure is different from others?

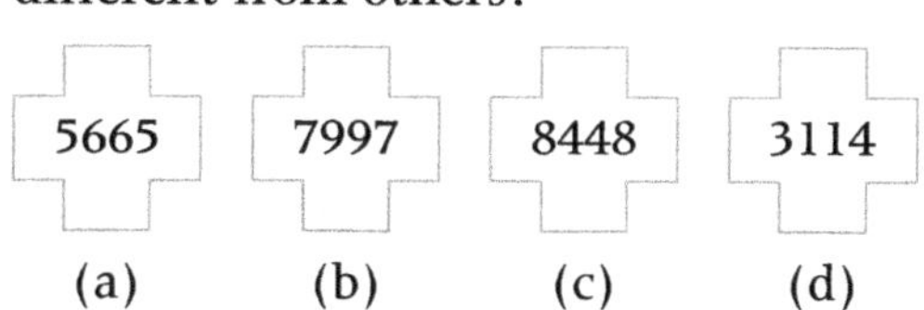

    (a)   (b)   (c)   (d)

27. Study the pattern of alphabets printed on the following piece of paper.
    How many alphabets will be there in Row 10?

Row	Numbers
1	D
2	E F G
3	H I J K L
4	M N O P Q R S
5	T U V W X Y Z A B

    (a) 18   (b) 19   (c) 20   (d) 21

28. In a certain code language 'pro not bos' means 'sky is pink', 'vog dor not' means 'avoid pink habit' and 'dor bos yet' means 'please avoid sky'. Which of the following means 'habit' in that language?

    (a) vog   (b) not   (c) dor   (d) bos

29. Four groups of letters are given-one of these groups is different from the other three. Find the odd one.

    (a) JOEHNJ   (b) LZKMSL
    (c) GWOURV   (d) GFXPMG

30. Observe the following diagram carefully.

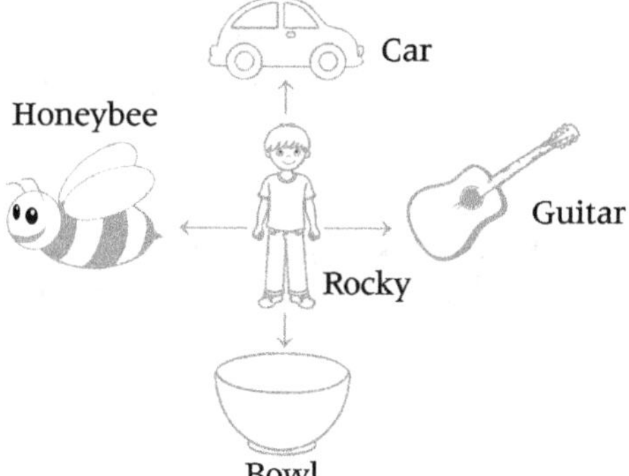

    In the above figure, Rocky is facing the car. If he turns 90° to his right, then in which object will he face?

    (a) Guitar   (b) Honeybee
    (c) Bowl   (d) Car

31. Which is the third number to the left of the number which is exactly in the middle of the following sequence of the members?

3 1 2 3 4 5 6 7 8 9 2 4 6 8 9 7 5 3 1 9 8 7 6 5 4

(a) 6   (b) 9
(c) 2   (d) 4

32. How many such pairs of letters are there in the word 'CORPORATE' each of which has as many letters in the same sequence between them in the word as in English alphabct?
(a) One   (b) Two
(c) Three   (d) More than three

33. Rakesh moves from his home to the mall straight in East direction with distance of 12 m. Then he turned left and walked for 2 m. Then he turns left again and walks straight for 12 m. How far is he from his home?
(a) 10 m   (b) 12 m
(c) 8 m   (d) 2 m

34. In a row of magician, if A who is tenth from the left and B who is ninth from the right interchange their positions, B becomes fifteenth from the left. How many boys are there in the row?
(a) 23   (b) 27
(c) 28   (d) 30

35. Shivani ranks eighteenth in a class of 60 students. What is her rank from the last?
(a) 40th   (b) 41th
(c) 43rd   (d) 44th

36. If 'G' stands for '+', 'H' stands for '−', 'I' stands for '×' and 'Q' stands for '÷', then 14 I 10 G 42 Q 2 H 8 = ?
(a) 150   (b) 153
(c) 160   (d) 165

37. Which letter will replace the question mark?

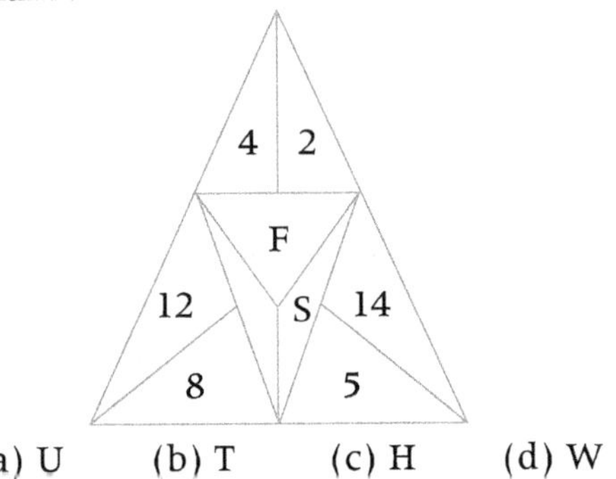

(a) U   (b) T   (c) H   (d) W

38. Select the alternative figure which embedded in figure (X).

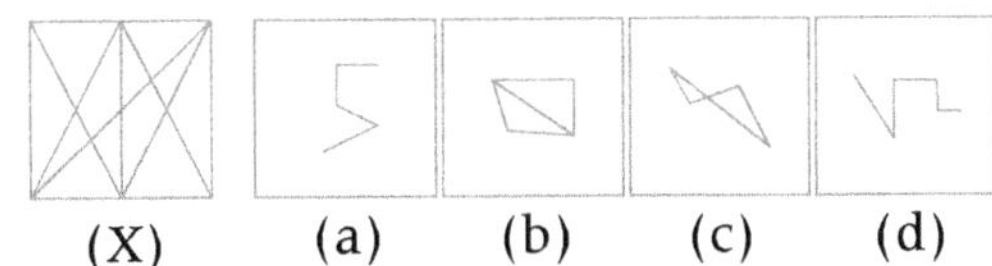

(X)   (a)   (b)   (c)   (d)

39. If the given interchanges are made in signs and numbers, which one of the four equations would be correct.
Given interchanges
Signs − and ÷ and numbers 8 and 16.
(a) $12 - 16 \div 8 = -12$
(b) $16 - 12 \div 8 = 11$
(c) $8 \div 16 - 4 = 14$
(d) $8 - 16 \div 12 = 14$

40. Identify the number which replaces the question mark (?)

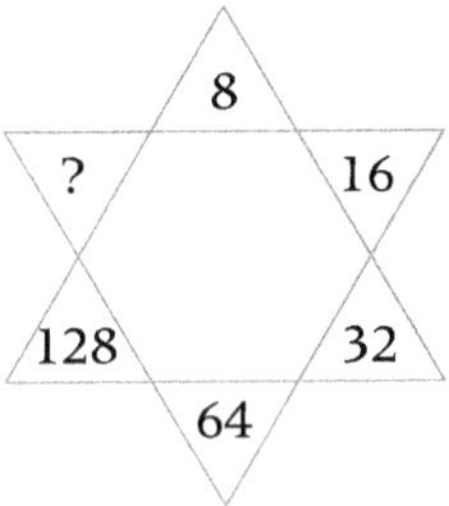

(a) 256   (b) 512
(c) 4   (d) 74

2 Marks Questions

Directions (Q. Nos. 41 and 42) Below some letters are given under each letter a small letter, a number and some symbols is written which is to be used as a code for the capital letter.

O	E	W	V	A	Y	E	D	R	Z	M
@	q	7	#	p	9	%	d	4	t	6

41. What is the code for 'OVER'?
(a) 4#@% (b) @4#%
(c) @#%4 (d) %4#@

42. '4%7p4d' is stands for which word?
(a) AWARD (b) REWARD
(c) OMADES (d) WARDMY

Directions (Q. Nos. 43 and 44) Study the following information carefully to answer the given questions.

Point V is 12 m South of point U. Point W is 24 m East of point V. Point X is 8 m South of point W. Point X is 12 m East of point Y and point Z is 8 m North of point Y.

43. If a man has to travel to point Y from point U which of the following points will he pass through first?
(a) Point W (b) Point X
(c) Point Z (d) Point V

44. If a man is standing at point W, how far is he and in which direction from point Z ?
(a) 12 m, West (b) 24 m, East
(c) 12 m, East (d) 24 m, West

Directions (Q. Nos. 45 and 46) Read the following information carefully and answer the questions given below.

Examine all the given statements.
In a class test of XYZ school Riya scored more than Arti. Arti scored less than Priya. Priya scored more than Riya. Pallavi scored more than Riya but less than Priya.

45. Who scored the highest marks?
(a) Riya (b) Pallavi
(c) Priya (d) Arti

46. Who score second lowest marks?
(a) Pallavi (b) Arti
(c) Riya (d) Priya

Directions (Q. Nos. 47 and 48) Study the following sequence carefully and answer the questions given below.

F 4 ¥ T 2 E % N G 7 @ R E N T # X β

47. Which of the following is the 10th to the right of 6th element from the right end of the sequence?
(a) T (b) # (c) 2 (d) X

48. If all the symbols are removed from the above sequence, which of the following will be the 8th from the left end?
(a) G (b) 7 (c) N (d) E

Directions (Q. Nos. 49 and 50) Study the following figure and answer the given questions based on this figure.

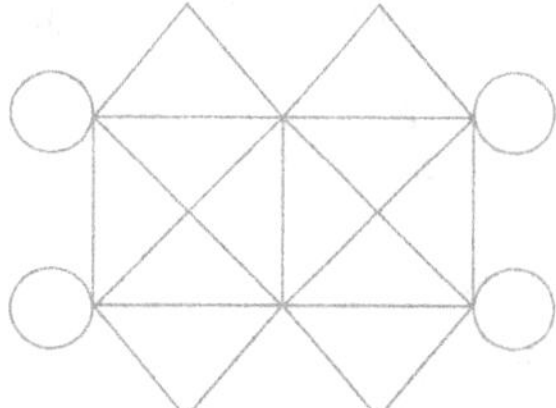

49. What is the minimum number of straight lines that is needed to construct the figure?
(a) 11 (b) 12 (c) 13 (d) 14

50. How many squares and circles does the figure contain?
(a) 5, 4 (b) 6, 3 (c) 7, 4 (d) 8, 3

Hints & Solutions

1. Matching Pairs

1. *(b)* As, a candle is made from wax, similarly a pot is made from clay.

2. *(a)* The baby of cat is known as kitten, similarly the baby of dog is known as puppy.

3. *(b)* As, dates are the part of calendar. Similarly, the words are the part of dictionary.

4. *(c)* The pattern is as follows:

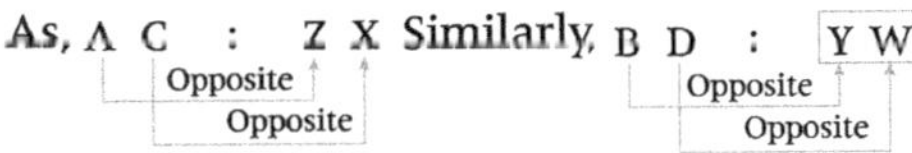

5. *(b)* The pattern is as follows:

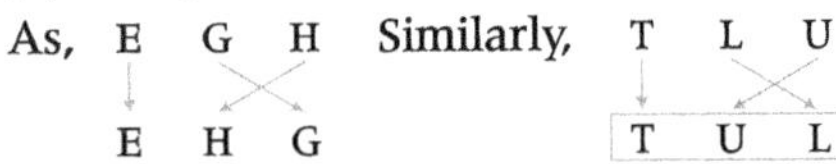

6. *(c)* The pattern in the balloon is as follows:

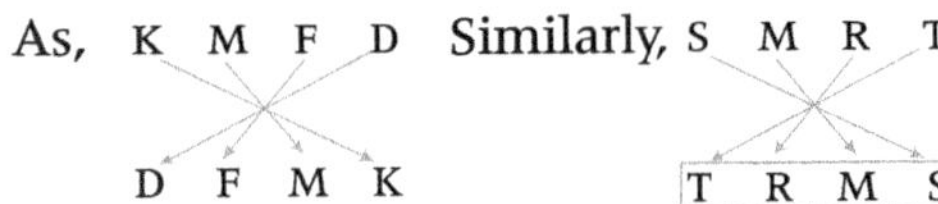

7. *(d)* As, $99 - 9 = 90$ and $80 - 9 = 71$
   Similarly, $100 - 9 = 91$

8. *(b)* As, $7 \times 7 + 1 = 49 + 1 = 50$
   Similarly, $9 \times 9 + 1 = 81 + 1 = 82$

9. *(c)* The pattern is as follows:

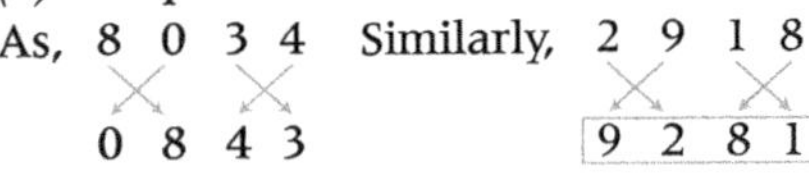

10. *(a)* As, the place value of G in English alphabetical order is 7.
    Similarly, the place value of J is 10.

11. *(c)* As, the number of wheels in a car is four. Similarly, the number of wheels in an auto rickshaw is three.

12. *(a)* The inner shape of first figure in the first pair, i.e. triangle is carried forward as the second figure. Similarly, in the second pair, the inner square of first figure will be carried forward as the second figure.

13. *(c)* In first pair, the triangle is turned upside down. Similarly in second pair, the 'A' shaped figure will be turned upside down.

14. *(b)* In first pair, the arrow is rotated 90° in anti-clockwise direction . Similarly, in second pair, the rectangle will be rotated 90° in anti-clockwise direction .

15. *(c)* In first pair, the sequence of elements in the first figure is reversed to obtain the second figure. Similarly, the sequence of elements in first figure of second pair will be reversed to obtain the second figure.

16. *(c)* The first figure is rotated 180° to obtain the second figure. On following the same pattern in the second pair, option figure (c) will complete the second pair.

17. *(a)* The pattern is as follows:
    As, $T \xrightarrow{+3} W$ Similarly, $P \xrightarrow{+3} S$
    $P \xrightarrow{+1} Q$ $L \xrightarrow{+1} M$
    $Q \xrightarrow{+5} V$ $M \xrightarrow{+1} R$

18. *(b)* The pattern is as follows:

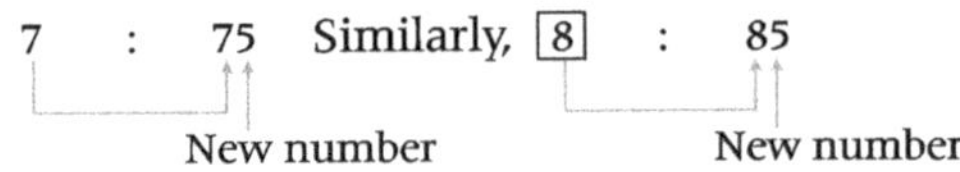

19. *(b)* In the left pair, second word is the mirror image of the first word.

20. *(b)* As, $B \rightarrow (2)^2 \rightarrow 4$ ($\because$ Place value of B is 2)
    Similarly, $D \rightarrow (4)^2 \rightarrow 16$
    ($\because$ Place value of D is 4)

21. *(c)* The relationship is $x : (x \times x + 8)$
    As, $7 \times 7 + 8 = 57$
    Similarly, $9 \times 9 + 8 = 89$

22. *(b)* The pattern is as follows :
    $$7 \; : \; 75 \quad \text{Similarly,} \; \boxed{8} \; : \; 85$$
    New number   New number

23. *(c)* In the second figure, the numbers are in (alphabetical order of letters + 1) of first figure.
    As, $U \rightarrow 21 + 1 \rightarrow 22$ $P \rightarrow 16 + 1 \rightarrow 17$
    $J \rightarrow 10 + 1 \rightarrow 11$ $C \rightarrow 3 + 1 \rightarrow 4$

24. *(d)* The small shaded circle gets unshaded and the small unshaded circle gets shaded. On following this pattern, figure (d) will complete the second pair.

25. *(b)* In the first pair, the bottom circle shifts upward and the shaded part gets unshaded and *vice-versa*. On following this pattern, option figure (b) will complete the second pair.

2. Odd One Out

1. *(d)* Ear, nose, tongue are sense organs but throat is not a sense organ. So, throat is odd one out.

2. *(d)* Here, curd, butter and cheese are obtained from milk but oil cannot be obtained from milk. So, oil is different from others.

3. *(a)* All except honey are produced by plant or tree. But honey is produced by bee. So, honey is odd one out.

4. *(d)* Except hammer, all others are used to cut. So, hammer is odd one out.

5. *(c)* The square has four sides, triangle has three sides and pentagon has five sides. But a Rectangle does not have five sides, it has four sides. So, rectangle : five is odd one out.

6. *(d)* The letters follow below pattern

A C E $'$ P R T$'$
$+2$ $+2$ $+2$ $+2$

U W Y and M N O
$+2$ $+2$ $+1$ $+1$

Here, except MNO all others follow same pattern. So, letters' group MNO is odd one out.

7. *(c)* The letters follow below pattern

E G I H , Q S U T
$+2$ $+2$ -1 $+2$ $+2$ -1

L N P Q and H J L K
$+2$ $+2$ $+1$ $+2$ $+2$ -1

Except LNPQ, all others follow similar pattern, so it is odd one out.

8. *(b)* Except 26, all others are multiples of 6. So, 26 is odd one out.

9. *(c)* The pattern is as follows

$3 \times 3 = 9$ and $9 + 1 = 10$

$2 \times 2 = 4$ and $4 + 1 = 5$

$4 \times 4 = 16$ and $16 + 1 = 17$

But $\qquad 5 \times 5 = 25$

and $\qquad 25 + 1 = 26 \neq 20$

So, spectacle (c) is different from others.

10. *(d)* Here, numbers represent the positional values of the given letters according to English alphabetical series but in option (d), 26 is given but the positional value of Y is 25.

So, $\dfrac{26}{Y}$ is odd one out.

11. *(c)* In all the figures, except figure (c), there are 5 straight lines. But in figure (c), there are 6 straight lines. So, figure (c) is odd one out.

12. *(d)* In all the figures except figure (d), the bottom shape is same. But in figure (d), it is different. So, figure (d) is odd one out.

13. *(c)* In all the figures, except figure (c) the shaded portion in both the shapes are in opposite direction but in figure (c), the shaded portion in both the shapes are in same direction. So, figure (c) is odd one out.

14. *(c)* In all the figures except figure (c), the two arrows are pointing in one direction and other two arrows are pointing in opposite direction. But in figure (c), the three arrows are pointing in one direction and one arrow is pointing in opposite direction.
So, figure (c) is odd one out.

15. *(d)* Except cube (d), all others have same elements. But in cube (d), an oval is missing.
So, cube (d) is odd one out.

16. *(d)* In all the figures except (d), the shape formed between the given two shapes is same as the original shape.

So, figure (d) is odd one out.

17. *(b)* The number of sides in figure (b) is even, while it is odd in other figures. So, figure (b) is odd one out.

18. *(d)* Except Pluto all others are planets. But pluto is not a planet.

So, Pluto is different from others.

19. *(a)* 03, 07 and 05 are the prime numbers, but 09 is not a prime number. So, 09 is odd one out.

20. *(c)* The numbers follow below pattern

$2 + 3 = 5, 1 + 4 = 5,$

$3 + 5 = 8 \neq 9$

and $\qquad 4 + 4 = 8$

So, 359 does not belong to the group.

21. *(a)* In all the numbers except 8516, the four digits are same, i.e. 2, 4, 7 and 9.

So, 8516 is odd one out.

22. *(d)* In all the necklaces except (d), the beads are same. But in necklace (d), a unshaded circle bead is replaced with another shaded bead. So, it is different from others.

23. *(c)* Let A = 1, B = 2, C = 3 …… Y = 25, Z = 26

from

Option (a) H = 8, 8 + 9 = 17

Option (b) F = 6, 6 + 13 = 19

Option (c) L = 12, 12 + 4 = 16 ≠ 19

Option (d) U = 21, 21 + 2 = 23

So, option (c) is odd.

3. What Comes Next?

1. *(a)* The pattern is as follows:

$$T \xrightarrow{-2} R \xrightarrow{-2} P \xrightarrow{-2} N \xrightarrow{-2} L$$
$$\xrightarrow{-2} J \xrightarrow{-2} (H)$$

So, H will complete the series.

2. *(d)* The pattern is as follows:

$$K \xrightarrow{-1} J \xrightarrow{-2} H \xrightarrow{-1} G$$
$$\xrightarrow{-2} E \xrightarrow{-1} D \xrightarrow{-2} (B) \xrightarrow{-1} (A)$$

So, the next two letters are B and A.

3. *(b)* The pattern is as follows :

B T G Q L N Q K V H

with −3 between alternate letters and +5 between alternate letters.

So, VH will complete the series.

4. *(d)* The numbers follow below pattern

15 17 20 24 |29|
  +2 +3 +4 +5

So, 29 will replace the question mark.

5. *(d)* The pattern is as follows

$$1 \xrightarrow{\times 2} 2 \xrightarrow{\times 3} 6 \xrightarrow{\times 4} 24$$
$$\xrightarrow{\times 5} \boxed{120} \xrightarrow{\times 6} 720$$

So, the missing number is 120.

6. *(c)* The series follows below pattern

$$53670 \xrightarrow{+100} 53770$$
$$\xrightarrow{-200} 53570 \xrightarrow{+100} 53670$$
$$\xrightarrow{-200} \boxed{53470}$$

So, 53470 will complete the pattern.

7. *(b)* The pattern is as follows :

8 20 9 19 10 18 ⑪

with −1 in the second series (20→19→18) and +1 in the first series (8→9→10→11).

Here, two series are given. In first number series, 5 is added each time. In second number series, 6 is subtracted each time.

So, 23 will replace the question mark.

8. *(d)* The numbers follow below pattern

$$2 \xrightarrow{\times 3} 6 \xrightarrow{\times 3} 18 \xrightarrow{\times 3} 54 \xrightarrow{\times 3} \boxed{162}$$
$$9 \xrightarrow{+6} 15 \xrightarrow{+6} 21 \xrightarrow{+6} 27 \xrightarrow{+6} \boxed{33}$$

So, $\dfrac{162}{33}$ will complete the series.

9. *(a)* The pattern is as follows

$$3 \xrightarrow{\times 2} 6 \xrightarrow{\times 2} 12 \xrightarrow{\times 2} 24 \xrightarrow{\times 2} \boxed{48}$$
$$D \xrightarrow{+3} G \xrightarrow{+3} J \xrightarrow{+3} M \xrightarrow{+3} \boxed{P}$$

So, $\boxed{48\ \ P}$ will continue the series.

Hence, option (a) is correct.

10. *(a)* The pattern is

$$4 \xrightarrow{+3} 7 \xrightarrow{+4} 11 \xrightarrow{+5} 16 \xrightarrow{+6} \boxed{22} \xrightarrow{+7} 29$$
$$Z \xrightarrow{-2} X \xrightarrow{-2} V \xrightarrow{-2} T \xrightarrow{-2} \boxed{R} \xrightarrow{-2} P$$

So, 22R will complete the series.

Hence, option (a) is correct.

11. *(a)* Here, 5 letters i.e., PQRST are repeated

P Q R S T	P Q R S T	P Q R S T ......
1 2 3 4 5	6 7 8 9 10	11 12 13 14 15

So, the letter at 91th position will be P as follows

P	Q	R	S	T
91	92	93	94	95

Hence, option (a) is correct.

12. *(c)* Number of circles in pattern 1 = 3

$$\Rightarrow 2 \times 1 + 1$$

Number of circles in pattern 2 = 5 $\Rightarrow 2 \times 2 + 1$

Number of circles in pattern 3 = 7 $\Rightarrow 2 \times 3 + 1$

Number of circles in pattern 4 = 9 $\Rightarrow 2 \times 4 + 1$

∴ Number of circles in pattern 98 = 2 × 98 + 1

$$= 197$$

Hence, option (c) is correct.

13. *(d)* Here, difference between each consecutive number in each column is 4.

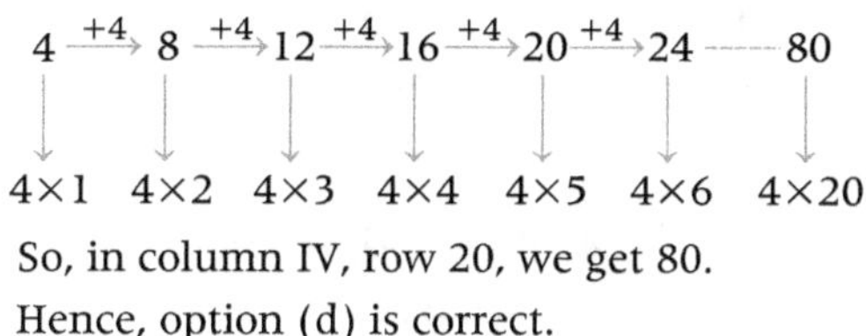

So, in column IV, row 20, we get 80.

Hence, option (d) is correct.

14. *(b)* Starting from left, fifth design is same as first design. So, the sixth and seventh designs will be same as second and third designs, respectively. On following this pattern, option figure (b) will complete the frill.

15. *(c)* Each time the line with the circle is shifting $\frac{1}{2}$ part downwards and the circle becomes unshaded and shaded alternately. So, the next figure will be figure (c).

16. *(b)* The fish is rotating 45° in clockwise direction in each step. And, the circle becomes two in first step and then become one in next step. So, option figure (b) will be the next figure.

17. *(c)* The circle is moving from one corner to other in clockwise direction. And, the square reduces its size from figure (1) to (2) and (2) to (3).

The same process will continue after figure (3).

So, option figure (c) will come next.

18. *(c)* Each time, figure rotates 90° in anti-clockwise direction and an unshaded and a shaded triangle is added alternately. On following this pattern option figure (c) will continue the given sequence.

19. *(b)* In each step, dot is moving $\frac{1}{2}$ step in anti-clockwise direction. The curved and straight lines are moving 1 step in clockwise direction.

On following this pattern, option figure (b) will complete the series.

20. *(b)* The letters follow below pattern

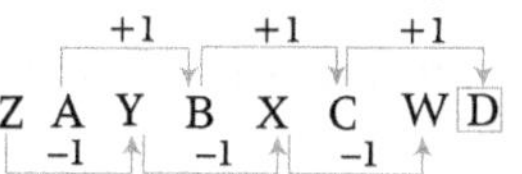

The above pattern consists of two series.

Here, in first series 1 is subtracted each time. In second series, 1 is added each time. So, D will replace the question mark.

21. *(c)* The numbers follow below pattern
$$5 \xrightarrow{+6} 11 \xrightarrow{+9} 20 \xrightarrow{+6} 26 \xrightarrow{+9} 35 \xrightarrow{+6} 41$$
Number '41' will be displaced by the LED 6.

22. *(b)* Let ☺ = X and ☹ = Y

So, the pattern is given as

$$\underbrace{X\,Y\,Y\,X\,Y}_{I} \quad \underbrace{X\,Y\,Y\,XY}_{II}$$

Hence, option (b) is correct.

23. *(d)* The number of dots in each figure can be written as

$$\underset{+2}{1}\ \underset{+3}{3}\ \underset{+4}{6}\ \underset{+5}{10}\ \underset{+6}{15}\ 21$$

Here, in each step 2, 3, 4, ... dots are added. So, in figure (6), there will be 21 dots.

24. *(b)* Numbers in first row = 4, Numbers in second row = 6, Numbers in third row = 8

So, the pattern is as follows

Row1	Row2	Row3	Row4	Row5	Row6
4	6	8	10	12	14

with +2 between each.

Row6	Row7	Row8	Row9	Row10
14	16	18	20	22

with +2 between each.

∴ There will be 22 numbers in row 10.

Hence, option (b) is correct.

25. *(b)* In each step, the hour hand is moving 1 h spaces forward and the minute hand is moving 10 min forward. So, in figure (v), the hour hand will point towards 4 and the minute hand will point towards 11.

4. Coding-Decoding

1. *(b)* Here, the letters of word are reversed to obtain the code. So, the code for DELHI is IHLED.

2. *(c)* The pattern is as follows:

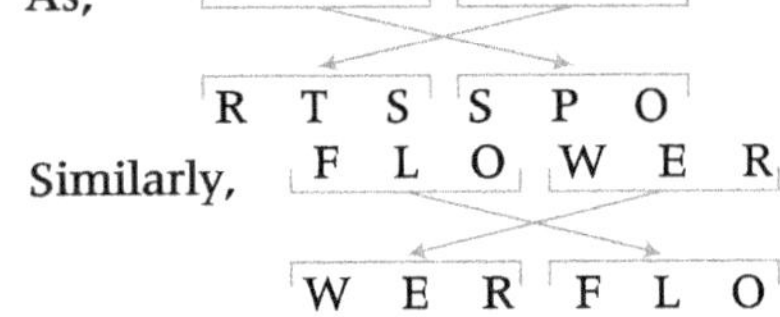

As,

R	E	S	U	L	T
+1	+1	+1	+1	+1	+1
S	F	T	V	M	U

Similarly,

F	I	R	S	T
+1	+1	+1	+1	+1
G	J	S	T	U

3. *(d)* The pattern is as follows:

As,

Q	V	O	J	T	I
−1	−1	−1	−1	−1	−1
P	U	N	I	S	H

Similarly,

S	F	X	B	S	E
−1	−1	−1	−1	−1	−1
R	E	W	A	R	D

4. *(a)* The pattern is as follows:

As, S P O R T S → R T S S P O

Similarly, F L O W E R → W E R F L O

5. *(d)* The pattern is as follows:

As,

8	5	3	4	9
−2	−2	−2	−2	−2
6	3	1	2	7

Similarly,

6	7	3	4
−2	−2	−2	−2
4	5	1	2

6. *(b)* As, $A = 1$ (Positional value)

and $ACE = 1 + 3 + 5 = 9$

Similarly, $ART = 1 + 18 + 20 = 39$

7. *(c)* The given codes can be represented as

Letters	M	O	T	H	E	R	L	A	N	D
Codes	9	2	0	6	3	1	4	7	5	8

Here, $N \to 5$, $O \to 2$, $R \to 1$, $T \to 0$, $H \to 6$

So, the code for NORTH is 52106.

8. *(b)* The given codes can be represented as

Numbers	8	3	6	5	4	2
Letters	G	A	R	D	E	N

Here, $5 \to D$, $4 \to E$, $3 \to A$, $6 \to R$

So, 5436 stands for DEAR.

9. *(d)* Here, $G \to 19$, $I \to 4$,

$N \to 8$, $E \to 10$

and $R \to 22$

So, the code for GINGER is

$19 - 4 - 8 - 19 - 10 - 22$.

10. *(b)* Here, the positional values of the letters (in English alphabetical order) are added to obtain the number.

As, RAHUL $\to 18 + 1 + 8 + 21 + 12 = 60$

SUNNY $\to 19 + 21 + 14 + 14 + 25 = 93$

Similarly, ROHIT $\to 18 + 15 + 8 + 9 + 20 = 70$

So, the jersey number of Rohit will be 70.

11. *(c)* The given codes can be represented as

Letters	B	R	I	N	G	O	U	D
Symbol codes	$	!	©	@	#	%	?	+

Here, $B \to \$$, $R \to !$, $O \to \%$, $D \to +$

So, the code for BROOD is $! %%+.

12. *(c)* We know that, the national flower of our country is Lotus. But, here Lotus is called cake. So, the national flower of India is cake.

13. *(c)* We know that, the India Gate is situated in New Delhi. But here, New Delhi is called as Patna. So, the capital of India is Patna.

14. *(a)* IPL 2020 is won by 'Mumbai Indians'. But here, Mumbai Indians is called Chennai Super Kings. So, Chennai Super Kings won IPL 2020.

15. *(b)* The formula of Distance = Speed × Time. But here, speed means slow and time means fast.

∴ Distance = Slow × Fast

16. *(b)* According to the given information.

(1) 2 [3] → bright [little] (boy)

(1) 4 5 → tall big (boy)

6 [3] 7 → beautiful [little] flower

∴ 2 = bright

17. *(d)* From the given table, we get
B → 1, I → 4, T → 9, E → 8
So, the code for BITE is 1498.

18. *(b)* From the given table, we get
A → 0, R → 6, I → 4, H → 3, N → 7, T → 9
So, the code for ARIHANT is 0643079.

19. *(a)* The given codes can be represented as

Numbers	1	5	6	3	7	4
Codes	S	%	<<	+	#	?

Here, 4 → ?, 3 → +, 5 → %, 6 → <<, 7 → #, 1 → S
So, the correct code of 435671 is ?+%<<#S.

20. *(c)* 2 → I, 4 → N and 9 → S
So, here, no condition is applicable. So, the code is IINS.

21. *(c)* 6 → B, 0 → A, 1 → R and 2 → I. Since, last number is even.

Here, condition (ii) is applicable, so the code is BAR©.

5. Alphabet Test and Words Sequence Test

1. *(d)* Letter 'D' will complete both the words as CLOUD and DARK.

2. *(b)* Letter 'A' will complete both the words as REWARD and AWARE.

3. *(b)* Only the word 'INTUTION' can be formed from the letters of the given word INSTITUTION.

4. *(c)* The word 'NEVER' cannot be formed from the letters of the given word UNIVERSITY. Because the letter E is occuring only once in UNIVERSITY.

5. *(d)* Only the word PHOTO can be formed from the letters of the given word APOSTROPHE.

6. *(b)* The word ENERGY cannot be formed from the letters of the given word TREATMENT. Because the letters G and Y are not present in the word TREATMENT.

7. *(b)* The correct combination is 2Q i.e., Caretaker.

8. *(b)* By using given letters, one meaningful word can be made which is PREY.

9. *(b)* The letters of the word PARAMETERS after arrangement will form a word SRETEMARAP.
So, the letter come before the letter 'M' will be 'E'.

10. *(b)* According to the question,
K P C W [K P W] N K G P W W P H K V P W Z P
So, there is only one P in the above sequence which is followed by W and preceded by K.

11. *(b)* According to the question,

Z Y X W V U T S R Q P O N M L K J I H G F E D C B A

3rd to the left — 11th from right

So, the required letter is N.

12. *(d)*   Forward

J O U R N E Y

Backward

There are three pairs i.e.
JN, UY and EJ

13. *(b)*   R   V   Z   D
STU   WXY   ABC

Here, the gap of '3' letters are given between each letter.

14. *(a)*   S   Y   D   H   K
TUVWX   ZABC   EFG   IJ

Here, gap of letters decreases as 5, 4, 3, 2.

15. *(a)* The arrangement of words is as follows:
Haste - 2, Heart - 3, Heedful - 1,
Hiemal - 5, Horse - 4

16. *(c)* The meaningful order of the words is

Illness → Doctor → Consultation

→ Treatment → Recovery, i.e. 2, 3, 1, 4, 5.

17. *(c)* The meaningful word is N U M B E R.

4 6 2 1 5 3

18. *(d)* The correct combination is 3P i.e. Become.

19. *(c)* The meaningful word can be formed, i.e. ACTION.

The third letter of the word ACTION is 'T'.

20. *(b)* According to the question,

X M N (D) F P R S T D (D) F O C E D F B T E D K

So, there are 2 D's in the above sequence which is followed by F but not preceded by E.

21. *(c)* According to the question,

$$\begin{array}{ccccccc} 3 & 8 & 1 & 14 & 14 & 5 & 12 \\ C & H & A & N & N & E & L \end{array}$$

∴ Such pairs are LN and AC.

22. *(c)* According to the question,

A B C D E F G H I (J) K L M N O P Q (R) S T U V W X Y Z

10th   8th

So, R is 8th letter to the right of 10th letter from the left.

23. *(a)* According to the question,

B A D C F E H G J I L K N M (P) O R Q T S V U X W Z Y

12th

So, P is 12th letter from the right end in the above sequence.

6. Ranking Test

1. *(d)* From the given figure it is clear that, there are four rungs above the rung on which Dinesh is standing.

So, the position of Dinesh from the top

$$= 4 + 1 = 5\text{th}$$

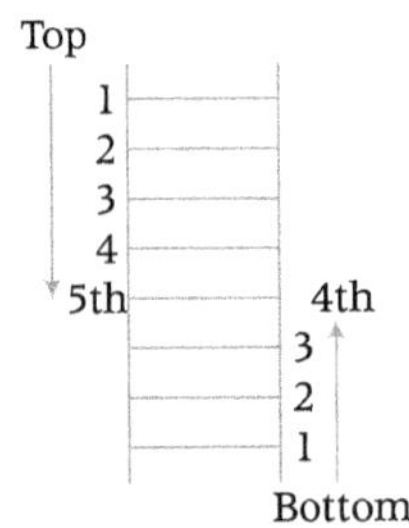

2. *(a)* The tree is 12th from both the ends, it means there are 11 trees to the left and 11 trees to the right of that tree.

So, the total number of trees $= 11 + 11 + 1 = 23$

3. *(c)* In a row of eight friends, Ojas is third from the left, it means there are two friends to the left of Ojas and $8 - 3 = 5$ friends to the right of Ojas.

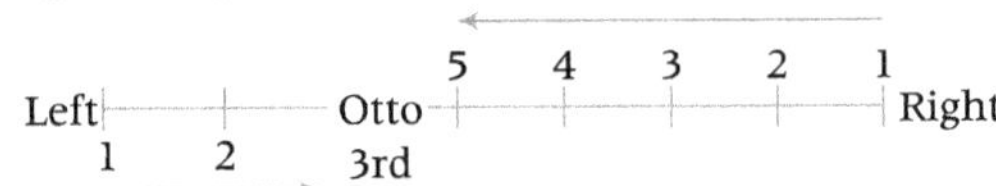

So, the position of Otto from the right end

$$= 5 + 1 = 6\text{th}$$

4. *(d)* Avni's rank is 22nd in 55 students. So, there are 21 students above Avni and $55 - 22 = 33$ students below Avni. So, the rank of Avni from the bottom $= 33 + 1 = 34$th

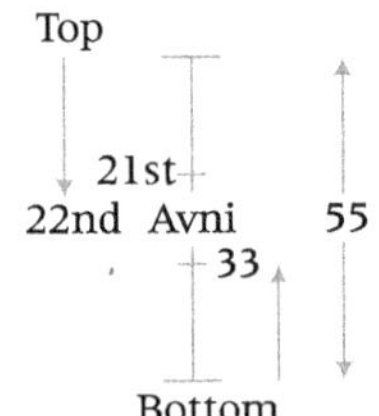

5. *(a)* The rank of duck toy from the left is 16th. It means, 15 toys are before duck toy and from the right its rank is 49th. It means, 48 toys are after the duck toy.

So, the total number of duck toys

$$= 15 + \text{duck toy} + 48$$

$$\Rightarrow 15 + 1 + 48 = 64$$

6. *(c)* Total number of boys in the line = Position of John from the left + Position of Joy from the right + Number of boys between John and Joy $= 13 + 20 + 4 = 37$

7. *(a)* Pallavi rank is 21st from the last and Komal is 8 ranks ahead of Pallavi.

So, Komal rank from the last = 21 + 8 = 29th

Now, Komal rank from the start
$$= 40 - 29 + 1 = 11 + 1$$
$$= 12th$$

8. *(c)* Joy rank is 22nd and Dev is 8 rank ahead of Joy.

So, Dev rank is (22 − 8) = 14th

Number of students behind Dev = 26 − 14
$$= 12$$

Thus, rank of Dev from the last = 12 + 1
$$= 13 th$$

9. *(a)* The position of green colour chair from the front is 14th.

The red colour chair is four positions behind the green colour chair.

So, the position of red colour chair from the front = 14 + 4 = 18 th

Now, position of red colour chair from the back = 40 − 18 + 1 = 22 + 1 = 23rd

10. *(d)* When Sakshat was shifted by three places towards his right side, then he occupies the middle position i.e. 13th position.

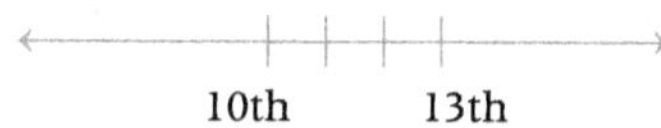

Thus, his original position from the left end of the row = 13 − 3 = 10 th

11. (b) For minimum number of persons, arrangement in the row will be given as follows

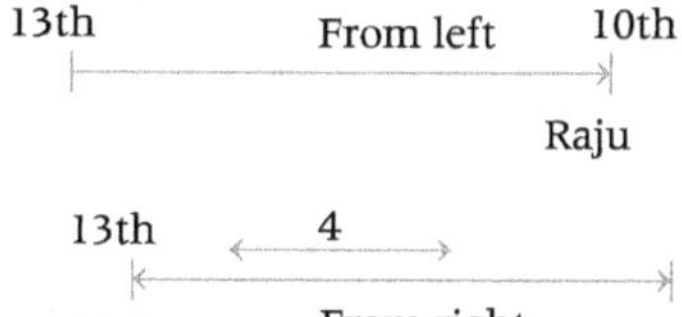

∴ Total number of persons = Sum of positions of both places − Number of places in middle − 2
$$= (10 + 13) - 4 - 2 = 17$$

12. *(a)* According to the question,

6th ⟶ 6th   9th ⟵
Gori   Arjun   Ziba

5 | 5 | 5 | 8

So, the number of students in a class
$$= 5 + 1 + 5 + 1 + 5 + 1 + 8 = 26$$

13. *(d)* According to the question,

Maya > Ankit > David, David > Anil [here, we use '>' for senior and '<' for junior] and Joy is the most senior. Now, we have

Joy > Maya > Ankit > David > Anil

Thus, Ankit is most junior.

14. *(d)* According to the question,

Rahul > Beena > Tiya and Tiya > Diksha > Jay [here, we use '>' for finishing before and '<' for finishing after]

So, we have

Rahul > Beena > Tiya > Diksha > Jay

Thus, Rahul won.

15. *(b)* Given, Total members = 16

Position from right = 7
$$Total = Left + Right - 1$$
$$16 = Left + 7 - 1$$
$$16 - 6 = Left$$
$$10th = Left$$

Hence, he is 10th from the left end.

16. *(b)* The chain has 46 hooks and a hook is 12th from the top, it means there are 11 hooks above that hook and 46 − 12 = 34 hooks below that hook.

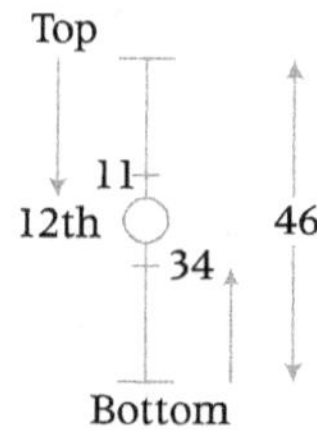

So, the position of that hook from the bottom
$$= 34 + 1 = 35th$$

17. *(b)* In a row of 28 books the rank of Maths book from the left is 18. So, there are 28 − 18 = 10 books to the right of Maths book.

And the rank of Reasoning book is 19th from the left. So, there are 28 − 19 = 9 books to the right of Reasoning book.

9 ⟵
Left ——— M — R ——— Right
⟶ 18th 19th ⟵
28

So, the rank of Maths book from the right end is 10 + 1 = 11 th. The rank of Reasoning book from the right end = 9 + 1 = 10 th

18. *(a)* The rank of Farah from the left end is 8th. It means, there are 7 girls to the left of Farah and her rank from the right end is 12th. So, there are 11 girls to the right of Farah.

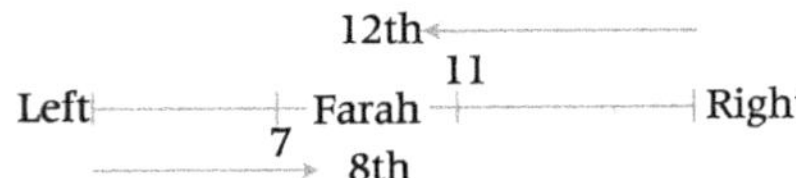

So, the total number of girls = 7 + Frieda + 11
$$= 7 + 1 + 11 = 19$$

So, the required number of girls to be added
$$= 30 - 19 = 11$$

19. *(a)* According to the question,

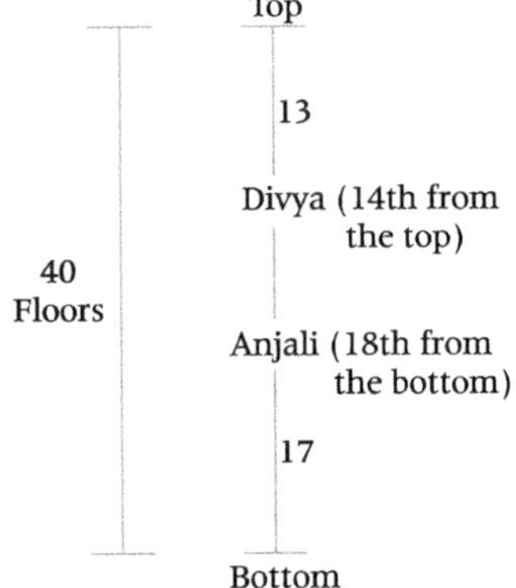

Number of floors = 40

Number of floors between Divya and Anjali
$$= 40 - (13 + \text{Divya} + \text{Anjali} + 17)$$
$$= 40 - (13 + 1 + 1 + 17) = 8$$

20. *(a)* According to the question,

Before

After,

Emily's new position is 19th from the left. But it is the same as Hari's earlier position, i.e. 10th from the right.

So, the total number of girls in the row
$$= 19 + 10 - 1 = 28$$

Now, Hari's new position is Emily's earlier position, i.e. 9th from the left. So, Hari's position from the right = 28 − 9 + 1 = 20th

7. Direction Sense Test

1. *(b)* From the adjoining figure it is clear that, the bus is moving in South-East direction.

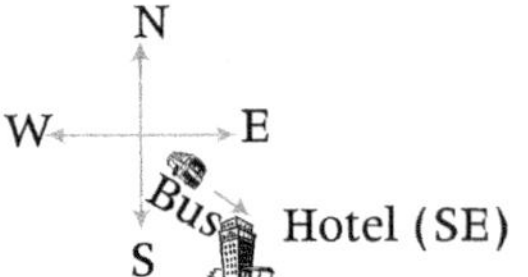

2. *(c)* According to the question, the opposite direction of South-East is North-West. So, James is facing North-West direction.

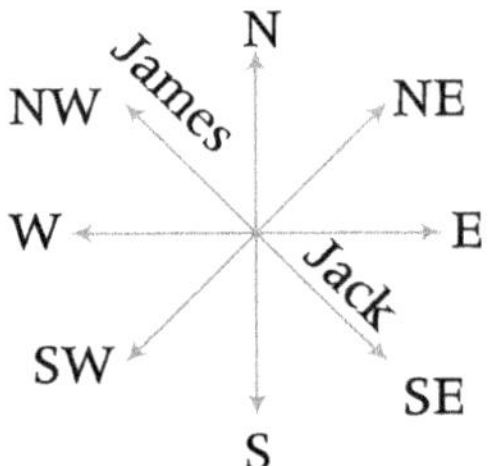

3. *(d)* Clearly, the garden is in North-East direction from Marie's present position.

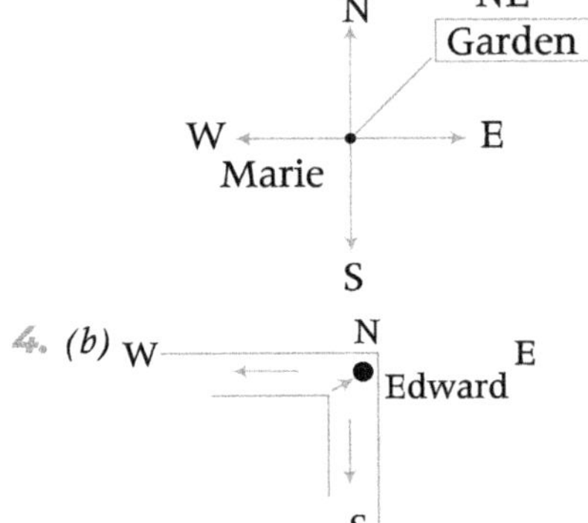

4. *(b)*

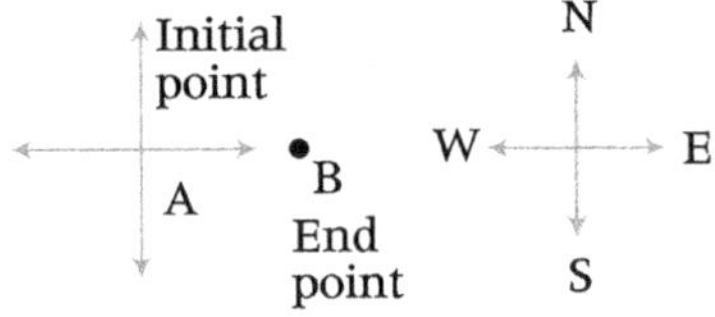

From the above diagram it is clear that, Edward will be moving in West direction after turning to his left.

5. *(a)* According to the question,

So, Adam has to move in East direction to reach at point B.

6. *(d)*

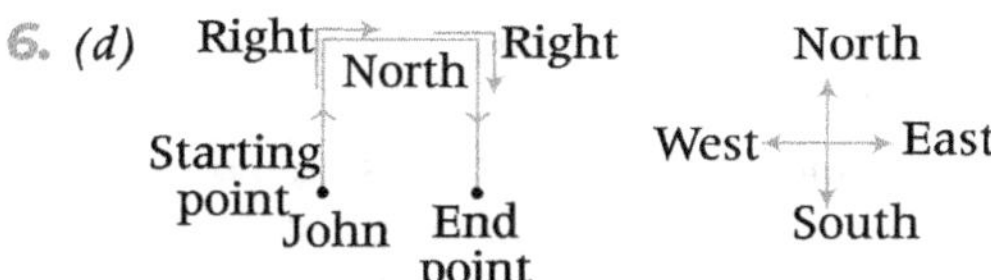

When we compare the above drawn direction diagram with the standard direction diagram, we find that John is moving in South direction.

7. *(b)* According to the question,

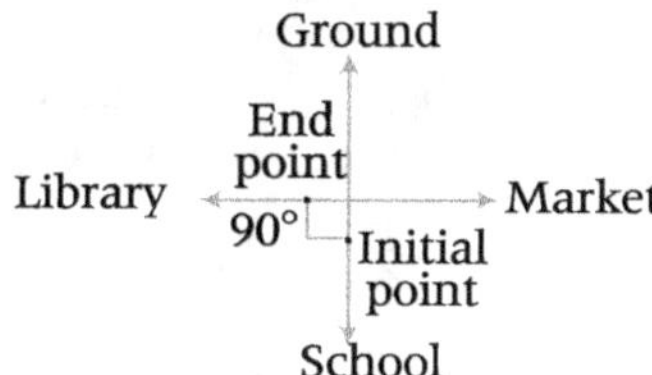

After turning 90° to the right, I will be facing the Library.

8. *(a)* According to the question,

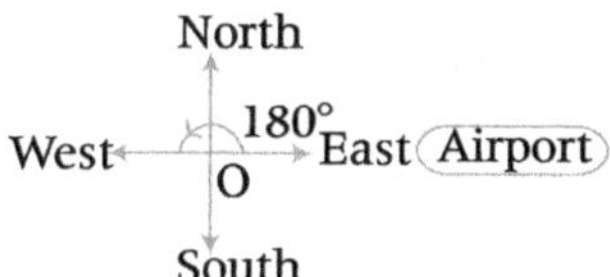

Clearly, the airport is in East direction. Paul turned 90° + 90° = 180° to face the West.

9. *(b)*

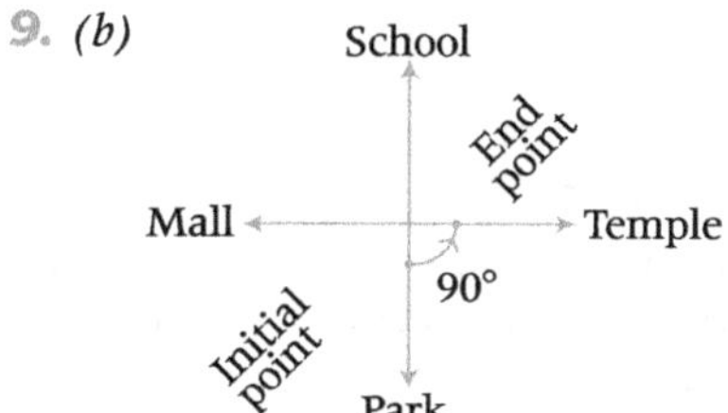

After turning 90° anti-clockwise, the boy faces the Temple.

10. *(a)*

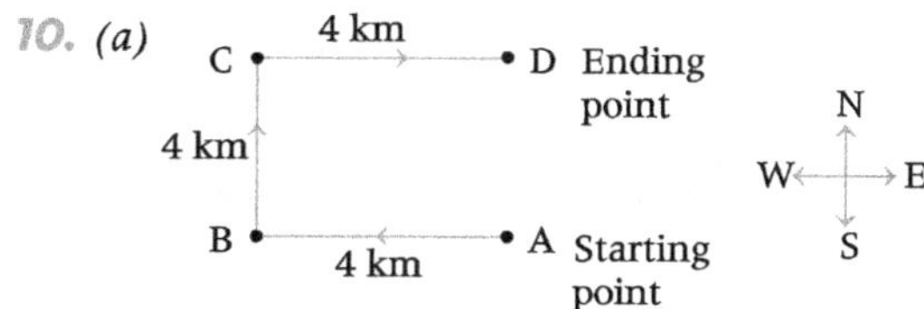

Clearly, the man is in North direction from his starting point.

11. *(c)* We have the direction graph as shown below

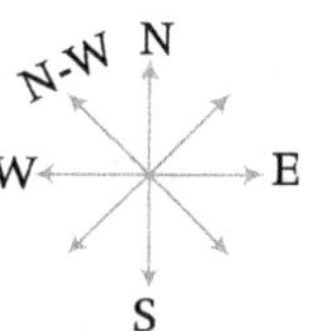

Now, as per the question, we have

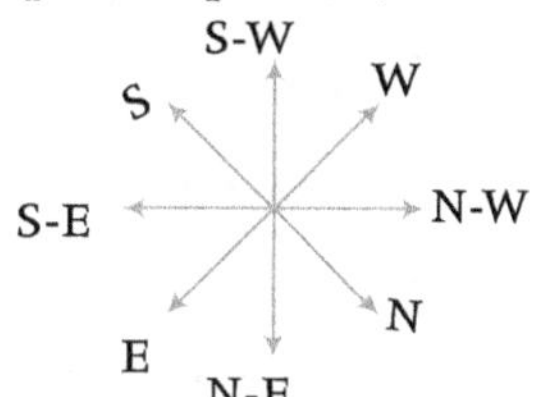

It is clear from the above diagram that, West will become South-East.

12. *(c)*

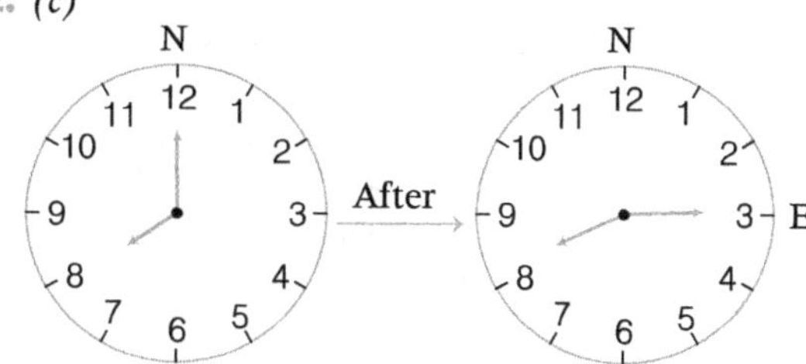

Clearly, after rotating 270° anti-clockwise the minute hand will point towards East direction.

13. *(d)* According to the question, direction diagram is as follows

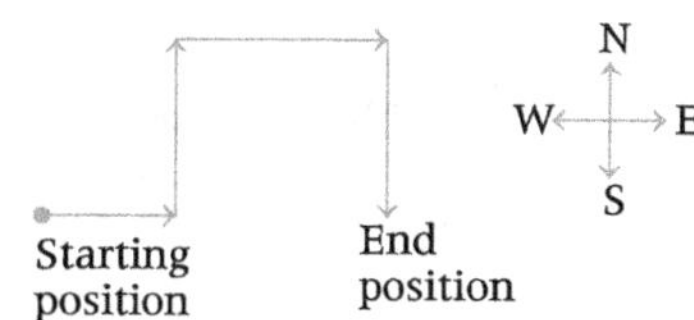

Hence, she is now in South direction.

14. *(d)*

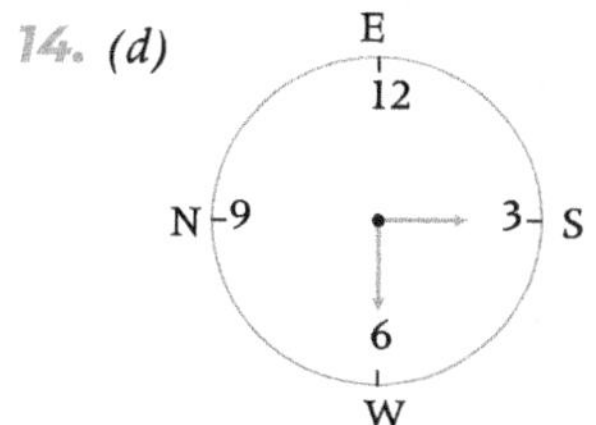

Clearly, the minute hand is in South direction.

15. *(b)* Total movement in one turn

$$= 3 \times 90 \,(\text{right}) - 90° \,(\text{left}) = 180° \,(\text{right})$$

So, to be in original direction i.e., 360° he has to take 2(90° × 2 = 180°) turns.

16. *(c)* Moving $\frac{1}{4}$th of the way around the track in clockwise direction.

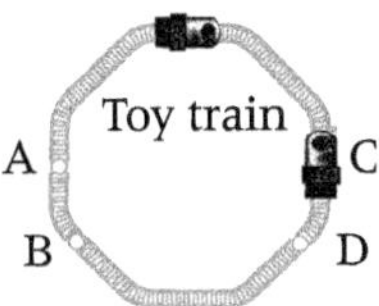

Here, the division of a track is in 8 equal parts. So, $\frac{1}{4}$th will be $\frac{8}{4}$ = 2 parts. Therefore, after moving 2 parts the train will reach close to the point C.

17. *(d)*

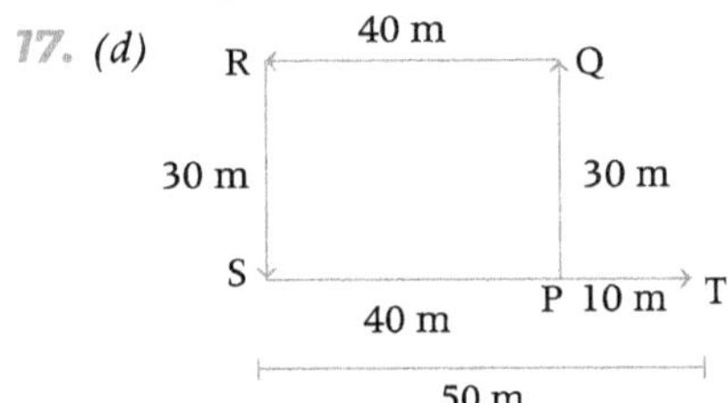

∴ Required distance, PT = ST − SP
$$= 50 - 40$$
$$= 10\,m$$

18. *(c)* According to the question,

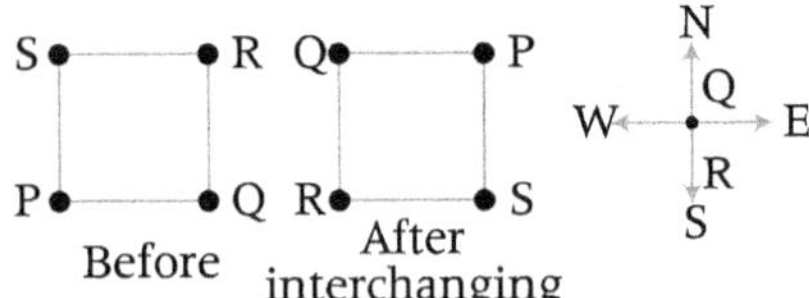

It is clear from the above diagram that, R is to the South of Q.

19. *(d)* From the adjacent diagram it is clear that, point B is in North-West direction of point O.

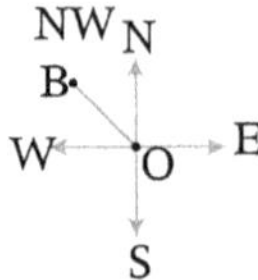

20. *(c)* Distance from Hina's house to bus stand
= 8 sides = 8 km

Distance from Remo's house to Post office
= 8 sides = 8 km

So, both are at the same distance.

21. *(d)* Two right angles means 90° + 90° = 180°

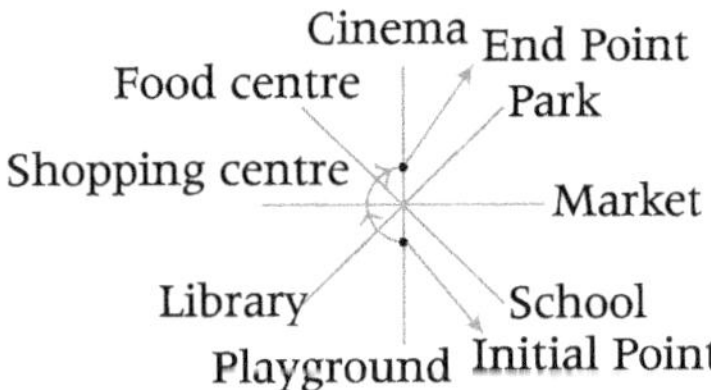

After turning 2 right angles, he is facing the cinema.

22. *(c)*

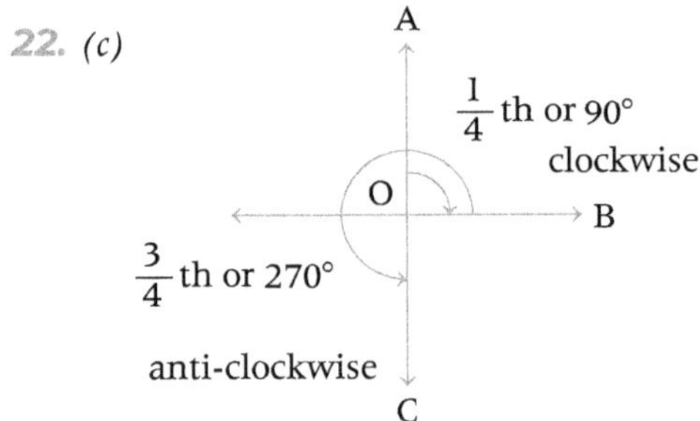

In the end Pihu was facing the OC direction i.e. South direction.

23. *(c)*

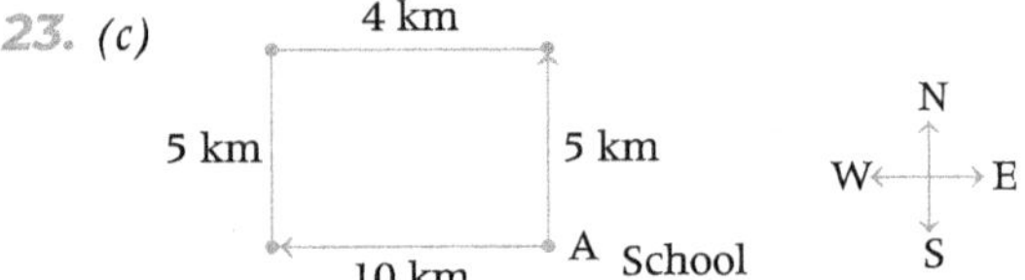

Clearly, Shruti is 10 km far away from her school and in West direction from school.

24. *(b)* Starting from point X to the end point Y, all the movements are given below

East, North-East, North, East, South, South-East, South, South-West, West, North, East, North, North-West, North and East.

Total number of directions
= 8 (i.e. East, West, North, South, North-East, North-West, South-East and South-West).

8. Mathematical Operations

1. *(b)* According to the question,

$? = 12 + 6 \div 3 - 2 \times 8$

$\quad\quad \downarrow \quad \downarrow \quad \downarrow \quad \downarrow$

$\quad\quad \div \quad - \quad \times \quad +$

$= 12 \div 6 - 3 \times 2 + 8$ (using VBODMAS rule)

$= 2 - 3 \times 2 + 8 = 2 - 6 + 8$

$= (2 + 8) - 6 = 4$

2. *(a)* According to the question,

$? = 54 \div 16 - 3 \times 6 + 2$

$\quad\quad \downarrow \quad \downarrow \quad \downarrow \quad \downarrow$

$\quad\quad - \quad \times \quad + \quad \div$

$= 54 - 16 \times 3 + 6 \div 2$ (using VBODMAS rule)

$= 54 - 16 \times 3 + 3$

$= 54 - 48 + 3$

$= 6 + 3 = 9$

3. *(d)* According to the question,

$? = 12 + (3 \times 1) + 4 - 1$

$\quad\quad \downarrow \quad \downarrow \quad \downarrow \quad \downarrow$

$\quad\quad \times \quad - \quad \times \quad +$

$= 12 \times (3 - 1) \times 4 + 1$ (using VBODMAS rule)

$= 12 \times 2 \times 4 + 1 = 96 + 1 = 97$

4. *(c)* According to the question,

$? = 7 - 10 \times 5 \div 6 + 4$

$\quad\quad \downarrow \quad \downarrow \quad \downarrow \quad \downarrow$

$\quad\quad + \quad \div \quad \times \quad -$

$= 7 + 10 \div 5 \times 6 - 4$ (using VBODMAS rule)

$= 7 + 2 \times 6 - 4 = (7 + 12) - 4 = 15$

5. *(a)* $? = 10 \times 5 \div 3 - 2 + 3$

$= 10 \div 5 + 3 \times 2 - 3$

$= 2 + 3 \times 2 - 3$

$= 2 + 6 - 3$

$= 8 - 3$

$= 5$

6. *(b)* According to the question,

Required answer

$= (15 \times 9) \div (12 \times 4) \times (4 \div 4)$

$\quad\quad \downarrow \quad\quad \downarrow \quad\quad \downarrow \quad\quad \downarrow \quad\quad \downarrow$

$\quad\quad - \quad\quad + \quad\quad - \quad\quad - \quad\quad +$

$= (15 - 9) + (12 - 4) - (4 + 4)$

(using VBODMAS rule)

$= 6 + 8 - 8 = 6$

7. *(a)* According to the question,

$? = 18\,C\ 14\,A\ 6\,B\ 16\,D\ 4$

$\quad\quad \downarrow \quad\quad \downarrow \quad \downarrow \quad\quad \downarrow$

$\quad\quad \times \quad\quad + \quad - \quad\quad \div$

$= 18 \times 14 + 6 - 16 \div 4$ (using VBODMAS rule)

$= 18 \times 14 + 6 - 4$

$= 252 + 6 - 4 = 258 - 4$

$= 254$

8. *(a)* According to the question,

$? = 4\,D\ 16\,A\ 5\,B\ 8\,C\ 5$

$\quad\quad \downarrow \quad\quad \downarrow \quad \downarrow \quad \downarrow$

$\quad\quad + \quad\quad \times \quad \div \quad -$

$= 4 + 16 \times 5 \div 8 - 5$ (using VBODMAS rule)

$= 4 + 16 \times 0.625 - 5$

$= 4 + 10 - 5 = 14 - 5 = 9$

9. *(b)* According to the question,

$? = 15\,B\ 3\,C\ 24\,A\ 12\,D\ 2$

$\quad\quad \downarrow \quad \downarrow \quad\quad \downarrow \quad\quad \downarrow$

$\quad\quad \div \quad + \quad\quad - \quad\quad \times$

$= 15 \div 3 + 24 - 12 \times 2$

$= 5 + 24 - 12 \times 2 = 5 + 24 - 24 = 5$

(using VBODMAS rule)

10. *(c)* As,

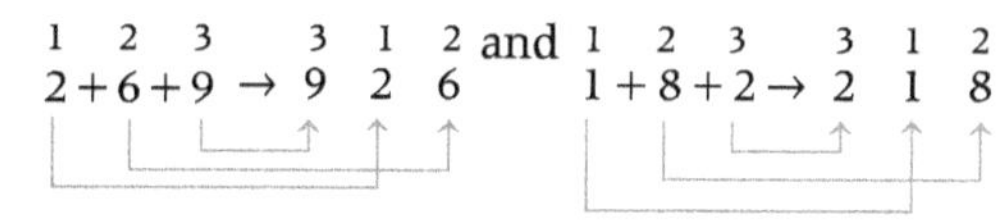

Similarly,

$\therefore ? = 143$

11. *(b)* As,

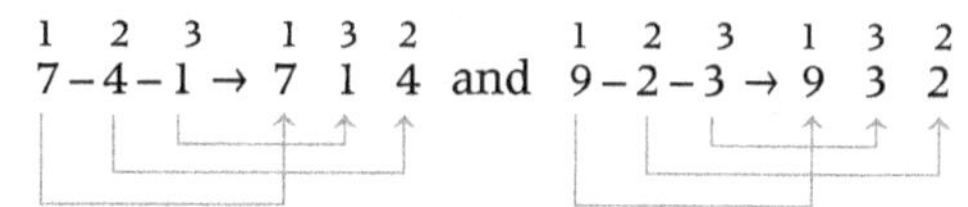

Similarly,

12. *(b)* As,

$\quad\quad\quad 4 \ \times \ 6 \ \times \ 2$

$\quad\quad -1 \downarrow \quad -1 \downarrow \quad -1 \downarrow$

$\quad\quad\quad 3 \quad\quad 5 \quad\quad 1$

and,

$$3 \times 9 \times 8$$

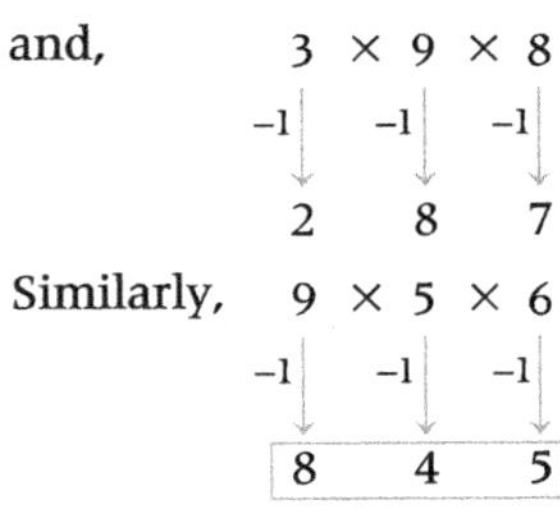

$$2 \quad 8 \quad 7$$

Similarly,

$$9 \times 5 \times 6$$

$$\boxed{8 \quad 4 \quad 5}$$

? = 845

13. *(c)* As,

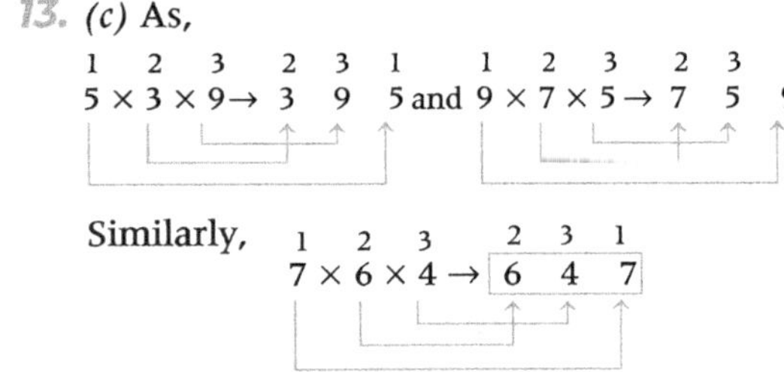

Similarly,

$$\begin{matrix} 1 & 2 & 3 & & 2 & 3 & 1 \\ 7 & \times 6 & \times 4 & \to & \boxed{6 & 4 & 7} \end{matrix}$$

$\therefore ? = 647$

14. *(c)* As,

$$\begin{matrix} 1 & 2 & 3 & & 2 & 3 & 1 \\ 4 & \times 6 & \times 9 & \to & 6 & 9 & 4 \end{matrix}$$

and

$$\begin{matrix} 1 & 2 & 3 & & 2 & 3 & 1 \\ 5 & \times 3 & \times 2 & \to & 3 & 2 & 5 \end{matrix}$$

Similarly,

$$\begin{matrix} 1 & 2 & 3 & & 2 & 3 & 1 \\ 7 & \times 8 & \times 2 & \to & \boxed{8 & 2 & 7} \end{matrix}$$

15. *(c)* As, $4 - 4 \Rightarrow 4 \times 4 = 16$

$$6 - 6 \Rightarrow 6 \times 6 = 36 \text{ and } 2 - 2 \Rightarrow 2 \times 2 = 4$$

Similarly, $5 - 5 \Rightarrow 5 \times 5 = 25$

16. *(d)* From option (d), we get,

$$64 \div 4 \times 5 + 8 = 88$$

On applying VBODMAS rule,

$$64 \div 4 \times 5 + 8 = 88$$
$$16 \times 5 + 8 = 88$$
$$80 + 8 = 88$$

17. *(b)* From option (b), we get,

$$32 - 16 \div 2 = 24$$

On applying VBODMAS rule,

$$32 - 16 \div 2 = 24$$
$$32 - 8 = 24$$

$$24 = 24$$

Hence, option (b) is correct.

18. (c) From option (c), we get,

$$70 \div 10 \times 20 < 30 \times 8$$
$$7 \times 20 < 240$$
$$140 < 240$$

Hence, option (c) is correct.

19. (b) On putting the given sign, we get,

$$40 + 32 \times 10 \div 20 - 16$$

By VBODMAS rule,

$$= 40 + 32 \times 10 \div 20 - 16$$
$$= 40 + 32 \times 1/2 - 16$$
$$= 40 + 16 - 16$$
$$= 40 - 0 = 40$$

Hence, option (b) is correct.

20. (c) Using the correct symbols, we have

$$= (20 \times 8) + (8 \times 8) - 12$$
$$= 160 + 64 - 12$$
$$= 224 - 12 = 212$$

Hence, option (c) is correct.

21. (c) By making the interchanges given in option (a).

$2 - 5 + 3 = 4$ or $0 \neq 4$, which is false

By making the interchanges given in option (b)

$3 - 2 + 5 = 4$ or $6 \neq 4$ (False)

By making the interchanges given in option (c)

$5 - 3 + 2 = 4$ or $4 = 4$ (True)

By making the interchanges given in option (d)

$3 - 5 + 4 = 2$ or $2 \neq 4$ (False)

Hence, option (c) is correct.

9. Inserting the Missing Character

1. *(b)* Either consider rowwise or columnwise, the multiplication of numbers in first and third blocks gives the value in the second block. Considering rowwise

As, $4 \times 3 = 12$

and $5 \times 3 = 15$

Similarly, $20 \times 9 = 180$

2. *(a)* In each column, the sum of the numbers in first three blocks gives the value in the fourth block

As $\qquad 8 + 20 + 2 = 30$

and $\qquad 2 + 9 + 11 = 22$

Similarly, $6 + 7 + 9 = 22$

So, 22 will replace the question mark.

3. *(d)* The pattern is as follows:

$$9 \times 7 = 63$$

and $\qquad 13 \times 7 = 91$

Similarly, $17 \times 4 = 68$

So, 68 will replace the question mark.

4. *(d)* The pattern is as follows:

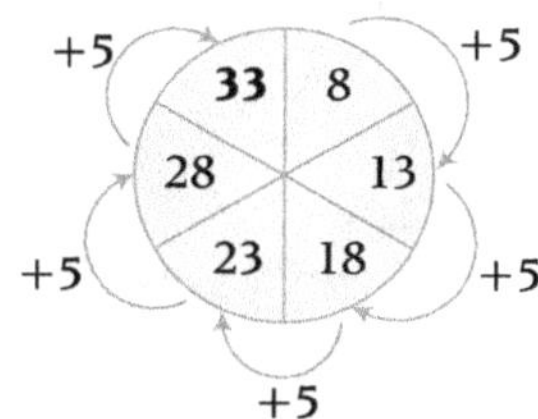

So, 33 will replace the question mark.

5. *(b)* The sum of all the numbers at the corner is multiplied by 2 to obtain the middle number.

As, $\qquad (10 + 4 + 3 + 5) \times 2 = 22 \times 2 = 44$

and $\qquad (8 + 2 + 1 + 7) \times 2 = 18 \times 2 = 36$

Similarly, $(9 + 3 + 12 + 1) \times 2 = 25 \times 2 = 50$

So, 50 will complete the third figure.

6. *(d)* The pattern is as follows:

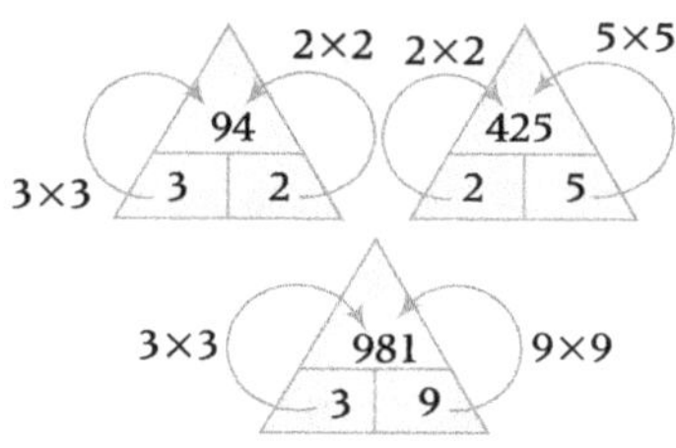

So, 981 is the missing number.

7. *(a)* The pattern is as follows :

As, $\qquad 7 + 3 + 4 + 4 = 18$

$\qquad\qquad 9 + 8 + 1 + 15 = 33$

Similarly, $13 + 3 + 5 + 7 = 28$

Hence, option (a) is correct.

8. *(b)* The pattern is as follows

As, $(6 \times 6) + (4 \times 4) = 36 + 16 = 52$

and $(4 \times 4) + (9 \times 9) = 16 + 81 = 97$

Similarly, $(7 \times 7) + (1 \times 1) = 49 + 1 = 50$

So, 50 will replace the question mark.

9. *(a)* The pattern is as follows :

As, $\qquad\qquad 8 + 3 + 6 = 17$

$\qquad\qquad\qquad 9 + 9 + 2 = 20$

Similarly, $12 + 8 + 16 = 36$

Hence, option (a) is correct.

10. *(c)* Consider rowwise,

In row I $\quad$ B $\xrightarrow{+2}$ D $\xrightarrow{+2}$ F

In row II $\quad$ D $\xrightarrow{+2}$ F $\xrightarrow{+2}$ H

In row III $\quad$ F $\xrightarrow{+2}$ H $\xrightarrow{+2}$ [J]

So, J will replace the question mark.

11. *(a)* The pattern is as follows:

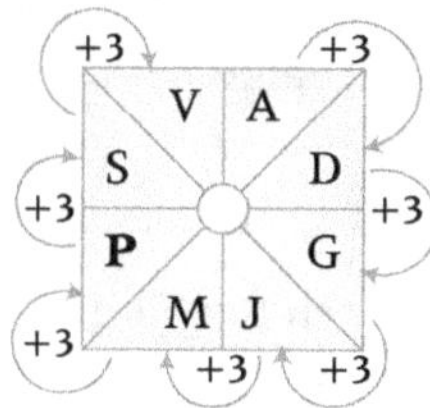

So, P will replace the question mark.

12. *(a)* The pattern is as follows

As, $4 + 4 = 8$, positional value of H in English alphabetical order.

$7 + 3 = 10$, positional value of J in English alphabetical order.

Similarly, $5 + 2 = 7$, positional value of G in English alphabetical order.

So, G will replace the question mark.

13. *(a)*

$\therefore P = 5$ and $Q = 4$

14. *(d)*

X	6	4	8
3	18	12	24
4	24	16	32

$\therefore$? $= 16$

15. *(a)* As, ☆ =10 sides

$\Rightarrow 10 \times 3 = 30$

and ⌂ = 5 sides $\Rightarrow 5 \times 3 = 15$

Similarly, △ = 3 sides

∴ $\qquad 3 \times 3 = 9$

16. *(d)* The pattern is as follows

$4 \times 3 = 12, 6 \times 4 = 24, 8 \times 5 = 40, 10 \times 6 = 60,$
$12 \times 7 = 84, 14 \times 8 = 112, 16 \times 9 = 144$

So, 144 will complete the given number puzzle.

17. *(a)* The pattern is as follows

As, $\qquad 3 + 5 = 8 = H$

$\qquad\qquad$ (Place value of H is '8')

for numerical value $= 8 \times 2 = 16$

We get = H16

Similarly, $\qquad 4 + 1 = 5$

$\qquad\qquad$ (Place value of E is '5')

For numerical value $= 5 \times 2 = 10$

We get = E10

Hence, option (a) is correct.

18. *(d)* Here, in each row and column, letters A, B and C must appear once.

So, the missing letter is C.

The numbers follow below pattern columnwise,

In column I, $2 \times 6 = 12$

In column II, $7 \times 9 = 63$

Similarly, in column III,

$\qquad 8 \times 4 = 32$

So, 32C will replace the question mark.

19. *(b)*

$$
\begin{array}{ccc}
& 20 & \leftarrow 11+9 \\
& 11 \quad 9 & \\
5+6 & & 6+3 \\
& 5 \quad 6 \quad 3 &
\end{array}
$$

∴ P = 6 and Q = 20

20. *(a)*

X	10	8	12
8	80	64	96
4	40	32	48

∴ ? = 8

10. Hidden Figures

1. *(a)* The given alphabet is hidden in option figure (a) as shown.

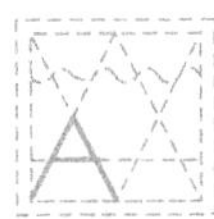

2. *(c)* The given small shape (X) is hidden in larger shape (c) as shown.

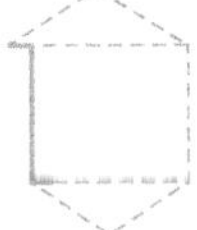

3. *(d)* The given figure (X) is hidden in option figure (d) as shown.

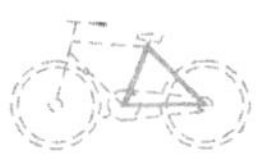

4. *(c)* The given figure (X) is hidden in option figure (c) as shown.

5. *(d)* The given shape (X) is hidden in option figure (d) as shown.

6. *(d)* The given figure (X) is hidden in option figure (d) as shown.

7. *(d)* The given figure (X) is hidden in option figure (d) as shown.

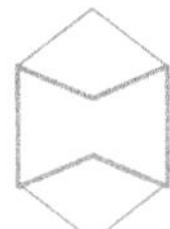

8. *(a)* The given figure (X) is hidden in option figure (a) as shown.

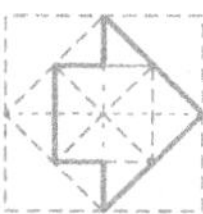

9. *(b)* The option figure (b) is exactly embedded in figure (X) as shown.

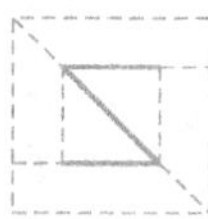

10. *(a)* The option figure (a) is hidden in the given figure (X) as shown.

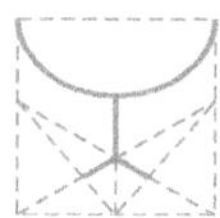

11. *(c)* Option figure (c) is hidden in the given figure (X).

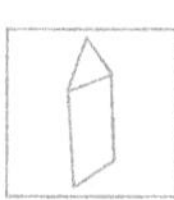

12. *(d)* Option figure (d) is hidden in the given figure (X).

13. *(a)* Option figure (a) is hidden in the given figure (X).

14. *(a)* Option figure (a) is hidden in figure (X).

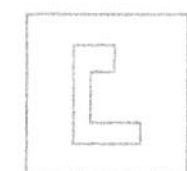

15. *(b)* Option figure (b) is hidden in figure (X).

11. Mirror Images

1. *(c)*

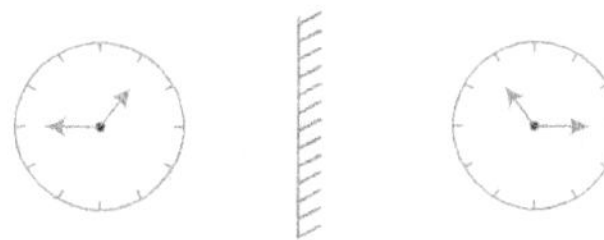

Original image   Mirror   Mirror image

2. *(d)*

Original image   Mirror   Mirror image

3. *(d)*

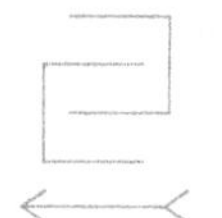 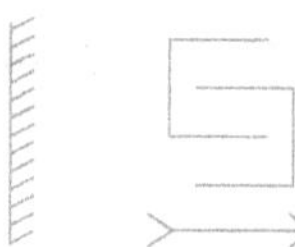

Original image   Mirror   Mirror image

4. *(b)*

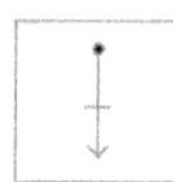 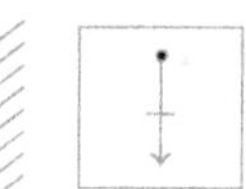

Original image   Mirror   Mirror image

5. *(a)*

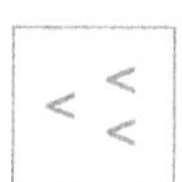 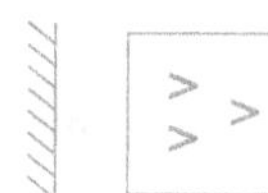

Mirror image   Mirror   Original image

6. *(d)*

Mirror image   Mirror   Original image

7. *(a)*

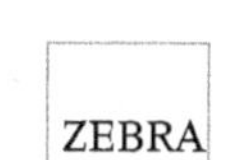

Original image   Mirror   Mirror image

8. *(d)*

Mirror image   Mirror   Original image

9. *(a)*

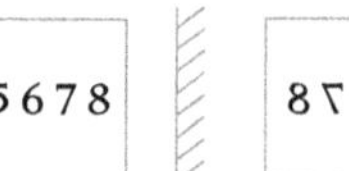

Original image   Mirror   Mirror image

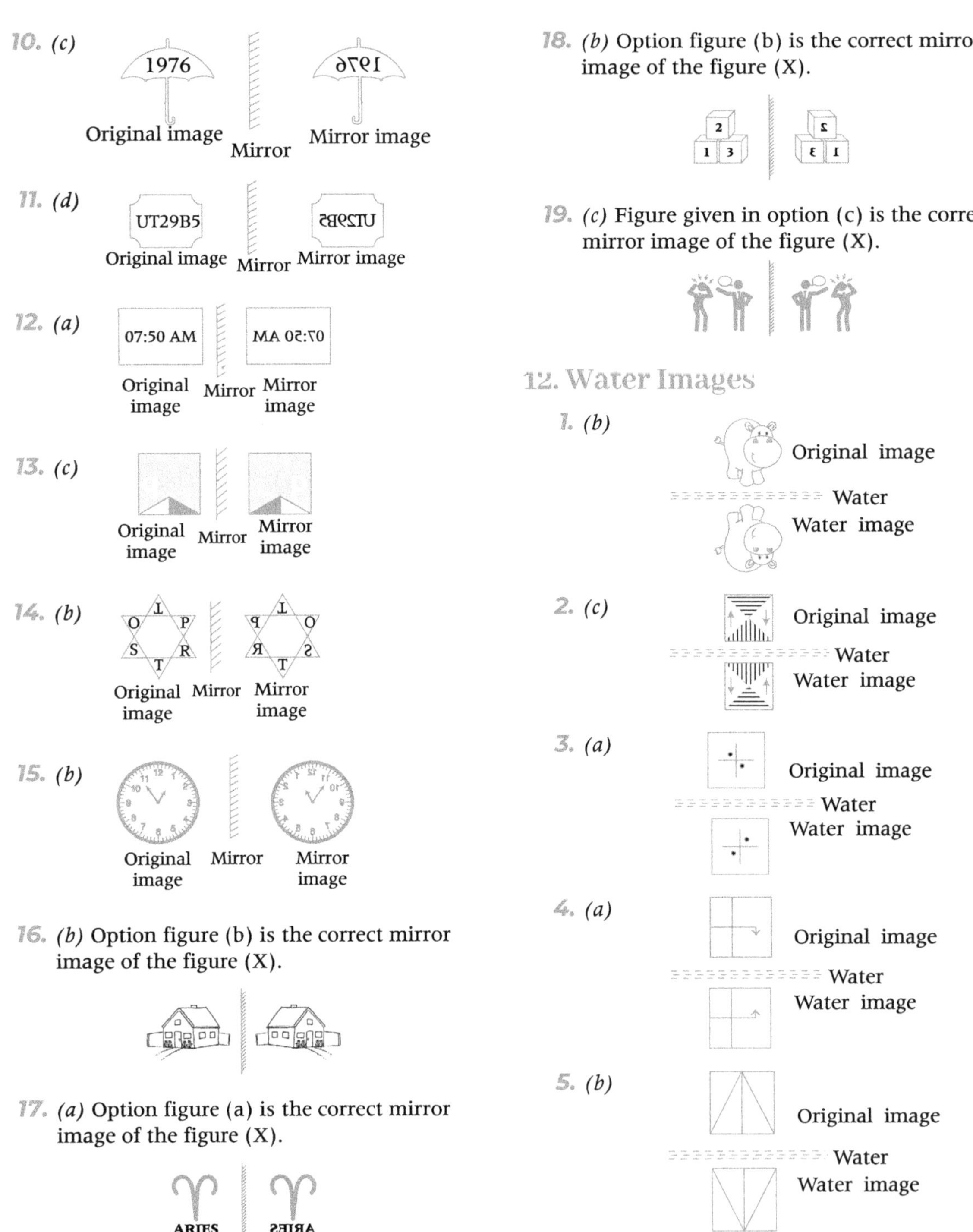

10. (c)

Original image   Mirror   Mirror image

11. (d)

Original image   Mirror   Mirror image

12. (a)

Original   Mirror   Mirror
image   image

13. (c)

Original   Mirror   Mirror
image   image

14. (b)

Original   Mirror   Mirror
image   image

15. (b)

Original   Mirror   Mirror
image   image

16. (b) Option figure (b) is the correct mirror image of the figure (X).

17. (a) Option figure (a) is the correct mirror image of the figure (X).

18. (b) Option figure (b) is the correct mirror image of the figure (X).

19. (c) Figure given in option (c) is the correct mirror image of the figure (X).

12. Water Images

1. (b)

Original image
Water
Water image

2. (c)

Original image
Water
Water image

3. (a)

Original image
Water
Water image

4. (a)

Original image
Water
Water image

5. (b)

Original image
Water
Water image

6. *(d)*

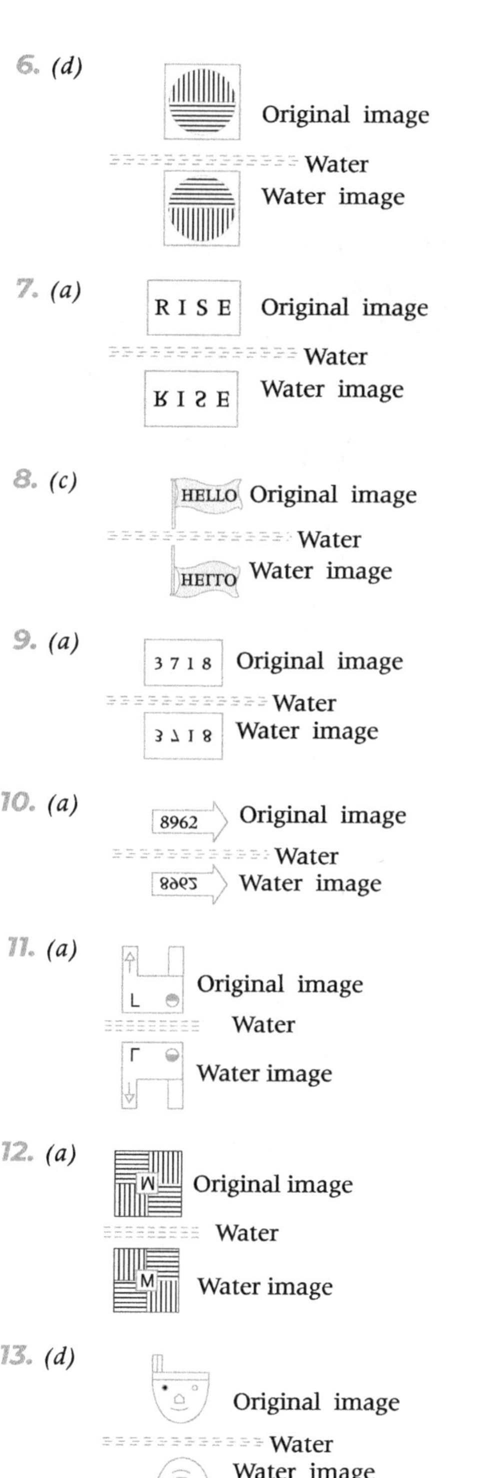

Original image

Water

Water image

7. *(a)* R I S E — Original image

Water

Water image

8. *(c)* HELLO — Original image

Water

Water image

9. *(a)* 3 7 1 8 — Original image

Water

Water image

10. *(a)* 8962 — Original image

Water

Water image

11. *(a)* Original image

Water

Water image

12. *(a)* Original image

Water

Water image

13. *(d)* Original image

Water

Water image

14. *(a)*

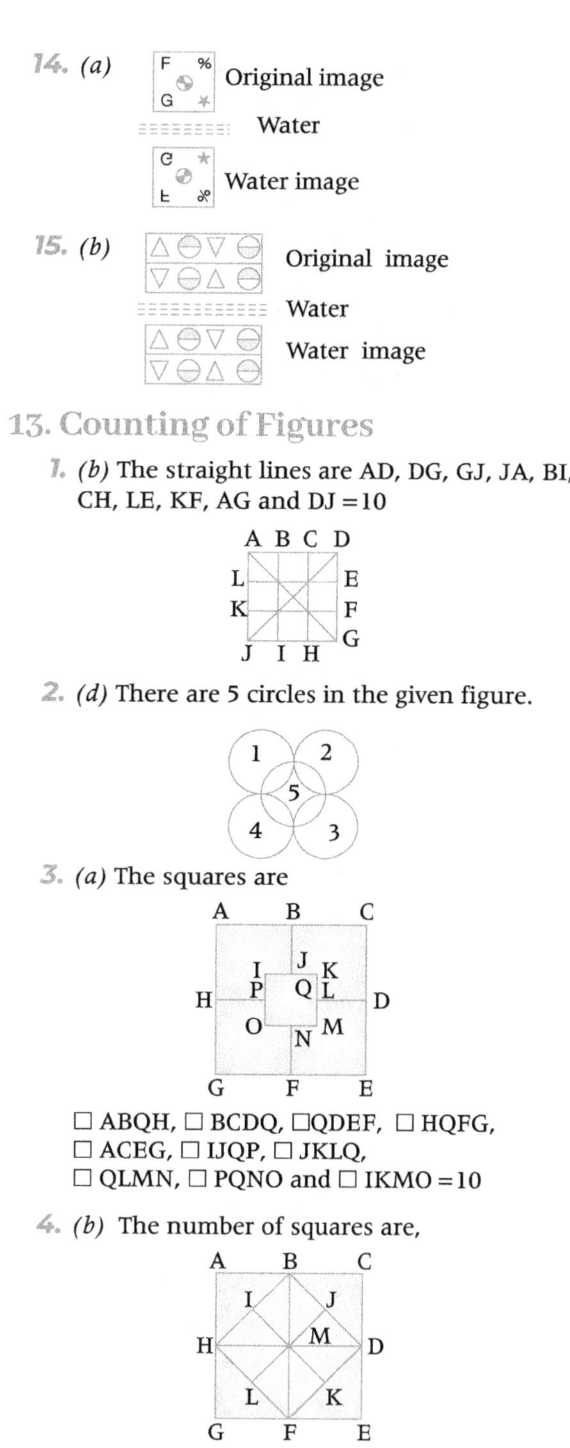

Original image

Water

Water image

15. *(b)* Original image

Water

Water image

13. Counting of Figures

1. *(b)* The straight lines are AD, DG, GJ, JA, BI, CH, LE, KF, AG and DJ = 10

2. *(d)* There are 5 circles in the given figure.

3. *(a)* The squares are

□ ABQH, □ BCDQ, □ QDEF, □ HQFG, □ ACEG, □ IJQP, □ JKLQ, □ QLMN, □ PQNO and □ IKMO = 10

4. *(b)* The number of squares are,

□ ABMH, □ BCDM, □ HMFG □ MDEF, □ ACEG, □ BJMI, □ JDKM, □ MKFL, □ IMLH and □ BDFH = 10

5. *(a)* The number of triangles are
ΔAGF, ΔDIF, ΔABE, ΔIED,
ΔHCD, ΔBEC, ΔIFD and ΔABC = 8

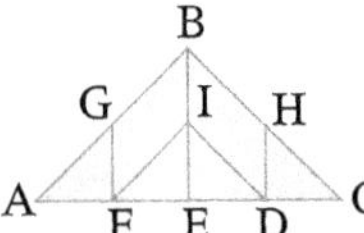

6. *(d)* The number of rectangles are

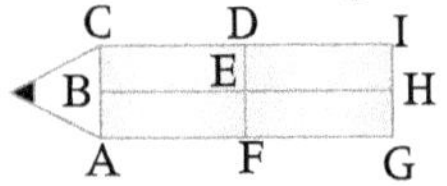

☐ABEF, ☐BCDE, ☐FEHG, ☐EDIH,
☐ABHG, ☐BCIH, ☐ACDF, ☐FDIG
and ☐ACIG = 9

7. *(a)*

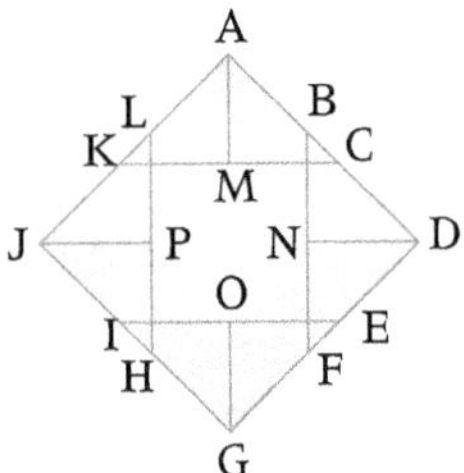

The straight lines are AD, DG, GJ, JA, LH,
BF, KC, IE, AM, ND, OG and JP = 12

8. *(c)* The triangles are

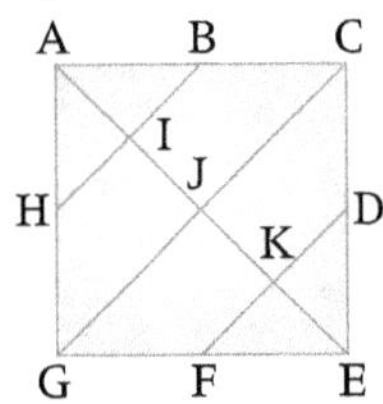

ΔABI, ΔAHI, ΔABH, ΔDKE, ΔFKE, ΔDFE,
ΔEGJ, ΔGJA, ΔACG, ΔACE, ΔEJC, ΔEGC
ΔCEG and ΔEGA = 14

9. *(a)* Using three dots at a time from the
given five dots, only 6 triangles can be
drawn

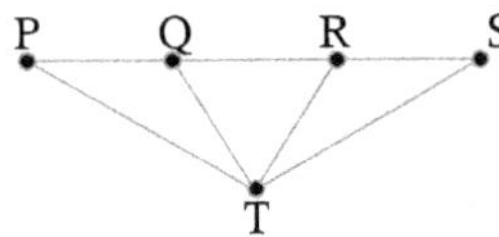

The triangles are ΔPQT, ΔQRT, ΔRST, ΔPRT,
ΔQST and ΔPST.

10. *(d)*

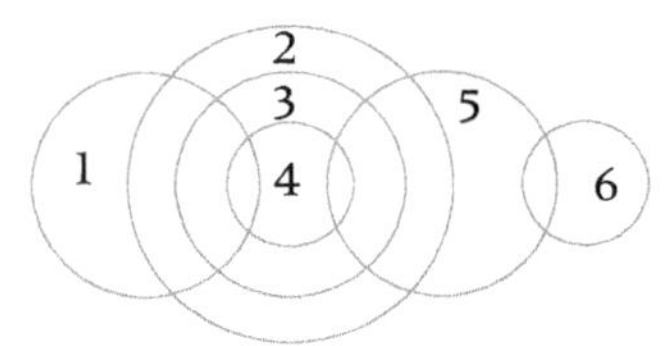

There are 6 circles in the above figure.

11. *(b)* The straight lines are
AC, CE, EG, GA, AI, CK, EM, GO,
FB, HD, BH, BD, DF, FH, IK, KM, MO and
OI = 18

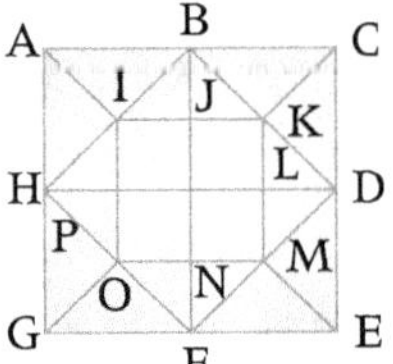

12. *(b)*

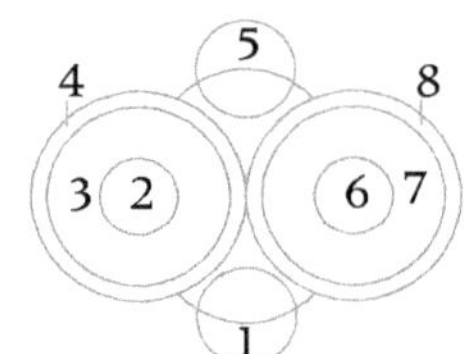

So, there are 8 circles in the above figure.

Sol. *(Q. Nos. 13 and 14)*

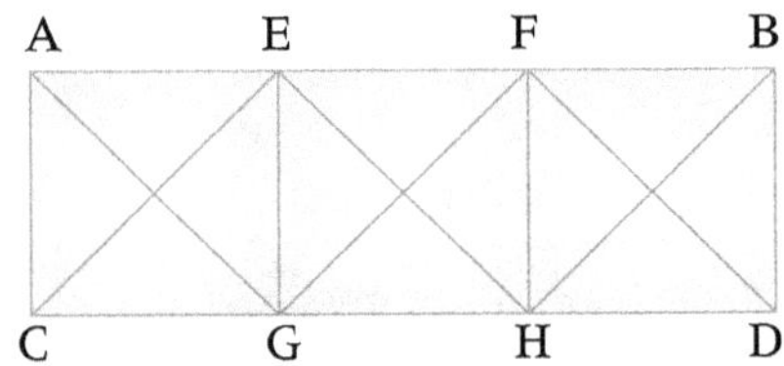

13. *(b)* The straight lines are
AE, EF, FB, AB, DH, HG, GC, AC, EG, FH, BD
and CD = 12

14. *(c)* The squares are ☐ACGE, ☐EGHF,
☐FHDB

15. *(d)*

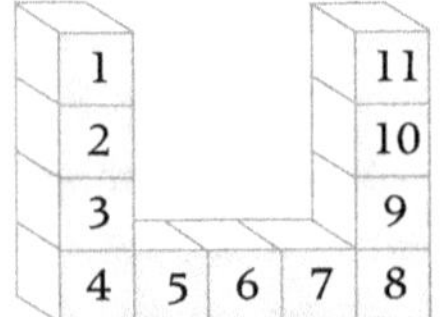

Clearly, there are 11 cubes in the above
figure.

Practice Set 1

1. *(d)* Letter 'T' will complete bothe the given words as RUS**T** and **T**OP.

2. *(d)* In first pair, the second figure is the mirror image of first figure. So, option figure (d) will complete the second pair because it is the mirror image of first figure given in second pair.

3. *(c)* The parking spots numbers follow below pattern

$$2 \xrightarrow{+3} 5 \xrightarrow{+4} 9 \xrightarrow{+5} 14 \xrightarrow{+6} \boxed{20} \xrightarrow{+7} 27$$

So, the car is standing on parking spot number 20.

4. *(c)* In all the figures, except figure (c) the small white circle in the larger circle is missing. So, figure (c) is different from others.

5. *(b)* We know that, the colour of leaf is green. But here, green is called carrot. So, the colour of leaf is carrot.

6. *(d)* It is clear from the adjacent diagram that, after turning 180° clockwise, Julia will face the park.

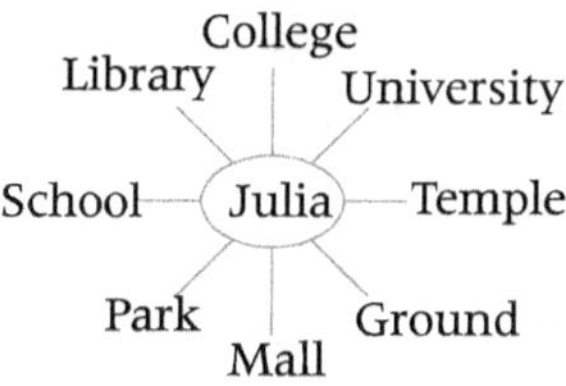

7. *(b)* The only word 'PRINT' can be formed from the given word CORPORATION.

8. *(a)* In a row of 35 boys, the rank of Danny is 16th from the left. It means, there are $35 - 16 = 19$ boys to the right of Danny.

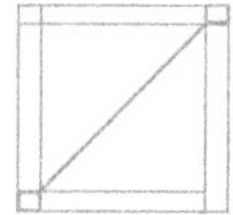

So, the rank of Danny from the right is $19 + 1 = 20$ th.

9. *(c)* The given figure (X) is embedded in figure (c) as shown below

10. *(b)* The pattern is as follows:
In figure I, $8 \times 4 \times 2 \times 3 = 192$
In figure II, $5 \times 9 \times 4 \times 4 = 720$
Similarly, in figure III, $9 \times 3 \times 5 \times 1 = 135$

11. *(c)* The correct mirror image of the given combination is

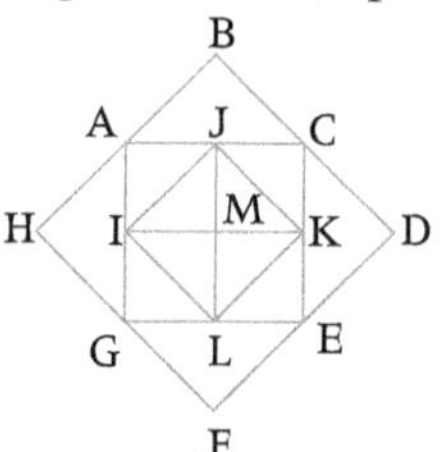

12. *(c)* The order of given animals according to their order in increasing order is
Ant → Mouse → Dog → Horse → Giraffe,
i.e. 3, 5, 1, 2, 4

13. *(b)* The given figure can be represented as

The squares formed are,
☐BDFH, ☐ACEG, ☐IJKL, ☐AJMI, ☐JCKM, ☐MKEL, ☐IMLG = 7

14. *(b)* The given information can be represented as

Food Person	Burger	Ice-cream	Pizza
Lina	✔	✗	✔
Anna	✔	✗	✗
Kari	✗	✔	✔
Paul	✔	✔	✗

Clearly, Karl likes pizza and ice-cream.

15. *(c)* The working place of 'Lawyer' is court, similarly the working place of a Scientist is Laboratory.

16. *(b)* The letters follow the below pattern

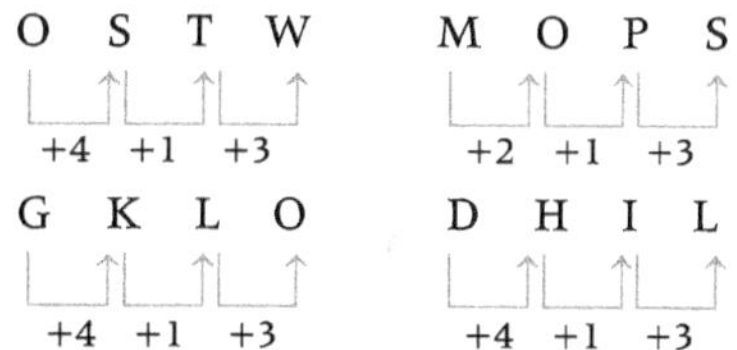

It is clearly seen that except 'MOPS' all others follow the similar pattern.

17. *(d)* As,

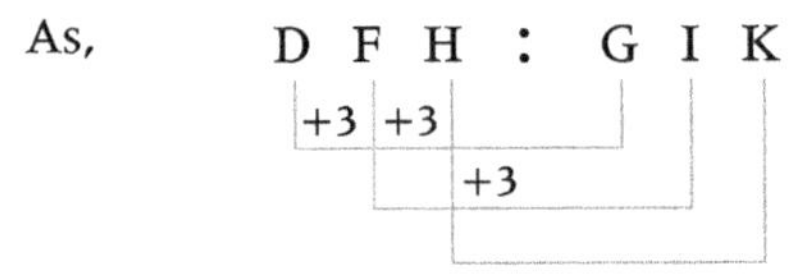

Similarly,

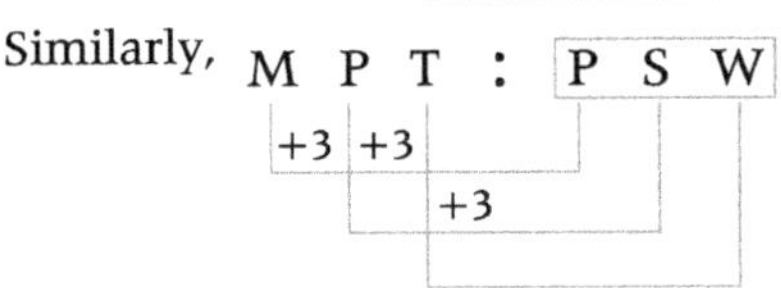

So, P 11 R 9 T 7 is related to Q 10 S 8 U 6.

18. *(d)* Except option (d), all the co-related to each other in some way.

19. *(c)* Except option (c), all are related in same way.

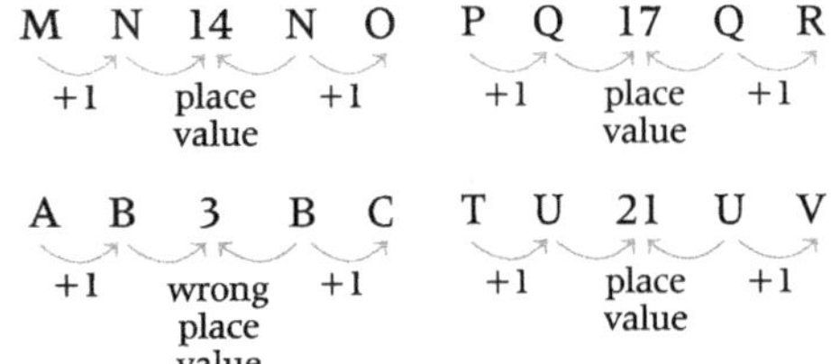

20. *(c)* The pattern follows by the fish

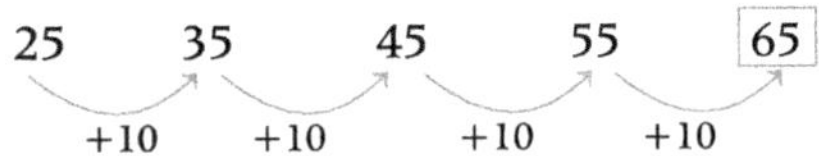

Hence, 65 will come at the place of question mark.

21. *(d)* The pattern is as follows

As,

$$7 \quad 8 \quad 5 \quad 4 \quad 9$$
$$-2 \quad -2 \quad -2 \quad -2 \quad -2$$
$$5 \quad 6 \quad 3 \quad 2 \quad 7$$

Similarly,

$$3 \quad 5 \quad 9 \quad 2 \quad 6$$
$$-2 \quad -2 \quad -2 \quad -2 \quad -2$$
$$1 \quad 3 \quad 7 \quad 0 \quad 4$$

22. *(d)* MAGNET can be formed from the letters of given word.

23. *(b)* The pattern is as follows

As,

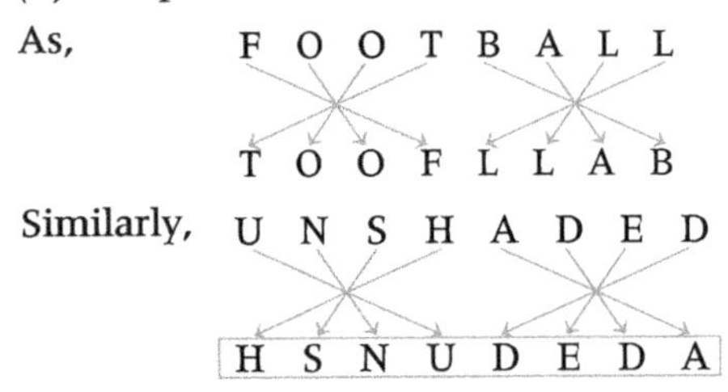

24. *(b)* There are two D's i.e., NDX and DDX. Hence, option (b) is correct.

25. *(c)* The pattern is

As,

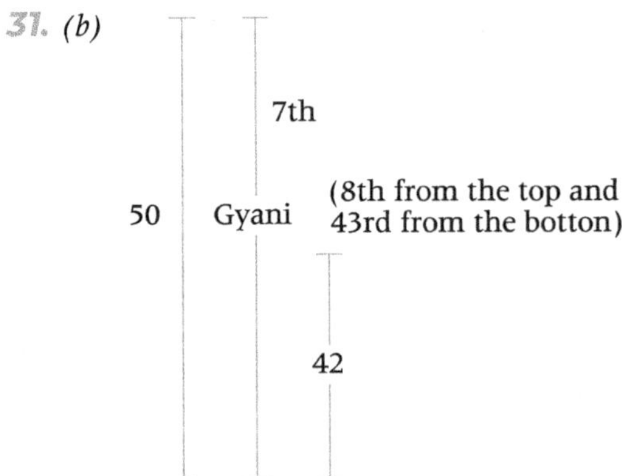

So, PSW will complete the second pair.

26. *(d)* Except option (d), all are the name of different flowers.

27. *(b)* The pattern is

$$5 \xrightarrow{+5} 10 \xrightarrow{+5} 15 \xrightarrow{+5} 20$$
$$10 \xrightarrow{+3} 13 \xrightarrow{+3} 16 \xrightarrow{+3} 19$$

So, the next term will be $\dfrac{20}{19}$.

28. *(c)* Here, the two words are given, i.e., ANGL? and ? GLE.

Now if we put 'E' in place of question mark, we get 'ANGLE' and 'EAGLE'.

Hence, option (c) is correct.

29. *(b)* Here, the first number is multiplied by 8 to get the second number.

As, $8 \times 8 = 64$, similarly, $19 \times 8 = 152$

So, 152 will replace the question mark.

30. *(c)* Except '35' all are multiple of '9'.

31. *(b)*

So, Gyani's rank from the bottom in the class is 43rd.

32. (c) As,

$$5 \times 7 \times 4 = 7\ 4\ 5$$

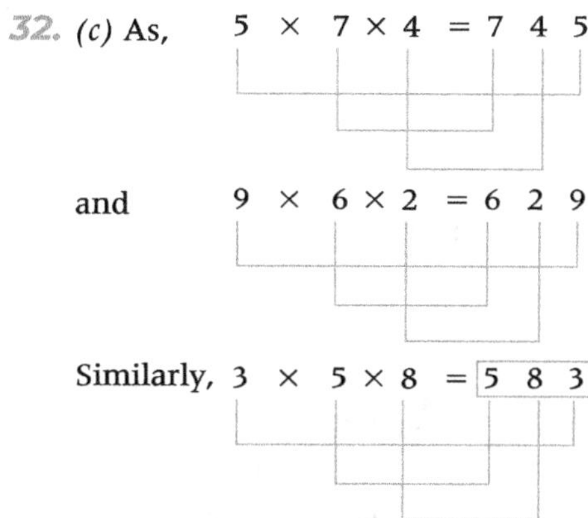

and

$$9 \times 6 \times 2 = 6\ 2\ 9$$

Similarly, $3 \times 5 \times 8 = \boxed{5\ 8\ 3}$

Hence, option (c) is correct.

33. (c) From the direct code method we get,

E	G	Y	P	T	R	N
9	3	4	5	6	8	1

∴ The code for TREE is 6899.

34. (d) The descending order of weights is shown below

$$VW > RS > PQ > TU$$

It is clear 'VW' is the heaviest.

35. (c) According to the question,

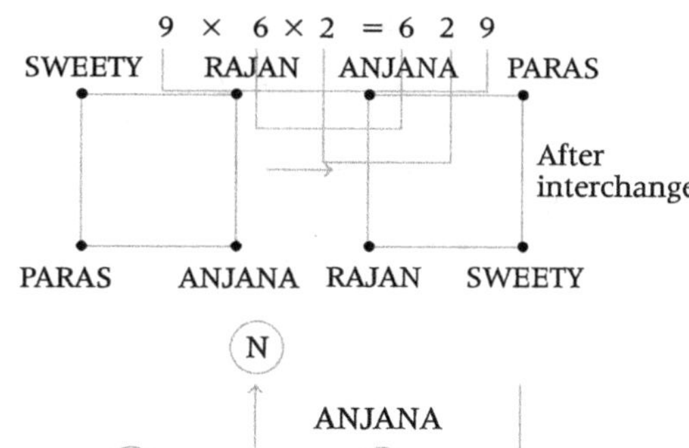

It is clear from the above diagram that, RAJAN is to the South of ANJANA.

36. (c) Change the symbols according to the question

$$? = 36 \times 10 \quad \div \quad 10 + 12$$
$$\downarrow \qquad \downarrow \qquad \downarrow$$
$$(-) \qquad (+) \qquad (\times)$$

$? = 36 - 10 + 10 \times 12$ (Using VBODMAS rule)

$? = 36 - 10 + 120$

$? = 156 - 10 = 146$

Hence, option (c) is correct.

37. (b) Here, in each row and column, letters P, J, and T must appear once.

So, the missing letter is T. Also, the numbers follow below pattern rowwise,

In row I, $3 \times 4 = 12$

In row II, $7 \times 2 = 14$

In row III, $9 \times x = 27 \Rightarrow x = \dfrac{27}{9} = 3$

So, $x = 3$

Hence, the missing pair will be T3.

38. (d) In figure (d) the given figure (X) is hidden.

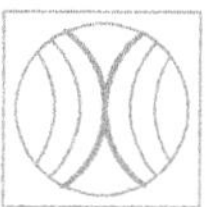

39. (c) The missing number is

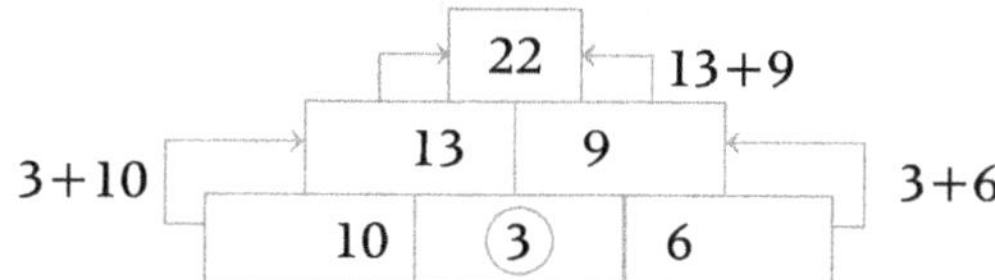

Here, we can see that the addition of numbers

As, $10 + 3 = 13$

and $3 + 6 = 9$

Similarly, $13 + 9 = 22$

40. (d) On close observation, we find that figure (X) contains figure (d) shown below

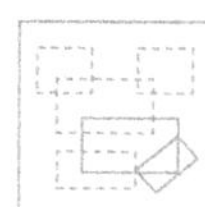

Hence, the answer is (d).

Sol. (Q. Nos. 41 and 42) From the given information we get the codes for each word as

you   are   good   pot   dot   not

good   and   bad   dot   tot   qot

thay   are   bad   tot   not   sot

41. *(c)* The code for 'they' is 'sot'.

42. (a) The code for 'bad' is 'tot'.

Sol. (Q. Nos. 43 and 44)

43. *(b)* The letter third to the right of sixteenth letter from left corner is Nineteenth letter from the left corner i.e., 'E'.

44. *(d)* There are four E's i.e.,

Two ER, EN, EM.

Hence, option (d) is correct.

Sol. (Q. Nos. 45 and 46) The huts are located as shown in the adjoining figure.

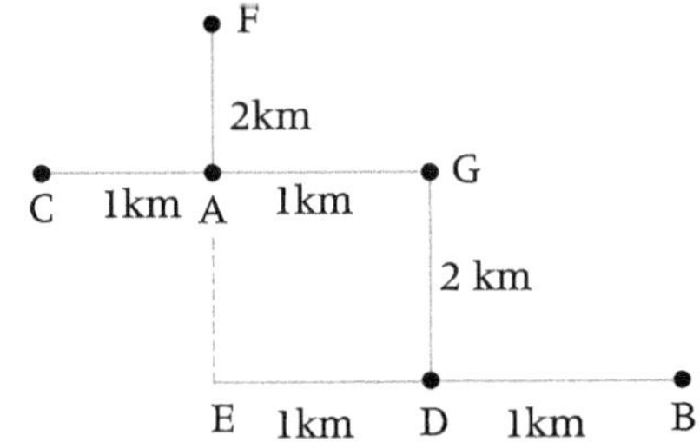

45. *(d)* Clearly, A is in middle of G and C

46. *(a)* Required distance = FE = FA + AE
$$= FA + GD$$
$$= (2 + 2)\ km = 4\ km$$

Sol. (Q. Nos. 47 and 48)

47. *(d)* There are total 13 triangles in the given figure.

48. *(d)* There are total 4 circles are present in the given figure.

Sol. (Q. Nos. 49 and 50)

49. (c) Sam is fourth to the right of fifth person from the left end.

50. *(b)* Pintu is third left of computer when telephone and computer changes its position to each other.

Practice Set 2

1. *(c)* As, $565 - 20 = 545$
Similarly, $864 - 20 = 844$
So, 844 will complete the second pair.

2. *(c)* The number of shaded circles is decreasing by one from figure (1) to (2) and figure (2) to (3). This process is repeating from figure (4) and the number of squares is same in each alternate figure.

One following this pattern, option figure (c) will replace the question mark.

3. *(a)* Except ears, all others are internal organs. So, ears are different from others.

4. *(b)* The codes can be represented as

Letters	W	A	T	C	H	E	R
Codes	7	2	4	5	3	6	9

Here, $E \to 6$, $T \to 4$, $C \to 5$
$$H \to 3, E \to 6, R \to 9$$
So, the code for ETCHER is 645369.

5. *(d)* The meaningful word is
T O U C H
4 1 3 2 5

6. *(b)* According to the question,
P $\boxed{R\ Q\ P}$ R P Q P $\boxed{R\ Q\ P}$ Q Q P R Q R P Q
So, there are two Q's, which are followed by P and preceded by R.

7. (c) From the given information,
We get
Joy > Tim > Brane > Rafle
Clearly, Rafle is the shortest.

8. (a) The arrangement of the given words according to dictionary is as follows:
Nubbin, Pain, Peach, Tabard, Temple,
i.e. 5, 2, 3, 1, 4.

9. *(b)* The movements of Casper can be shown as below

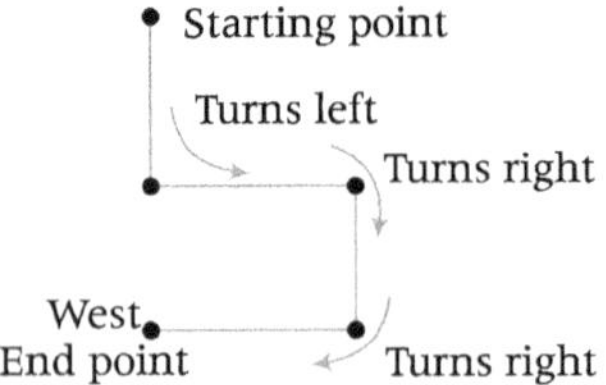

So, Casper is facing in West direction.

10. *(b)* The pattern is as follows:
In figure I, $(8 + 10) - 12 = 18 - 12 = 6$
In figure III, $(4 + 11) - 7 = 15 - 7 = 8$
Similarly, in figure II,
$$(6 + 12) - 8 = 18 - 8 = 10$$
Hence, the missing number is 10.

11. *(b)* The correct mirror image can be obtained as

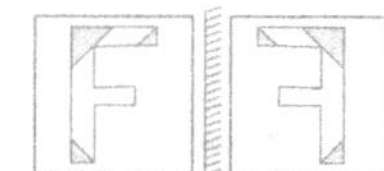

12. *(d)* The given figure (X) is hidden in figure (d) as shown below

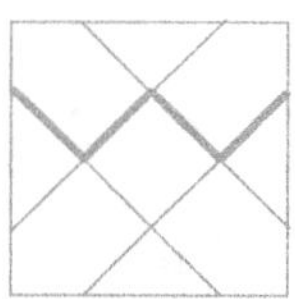

13. *(c)* The given figure can be represented as

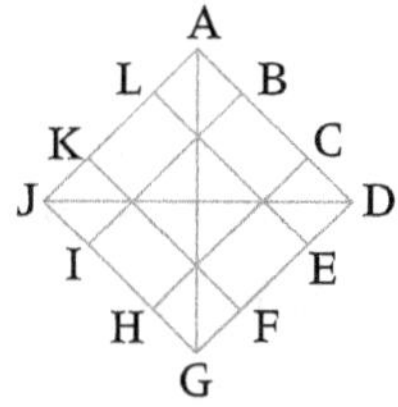

The straight lines are AG, JD, AD, DG, GJ, JA, LE, KF, BI and CH = 10

14. *(d)* As, for the Radio we need some listeners similarly, for the Drama we need some viewer to watch the drama.

15. *(d)*

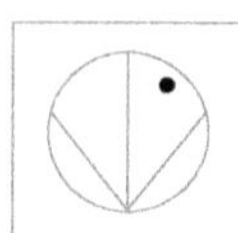

Figure (d) is odd from the other.

16. *(b)* Here,

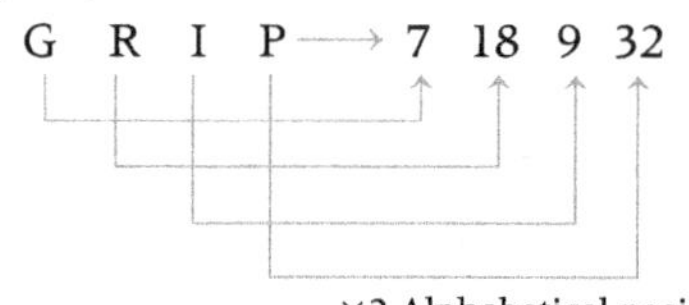

So, the code for DOLL is $ # * *

17. *(d)* The arrangement of words is as follows

Sporadic Sport Spouse Squash
    4   1   2   3

18. *(d)* As,

G R I P ⟶ 7 18 9 32

×2 Alphabetical position

Similarly,

L P D T ⟶ 12 16 4 40

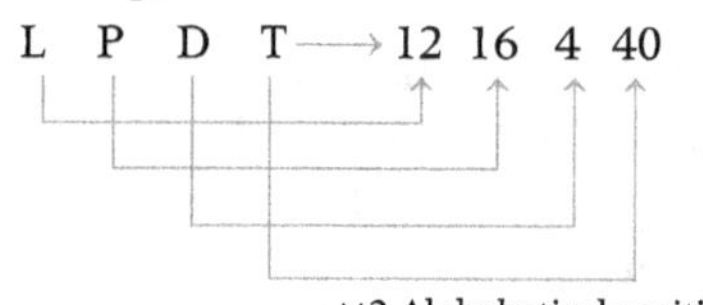

×2 Alphabetical position

19. *(b)* Except (b) all other are the part of calendar.

20. *(c)* The correct mirror image of the given word is

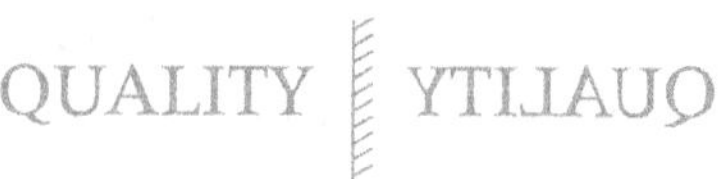

21. *(a)*

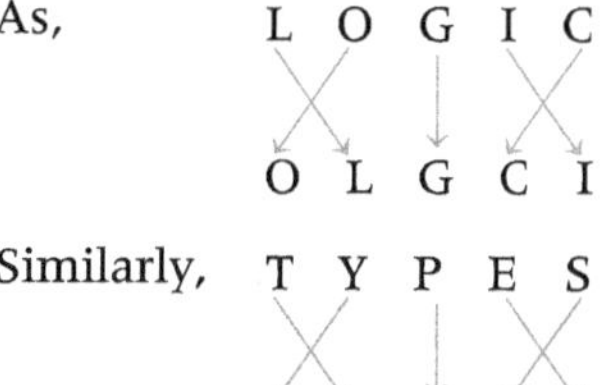

Hence, correct answer is option (a).

22. *(c)* Every number in each set is a perfect square
As, $16 = 4^2, 25 = 5^2, 100 = 10^2$
Similarly, $81 = 9^2, 64 = 8^2, 36 = 6^2$

23. *(a)* The given codes can be represented as

Numbers	2	5	7	9	4	3
Codes	&	%	@	#	*	!

So, the correct code for '4593' will be * % # !

24. *(a)* The pattern followed by the clock is as,

3:00 ——(+ 1 hr)⟶ 4:00 ——(+ 1 hr)⟶ 5:00 ——(+ 1 hr)⟶
6:00 ——(+ 1 hr)⟶ 7:00 ——(+ 1 hr)⟶ 8:00

25. *(b)* The letters of the word 'LOGIC' are follow the pattern as

As,   L O G I C
          O L G C I

Similarly, T Y P E S
            Y T P S E

So, TYPES written as 'YTPSE'.

26. *(d)* Number 3114 is the only number in which last digit is not repeated.

27. *(b)* Alphabets in first row = 1

Alphabets in second row = 3
Alphabets in third row = 5
So, the pattern is as follows
Row I = 1
Row II = 2 × 1 + 1 = 3
Row III = 3 × 1 + 2 = 5
Row IV = 4 × 1 + 3 = 7
⋮
Row X = 10 × 1 + 9 = 19
So in row 10 we get 19 alphabets.
Thus, '19' alphabets will be come in row '10'.

28. *(a)* We have,

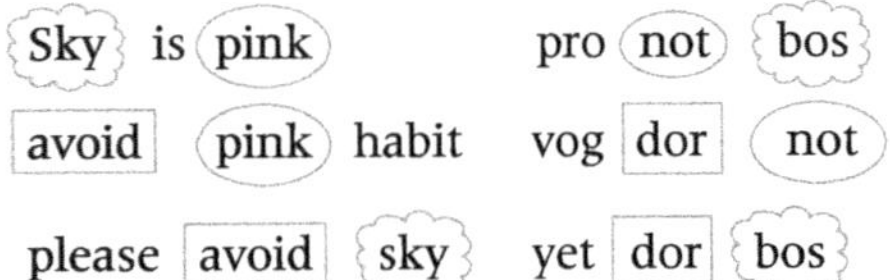

From the above arrangement, we get the
code for habit is 'vog'.

29. *(c)* In all other groups, begin and end with
the same letter.

30. *(a)*

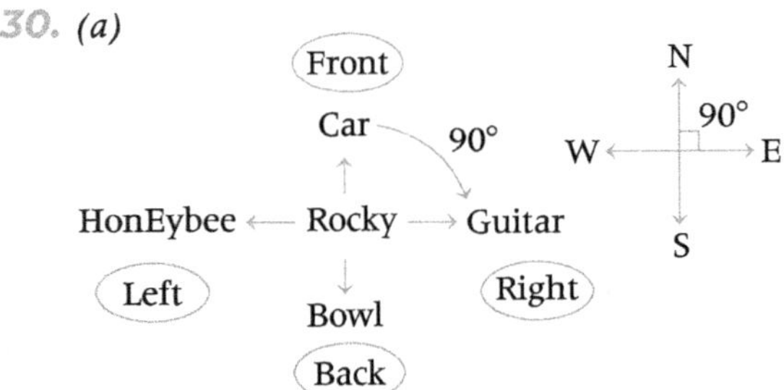

In the adjoining diagram. Rockey turns 90°
to his right. After turning, he faces Guitar.
Hence, option (a) is correct.

31. *(b)* There are total '25' numbers in the given
sequence.
So, middle number = 13 th number = 6
Clearly, the third number to left of (middle)
'6' is '9'.

32. *(d)*

C O R P O R A T E

There are 4 pairs i.e. PR, RT, PT and PO.

33. *(d)*

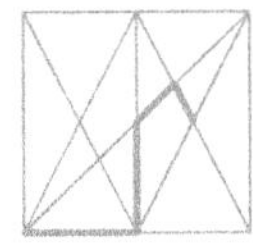

∴ Required distance = 2m

34. *(a)*

A
10th
Left
A
9th
Right
After interchanged
B
5th
Left

Total number of boys will be = 15 + 9 − 1 = 23

35. *(c)* Number of students behind Shivani
$$= 60 - 18 = 42$$
So, Shivani is 43rd from the last.

36. *(b)* Using the proper signs, we get
Given expression = 14 × 10 + 42 ÷ 2 − 8
(using VBODMAS rule)
= 14 × 10 + 21 − 8
= 140 + 21 − 8 = 161 − 8 = 153

37. *(b)* The pattern is as follows
As, 4 + 2 = 6 (Positional value of F)
14 + 5 = 19 (Positional value of S)
Similarly, 12 + 8 = 20 (Positional value of T)
So, 'T' will replace the question mark.

38. *(a)* Figure (a) embedded in figure (X).

39. *(c)* On interchanging − and ÷, and 8 and 16
in option (c) we get, 16 − 8 ÷ 4 = 14
16 − 2 = 14 which is true.

40. *(b)* The pattern is shown in adjacent figure.

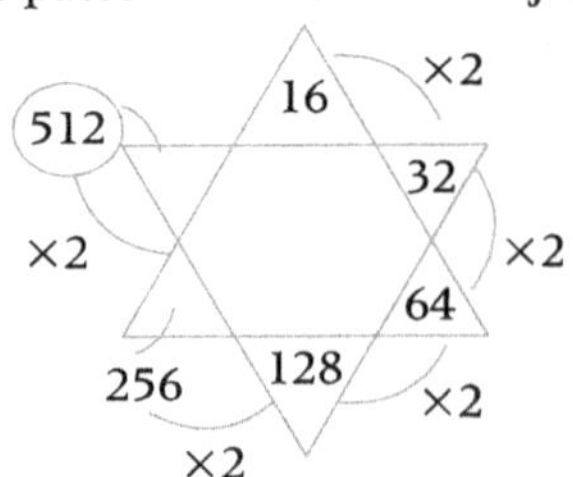

So, 512 will replace the question mark.

Sol. (Q. Nos. 41 and 42)

41. (c) The code for 'OVER' is '@#%4'.

42. (b) '4%7p4d' is stands for 'REWARD'.

Sol. (Q. Nos. 43 and 44)

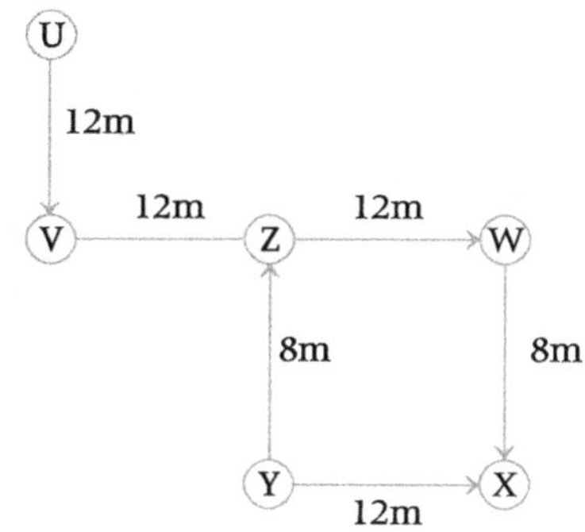

43. (c) He will pass through first point Z.

44. (c) The point W is 12 m East of point Z.

Sol. (Q. Nos. 45 and 46)

According to the question,

$$Riya > Arti \qquad ...(i)$$
$$Arti < Priya \qquad ...(ii)$$
$$Priya > Riya \qquad ...(iii)$$
$$Priya > Pallavi > Riya \qquad ...(iv)$$

On combining all the Eqs., we get

$$Priya > Pallavi > Riya > Arti$$

45. (c) Priya scored the highest marks.

46. (c) Riya scored second lowest marks.

The score of second lowest scorer may be 60.

Sol. (Q. Nos. 47 and 48)

47. (a) The element 10th to the right of 6th element from the right end is = 4th element from the right end i.e., 'T'.

48. (b) If we removed all the symbols, then we get the sequence.

F 4 T 2 E N G 7 R E N T X

8th element from left end. is '7'.

Sol. (Q. Nos. 49 and 50) The figure may be lebelled as shown.

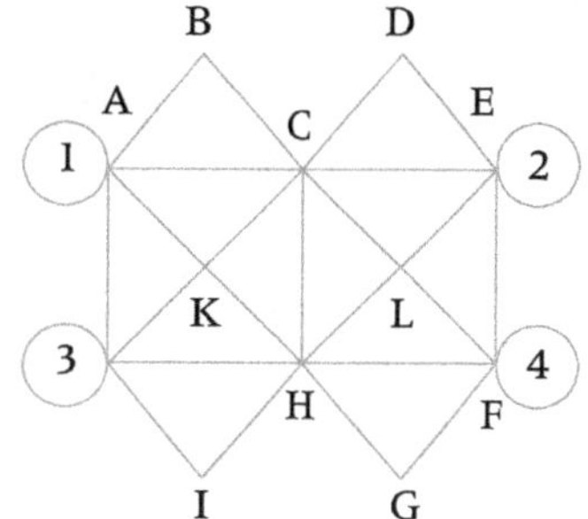

49. (b) The horizontal lines are AE and JF i.e. 2 in number.

The vertical lines are AJ, CH and EF i.e. 3 in number.

The slanting lines are AG, BF, JD, IE, DE, JI and FG i.e. 8 in number.

∴ Total number of straight lines needed to construct the figure = 2 + 3 + 8 = 13

50. (c) The squares composed of two components are ABCK, CDEL, JKHI, HLFG and KCLH i.e. 5 in number.

The square composed of four components each are ACHJ and CEFH i.e. 2 in number.

∴ Total number of squares in the figure
$$= 5 + 2 = 7$$

Now, on counting the circles we get total '4' circles.